SO-ALH-407

Mountain Weather

Weather gets everybody's attention outdoors. Jeff Renner's *Mountain Weather* will teach you how to see what's over the horizon.
—*Medford Mail Tribune*, **Medford, OR**

Provides user-friendly descriptions on cloud formation, wind patterns, snow conditions, and other weather conditions. Chapters on safety, thunderstorms and extreme weather are helpful for all outdoor adventurers.
—*Connecticut Post*, **Bridgeport, CT**

Provides vital and practical information for people who spend time in the outdoors . . . . Makes for good armchair reading as well.
—*Bend Bulletin*, **Bend, OR**

The book's graphics are easy to understand. The book also has tips laid out in easy-to-read boxes. It is a smart idea and worth a read.
—*Idaho Falls Post Register*, **Idaho Falls, ID**

The ultimate guide to surviving rapid weather changes up in the mountains . . . . Jeff Renner has packed this book with everything hikers need to know about the elements.
—*Atlanta Sports & Fitness*, **Atlanta**

Knowing the essentials of mountain weather can keep hikers, climbers, and birders out of trouble. And there's no need to have a meteorology degree when forecaster Jeff Renner shares strategies and tips . . . . Charts, illustrations, regional maps, and text are easy to follow, so hop on the learning curve and stay safe.
—*Olympian*, **Olympia, WA**

mountaineers
outdoor
basics

Mountain Weather

**Backcountry Forecasting
and Weather Safety for
Hikers, Campers, Climbers,
Skiers, and Snowboarders**

Jeff Renner

THE MOUNTAINEERS BOOKS

Dedication

Dedicated to my wife Sue and son Eric, with whom I have shared so many enjoyable hours in the mountains; to my mother Gloria and late father Russ who always encouraged my curiosity, love of learning, and spirit of adventure (even when they privately harbored reservations), and finally to all who are moved by the beauty of wild and high places . . . and seek both to enjoy and protect them.

THE MOUNTAINEERS BOOKS
is the nonprofit publishing arm of The Mountaineers Club, an organization founded in 1906 and dedicated to the exploration, preservation, and enjoyment of outdoor and wilderness areas.

1001 SW Klickitat Way, Suite 201, Seattle, WA 98134

© 2005 by Jeff Renner. All rights reserved

First edition; first printing 2005, second printing 2007, third printing 2010

No part of this book may be reproduced in any form, or by any electronic, mechanical, or other means, without permission in writing from the publisher.

Manufactured in the United States of America

Project Editor: Margaret Sullivan
Copy Editor: Heath Lynn Silberfeld / Enough Said
Cover and Book Design: The Mountaineers Books
Layout: Mayumi Thompson
Cartographer: Gray Mouse Graphics
Cover Photograph: © Royalty-Free/Corbis

Library of Congress Cataloging-in-Publication Data
Renner, Jeff.
   Mountain weather : backcountry forecasting and weather safety for
hikers, campers, climbers, skiers, snowboarders / Jeff Renner.— 1st ed.
      p. cm.
   Includes bibliographical references.
   ISBN 0-89886-819-X
   1. Mountain climate—Handbooks, manuals, etc. 2. Outdoor
recreation—Safety measures—Handbooks, manuals, etc. I. Title.
   QC993.6.R46 2004
   551.6914'3—dc22

                              2004029274

♻Printed on recycled paper
ISBN (paperback): 978-0-89886-819-7
ISBN (ebook): 978-1-59485-162-9

Contents

Preface   7

Acknowledgments   9

CHAPTER 1 MOUNTAIN WEATHER: AN INTRODUCTION   11

CHAPTER 2 MOUNTAIN WEATHER 101   21
  A Little Basic Meteorology   23

CHAPTER 3 MOUNTAIN THUNDERSTORMS 101   48
  Mountain Thunderstorms   60
  Thunderstorms and Fronts   62
  Post-Frontal Thunderstorms   64

CHAPTER 4 STRATEGIES FOR SAFETY AND SURVIVAL   66
  The Four A's of Thunderstorm Safety   67
  Other Thunderstorm Threats   76
  Thunderstorms and Flash Floods   76
  Thunderstorms and Wildfires   81

CHAPTER 5 MOUNTAIN WINDS   87
  Mountain Winds: The Big Picture   89
  Winds in the Upper Atmosphere   89
  Winds that Move over Mountains   92
  Winds in and through the Mountains   95
  Winds that Change from Day to Night   102
  Thunderstorm Winds   106
  Assessing Your Exposure to Wind   110
  Acting Safely in a Windstorm   112
  Aiding Others in a Windstorm   113
  Light Winds   115

CHAPTER 6 MOUNTAIN SNOW   116
From Sky to Ground: Understanding and Finding Good Snow   118
Snow on the Ground: When It's Risky, When It's Not   123
Glaciers and Weather   130

CHAPTER 7 PRE-TRIP WEATHER BRIEFINGS   133
Mountain Weather Sources: The Good, the Bad, and the Ugly   135
Strategies for Pre-Trip Weather Briefings   137
Weather Briefings for the Overachieving Outdoors Enthusiast   150
Following a Plan with a Purpose   153

CHAPTER 8 TRAIL NOTES: REGIONAL WEATHER GUIDANCE   163
Local Weather Wisdom: Not Just for Locals   163
The Far North: Alaska and the Yukon   165
The Canadian Coast Range and Rockies:
    British Columbia and Alberta   181
The Pacific Northwest Coast: Washington and Oregon   195
The Northern U.S. Rockies: Montana, Idaho, and Wyoming   211
The Pacific Southwest: California and Nevada   223
The Desert Southwest: Arizona, New Mexico, and West Texas   236
The Central U.S. Rockies: Colorado and Utah   249
The Northern Appalachians: New York to Quebec   263
The Central and Southern Appalachians:
    Pennsylvania to Alabama   279

Conclusion   295
Appendix I: Wind Chill   297
Appendix II: Heat Stress   298
Appendix III: Cloud Identification Chart   300
Appendix IV: Useful Conversions and Guidelines   302
Appendix V: Internet Resources   303
Appendix VI: Bibliography   304
Index   306

Preface

I have never been fond of early alpine starts. I recognize the reason for them and practice them but much prefer waiting until sunrise—or later—to exit my tent. Still, in the dark hours of the morning as we prepared to leave our base camp on Mount Baker for a summit attempt, I felt positively buoyant. To be certain, I was looking forward to our climb, though the hike in from the trailhead had been one of the soggiest any of us had endured in ages.

A break in the weather was possible. It was to be a brief break, but this climb was a fund-raiser for breast cancer research, and we wanted to reach the summit and maximize contributions for the charity. At first, the weather was good: light winds and no precipitation. We made good progress, slowing as we zigzagged around the many crevasses that mark this particular Northwest volcano. All too soon, the wind and the snow returned and built steadily. Despite the hard work of climbing, several members of our party began to show early signs of hypothermia. Shared clothing solved that problem, at least temporarily. Continuing in the face of now-howling wind, we reached the lip of the crater. Pellet-like graupel bounced painfully off exposed flesh, and the wind continued to build. Another thousand vertical feet stood between our rope teams and the true summit. Realizing the forecasted break in the weather had come and gone, and assessing the steadily deteriorating weather along with the borderline hypothermia of several party members, we reluctantly abandoned our summit attempt and returned to base camp.

Nothing unusual or profound characterizes this decision. Climbers, hikers, and other travelers in the backcountry make similar decisions all the time. We are not aware of them because these people never make "the news." Instead, we hear about the people who choose to press on while ignoring good information—or who do not obtain such guidance in the first place. In my work as a broadcast meteorologist, all too frequently I hear reports of weather-related climbing accidents that are due to a lack of basic weather knowledge, inadequate pre-trip planning, or insufficient vigilance on the mountain.

With my background as a commercial pilot and flight instructor, I realized that mountain travelers could avoid many accidents by using some of the same techniques pilots use to assess and monitor the weather before and during a flight. That has been the inspiration for this book.

I have worked to distill the essentials of mountain weather in the first six chapters, with particular attention paid to thunderstorms, thunderstorm safety, mountain winds, and snow and avalanche hazards. The seventh chapter walks you through the process of obtaining solid weather guidance before leaving on a trip. You will find detailed outlines and examples of how to analyze that information, which will enable you to make good "go" or "no go" decisions. Scattered throughout are numerous anecdotes that will bring these principles alive.

Chapter 8 is a field guide within a guide, organized into regional subsections for the major mountain areas of the United States and Canada. Each regional guide contains an overview of local climate, graphics showing the major storm tracks and areas most likely to get precipitation, and short lessons on important regional weather phenomena. A reference map for each region highlights local weather challenges likely to be problematic during specific seasons, followed by a summary to help you anticipate and avoid those challenges.

It would be easy to view this book solely as a guide to avoiding risky weather and hazardous situations in the mountains. Certainly I do not want you to find yourself in the mountains desperately wishing you were at home, but I would like to raise the bar a little: This book is also written to help you experience the greatest possible enjoyment in the beauty of the mountains—and to keep you from sitting at home wishing desperately that you were in the mountains.

I look forward to seeing you on the trail.

Jeff Renner
Sammamish, Washington

Acknowledgments

It would seem that broadcasting and book publishing share little in common. Certainly the shelf life of one of my weather broadcasts is generally measured at most in days, and occasionally in hours. In contrast, a book, and I hope this one in particular, will be of service for years. But like a broadcast, the cover of a book typically carries only one or two names; yet the content is the result of work contributed by many. That is no less true of this volume. For that reason, I'd like to take time to offer my thanks to those who in one way or another helped "co-author" this book.

The process of transforming a broadcaster into a writer isn't an easy one. Thanks are due to Mountaineers Books in general, and to Deb Easter, Margaret Sullivan, and Kathleen Cubley in particular. My copy editor, Heath Lynn Silberfeld, adeptly switched between the language of science and conversational grammar, and helped me do the same. Thanks to Marge Mueller for her usual wonderful job on translating concepts to graphics. Any shortcomings are my responsibility, not theirs. It was a pleasure and honor to work with each of them.

In researching some of the climbing and hiking accidents related to weather, I am indebted to the willingness of many to share their expertise and experiences. Reynold Jackson of the Grand Teton National Park was particularly generous and patient in describing the rescue of climbers struck by lightning in 2003.

Major thanks are due to my friend and colleague Rich Marriott for his guidance in preparing the section on snow and avalanche conditions, as well as Paul Baugher of the Northwest Avalanche Institute, Mark Moore of the Northwest Avalanche Center in Seattle, and Alan Jones of the Canadian Avalanche Association. Tom Haradan and Cindy Purcell of the National Park Service provided excellent detail on flash flood hazards; Dave Johnson and Bruce Keleman of the U.S. Forest Service were generous in explaining the fine points of wildfire behavior.

While it's possible to become well versed on the weather of one region, it's impossible for one meteorologist to be familiar with the complex weather patterns of all of the regions covered in this book. Although I've had the good fortune to hike, ski, or climb in all of the areas described, a few trips hardly confer expertise. That's why I am indebted to the meteorologists who generously shared their knowledge and experience with me, both as forecasters and outdoor enthusiasts who understand the impact of local weather patterns on outdoor activities. Ed LaChapelle, the dean of snow scientists in the United States, was instrumental in helping me compose the section on Alaska and the Yukon. Darryl Brown, Trevor Smith, and Jim Goosen of the Pacific Weather Center in Vancouver, British Columbia, and Gabor Fricska of Kelowna patiently shared their expertise in the weather patterns of the Canadian Rockies and Coast Mountains. Here in the Pacific Northwest, I turned to my friend and former professor Cliff Mass at the University of Washington, as well as friends and broadcast colleagues Rich Marriott of KING Television in Seattle and Matt Zaffino of KGW Television in Portland for additional perspectives on our wonderful but complex region.

Eugene Petrescu of the National Weather Service Forecast Office in Missoula, Montana, and Jim Woodmencey of Mountainweather.com in Jackson Hole were very helpful in sharing the intricacies of weather patterns in the northern Rockies. Professor Jim Steenburgh of the University of Utah and Eric Thaler of the National Weather Service Forecast Office in Boulder, Colorado, patiently steered me through the complexities of mountain weather in Utah and Colorado, with particular focus on ski conditions. Warren Blier of the National Weather Service Forecast Office in Monterey, California and Larry Schick, now of the U.S. Army Corps of Engineers, generously shared their knowledge of weather patterns in California and Nevada. Likewise, David Bright, formerly of the National Weather Service Forecast Office in Phoenix and now serving with the Severe Storms Prediction Center in Norman, Oklahoma, offered his considerable experience and knowledge of weather in Arizona and New Mexico.

Jim Mansfield of the National Weather Service Forecast Office in Gray, Maine, Anton Seimon of Columbia University, and the staff of the Mount Washington Weather Observatory in New Hampshire were very helpful in expanding my knowledge of the Northeast; it can exemplify extreme weather! Bryan Yeaton, host of the Observatory's Weather Journal radio program, offered me valuable tips for some enjoyable field research; i.e., hiking. Paul Knight, Pennsylvania State Climatologist and faculty member at Penn State, generously shared his expertise for his area of the Appalachians; so did Steve Keighton of the National Weather Service Office in Blacksburg, Virginia; Professor Gary Lackmann of North Carolina State University; and Lawrence Lee of the National Weather Service in Greer, South Carolina. Credit for helpful information goes to each, while responsibility for any errors is mine and mine alone.

Mountain Weather: An Introduction

l ife is rather like a tin of sardines—we're all of us looking for the key.
Alan Bennett in stage review,
Beyond the Fringe

The summer of 2003 had been unfailingly sunny over the northern Rockies. Severe clear Grand Teton National Park was no exception. The few clouds that appeared drifted through quickly, and what at first glance appeared to be a cloud often was smoke from wildfires farther north. On those rare occasions that a thunderstorm would form, only scattered spits of rain would fall, outnumbered by staccato bursts of lightning that flickered through the dry air. Such strikes had already ignited fires in Montana's Glacier National Park and Canada's Banff National Park in Alberta. So far, no wildfires had erupted in Grand Teton, but the vegetation was alarmingly dry.

The lack of bad weather in recent summers, particularly that of climbers' chief nemesis—thunderstorms—had strengthened a growing tendency to abandon the tradition of early alpine starts. That practice is aimed at getting up and down a mountain before the typical afternoon thunderstorms develop. "Early up, early down," goes the slogan. A visiting group of climbers from Idaho was no exception. It was well after sunrise on Saturday, July 26, when they finally assembled in the Garnet Canyon meadows for their planned climb of the Grand Teton.

The Grand, as it is sometimes called, is big—13,770 feet—though size alone cannot define the presence projected by this peak. More than fifty peaks just to the south in Colorado are taller than the Grand Teton. Yet from the ground or from the air, the Grand commands attention. It thrusts skyward from the even plains of Jackson Hole like a great incisor, a shark's tooth of gneiss forged in the basement of the North American continent. The Grand inspires superlatives in good weather, but in bad weather it can bite and bite hard. Long known as the greatest, "le grande" of the "Trois Tetons" or "Three Nipples," it was named by bewhiskered, fur-and-buckskin-clad trappers perhaps lacking gentler company for too long. The sheer gravitas of the Grand exerted a similar pull on some of the earliest alpinists to explore the Rockies. William Owen, Franklin Spalding, John Shive, and Frank Peterson are credited with the first successful ascent on August 11, 1898. More than thirty published routes now lead up the Grand. One of the most popular, the Exum Ridge route, was pioneered in 1931 by a lone teenager named Glenn Exum. That was the route the late-departing group from Idaho had selected. Some had climbed together before, others were neophytes, but all had been eagerly anticipating this trip for the past year. For some the focus was the climb, others were drawn by the grandeur of the Tetons, and all looked forward to simply spending time together. They divided into four rope teams: a mix of coworkers, friends, and family members.

Like most parties preparing to ascend a new peak, a mix of nerves and anticipation was present. The process of dividing into rope teams, reviewing the route, then organizing, sorting, and stowing gear, however, has a way of focusing attention on the objective instead of on apprehensions—or at least masking them temporarily. If the number in their group—thirteen—raised any superstitious concern, it was not obvious when a park ranger stopped by to mention the possibility of thunderstorms. Shortly after the ranger's visit, the Idaho climbers shouldered their packs and joined what was fast becoming a crowd heading up the trail. It was approximately 8:00 in the morning. The sun was now well above the horizon.

Meteorologists scrutinizing weather data at the National Weather Service office in Riverton, Wyoming, noted the beginnings of a shift away from the long-running dry spell. Winds at and above the summit of the Grand Teton were now from the south–southwest, and they were the warm winds that carried the same moist, unstable air that generates almost daily summer thunderstorms farther south in the Rockies. The satellite images used to analyze the amount of water vapor in the atmosphere showed a milky-white plume of humid air flowing from the Four Corners area—where Colorado, New Mexico, Arizona, and Utah meet—toward northwestern Wyoming. Those clues—together with the more arcane numbers and indices that are part of the meteorologist's daily dissection of the atmosphere—led to the prediction of something not seen recently in forecasts: thunderstorms. That caused the park ranger to visit the climbers' camps that morning. Although weather can pose life-threatening risks in the mountains, knowledge and good judgment can prevent most accidents.

To the uninitiated or incautious, the small dollops of clouds appearing near the Tetons by mid-morning seemed incapable of causing trouble. They were not imposing, they were not dark, and they certainly were not discharging any rain—not even a sprinkle. The steep shoulders of rock were, however, absorbing the steadily increasing warmth of the sun. Acting like oversized heating elements, they radiated some of that heat upward. Wily hawks and vultures had discovered those invisible thermals and were already soaring high, reconnoitering the ground below for the unwary or unlucky. Those same thermals were carrying additional moisture and heat to the confectionery-like cumulus clouds: more fuel for the atmospheric fireworks to come.

Reynold Jackson had noticed the shift in weather the day before while still on duty. A climbing ranger for Grand Teton National Park, he had earned his decades-long safety record by careful observation of the mountain environment, considerable skill, and realistic appraisal of risks. Reynold knew too well the costs of a cavalier or careless approach to high places, having led or participated in countless rescues. Although he was not prone to discuss it, the Department of the Interior had twice recognized his skill and dedication with an Award for Valor. Never really being off-duty in his job as head of Grand Teton National Park's helicopter rescue program, Reynold was nonetheless enjoying some rare leisure moments at home and at the time was in the horizontal rather than the vertical plane. Hopefully, this still mostly sunny day would not provide any urgent interruptions. Climbing rangers know that people—as much as, if not more than, the weather—can be unpredictable.

The sun was riding higher as the Idaho climbers completed a traverse toward the lower, north end of the broad ledge called Wall Street. The wide ramp was bathed in sunlight, leading to the most challenging pitches of the climb. A wait was in order, however. The good weather of the past week had attracted scores of climbers. Each party had to inch past the narrow terminus of Wall Street, get up the knobby rock of the Golden Stair, complete a scramble, and then face the crux of the climb, Friction Pitch. Given the crowd and more demanding pitches beyond Wall Street, the Idaho group had no alternative but to sit and wait their turn. It was then 11:00. As the delay stretched to two hours, conversation lagged. Though the wait provided plenty of time to ponder the challenges ahead, no one could later remember whether the changing sky was given due consideration. What had been fleecy

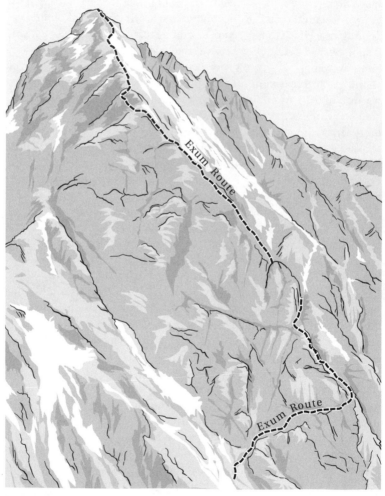

Exum Ridge Route, Grand Teton. Reprinted courtesy of A Climber's Guide to the Teton Range, *third edition, © 1996 by Leigh Ortenburger and Reynold Jackson*

puffs of fair-weather cumulus when they first arrived at Wall Street had undergone a stunning transformation, soaring first into gleaming, hard-edged pillars of water and ice, then broadening into brooding, battleship-gray towers waiting to erupt.

By 1:00 P.M., the last of the climbers ahead had exited the pitch leading upward from the ledge. Any discomfort with the looming presence of towering cumulus was perhaps offset by the lack of rain; nothing beyond a few spits fell. The top of the Grand was so close, and they had waited so long for this trip. The vistas of the Tetons, Yellowstone to the north, and their home state of Idaho to the west promised to become even more spectacular. One rope team after another started up. An hour and a half later, all thirteen Idaho climbers had successfully negotiated the Golden Stair and reached the hardest element of the climb: Friction Pitch. Friction climbing emphasizes finesse and trust more than strength. Missing are the hand and finger holds, cracks, chimneys, and knobs that mark many pitches and most climbs. Friction climbs are marked by mostly smooth, featureless rock. What matter are balance, position, and trusting the sticky soles of your climbing shoes to keep you attached, spiderlike, to the sheer slab. The technique can be both effective and exhilarating—if the rock is dry.

Friction Pitch on Grand Teton consists of a nearly 120-foot vertical slab. The towering storm cloud looming over the summit broke just as the rope teams were inching up the rock face. Gone was the relative protection of Wall Street. The drops were big and fell hard, greasing the pitch into a nonstick Teflon-like surface. Even the best technique resulted in skittering feet. The strain of maintaining traction—any traction—led to the shakes known by rock climbers as "sewing-machine leg." Clearly, it was time to turn back.

Rob and Sherika Thomas had just completed ascending the pitch when the sky opened up. Discouraged, but certain of the need to abandon the climb, Rob radioed down his decision. Given the nature of this pitch, getting down to a more protected position would take time—too much time. Climber Rod Liberal was effectively stranded halfway up the pitch. Sheets of rainwater pouring down the slab made it impossible for him to move. Just as Rod and the other climbers were pondering their next move, a pulsing, rhythmic buzz became audible over the downpour's din and rose to a sharp crescendo. A blinding flash of light filled the sky, engulfing the climbers, seeming to penetrate them. Every muscle in Rob Thomas's body convulsed violently; his mind, his will to survive, were trapped in a twitching, unresponsive cocoon of muscle and bone. Rob began to slide down the rock face, slowly gathering speed.

Sherika, who was stunned by the flash but untouched by the lightning bolt, instinctively grabbed for her husband. As soon as she felt her fingers close around him, Sherika pushed him against the wall. Perhaps 60 feet below, Rod Liberal had been blown off the rock face. Stunned, but still alive, he recognized that he was dangling upside down, his feet extended toward the sky. The three climbers immediately below Friction Pitch—Reagan Lembke, Justin Thomas, and Jacob Bancroft—had each been speared by that single bolt of lightning and were jerking uncontrollably as spasm after spasm overwhelmed their nervous systems. Each miraculously regained consciousness, unsure at first where they were or what had happened. Just as their situation became painfully clear, a soul-rending scream seemed to emanate from the mountain itself; it actually came from Clinton Summers. Rob Thomas had regained consciousness and had edged past an outcrop toward Clinton and Erica Summers. Erica was leaning against her husband, who was unable to move his legs. As Thomas reached them, Erica's lips seized his attention. They were swollen and discolored, in shades of black and blue. She was motionless. Rob lifted off her helmet as Clinton attempted to breathe life back into his young wife. The inside of the climbing helmet was melted and scorched. Clinton began chest compressions, but Erica did not respond. Not a gasp, no movement, just stillness. It was shortly after 3:30 in the afternoon.

Rob Thomas's father, Bob, had a cell phone and punched in 911. Mustering as much composure as possible, he outlined the group's predicament to the dispatcher. Bob had not finished stowing his cell phone when the dispatcher rang park rescue coordinator Brandon Torres. As Torres picked up the phone in his Lupine Meadows rescue cabin, he noticed it was pouring hard outside, huge drops bouncing off the ground. He was not surprised by a request for help in such conditions, but he was astounded by the magnitude of the problem. *A lightning strike on the Grand. CPR underway. Mass casualties at 13,000 feet.* One helicopter, then a second, were ordered for the rescue, plus a third to serve as an air ambulance to Idaho Falls. Off-duty rescue rangers were quickly paged, including Reynold Jackson. Within an hour of the initial call from Bob Thomas, the first helicopter, a Bell 206 with the call sign Two-Lima-Mike was circling the climbers. Pilot Laurence Perry maneuvered the craft while rangers Dan Burgette and Leo Larson took digital photos that would assist the rescue team in planning their approach. Perry, Burgette, and Larson landed 1400 feet below on a site called the Lower Saddle. Other rescuers were rapidly ferried to the makeshift helipad with the urgent realization that the sun was steadily sinking behind the thunderheads. Perhaps three hours were left to effect a mass rescue. The alternative was to leave the rain-soaked climbers, some critically injured, stranded on the mountain overnight. That included Rod Liberal, still dangling headfirst along the rock face, his climbing harness forcing him to gasp small breaths of air to stay conscious, each small inhalation requiring more effort as the webbing steadily tightened just below his diaphragm. It was questionable whether he could survive until sunset. Clinton Summers had reluctantly abandoned efforts to revive his wife. Below Friction Pitch, Reagan Lembke and Justin Thomas were secured by chance, their climbing rope snagged on a boulder. Bleeding and immobilized, both labored to maintain composure, to keep panic at bay. The climbing rangers also had to work to maintain focus. A successful rescue requires professional detachment, neither of which is always easy to muster. For years, rescues similar to this one required rangers to rappel from hovering helicopters, and that requires a long hover in thin air at high altitude. The alternative, now preferred, was for the rescuer to dangle from the end of a 100-foot-long static line. It is a thin line, little more than a third of an inch thick, but it is strong: It has to be.

Ranger Leo Larson, among the first to arrive at the scene, soon was securing himself to the static line. Renny Jackson was perched in the doorless helicopter as it carefully eased Larson off the ground and up toward the stranded climbers, a quarter of a mile above on the face of the Grand. The winds seemed to strengthen just as pilot Laurence Perry tried to delicately maneuver Larson toward the injured climbers, and dark clouds surged over the summit toward Exum Ridge. If the hope of imminent rescue momentarily masked the stranded climbers' pain and despair, both came surging back when Two-Lima-Mike withdrew a second time. Rod Liberal, still upside down in his harness, was now motionless, the grasp of the harness still holding him to the mountainside rapidly exceeding his own grip on life. What the Thomases and the rest of the party did not know was that two rangers, loaded with rescue and medical gear, were picking their way up the mountain. Fortunately, just minutes after the helicopter with Larson and Jackson landed back at the Lower Saddle, the cloud had lifted from the summit of the Grand. Then the rotors again bit hard into the thin air, and the crew ascended into the fading light for yet another rescue try.

This attempt succeeded, and within the next twenty minutes, five other rescuers joined Larson. These rangers confirmed what Clinton Summers already knew. His wife Erica was dead. A small moan from Rod Liberal, elicited by loud screams from his friends, convinced the climbing rangers he was not also gone. With daylight rapidly disappearing, the rescue team had to work swiftly. One after another, the injured climbers were evacuated. Liberal, the twelfth, was difficult to secure to a litter but surely would not survive a night on the mountain. Finally, shortly before 9:00 P.M. and within minutes of darkness, he was transferred to an air ambulance and flown to an Idaho Falls hospital. Erica Summers was removed from the Grand as the last vestiges of twilight faded from the sky. Although many of her companions needed extensive medical care, she was the only climber to die.

Clinton Summers probably did not feel lucky as he attended his wife's funeral in a wheelchair, interrupting lengthy treatments for extensive second-degree burns. Rod Liberal undoubtedly had difficulty smiling at his good fortune, enduring months of dialysis and therapy in a Salt Lake City hospital. Yet this group had in fact been incredibly lucky. Statistics suggest one in five people struck by lightning die. Despite being stranded near the summit of a very tall peak, only one of the thirteen climbers from Idaho Falls ultimately succumbed to that single, terrifying bolt of lightning. No first strike at a safe distance had occurred to alert them to their danger—only that strange buzzing seconds before the strike and the swelling clouds gathering above Wall Street ledge as they waited their turn to press for the summit. Had this accident occurred on most other major peaks in North America, Rod Liberal probably would not have survived. In fact, the entire party probably would have been stranded on the mountain overnight, with others almost certainly succumbing to hypothermia. The proximity of highly trained rescue climbers and medical personnel literally at the base of the peak prevented this accident from expanding into a massive tragedy. In fact, if this same accident had occurred just a few years before on the Grand—before lightweight, portable cell phones—it probably would have been the next day before rangers discovered that the climbers were missing.

Weather has always caused accidents in the mountains, but it was not always blamed for disappearances. Just a few centuries ago, venturing into the mountains for pleasure would have been considered sufficient reason for involuntary commitment to an asylum. Landscapes bent to human purpose were the ideal. Mountains were considered wastelands, unsightly "boils" on Earth's surface, dangerous places peopled by monsters or supernatural gods. Of those who entered high places, an appallingly large number were never heard from again. Fear of the mountains resulted in ignorance of the mountains, and ignorance is not conducive to safe travel in high places. Later in the eighteenth century,

Grand Teton (photo courtesy of Grand Teton National Park)

advancements in science led to curiosity and a different aesthetic. Whatever the sins of imperialism—and unquestionably there were many—it carried the imperative to explore and learn about mountains around the world. The truth was discovered at once to be both more serene and beautiful than the stuff of fable and myth, but the immensity of the forces at work could be sobering, if not terrifying. Historian Ariel Durant has said civilization exists by geological consent. Anyone who has spent much time in the mountains would amend that statement: Life in high places exists by meteorological consent.

That was certainly true on the Grand Teton late that afternoon on July 26, 2003. It is also true that more knowledge of summer thunderstorm behavior and certainly more caution could have prevented that accident. Of course, lightning is not the only threat posed by weather in the mountains. Flash floods, avalanches, and punishing winds are capable of causing extreme destruction; bitter cold and suffocating heat are additional dangers. By learning and following some basic principles, though, you are far less likely to become a statistic. That is the first purpose of this volume. Trails are peopled with hikers, climbers, and paddlers from eight to eighty and older. Many have spent the equivalent of years in the great outdoors without suffering a fate worse than a snoring tent mate or a botched meal. What draws them back, trip after trip, year after year, is the realization that wilderness brings great gifts, particularly in high places. All the world's great faiths place events of significance in the mountains: Moses received the Ten Commandments on Mount Sinai, Jesus ascended to heaven from Mount Olivet, Mohammed was visited by the Angel Gabriel on Mount Hira, and Mount Kailas in Tibet is central to Hindus and Buddhists alike. Native Americans have always recognized high peaks as places of great medicine, and frequently have chosen them for their personal vision quests. Ultimately, whether making a divine pilgrimage or simply attempting to recharge the human spirit, less timid souls have long recognized the importance of spending time in the wilderness, understanding that accepting its hazards with curiosity, appreciation, and judgment is profoundly enriching. That is the second purpose of this work: to help you venture into the backcountry with the confidence that comes from knowledge and good judgment.

A NOTE ABOUT SAFETY

Safety is an important concern in all outdoor activities. No book can alert you to every hazard or anticipate the limitations of every reader. The descriptions of techniques and procedures in this book are intended to provide general information. This is not a complete text on mountain weather forecasting technique. Nothing substitutes for formal instruction, routine practice, and plenty of experience. When you follow any of the procedures described here, you assume responsibility for your own safety. Use this book as a general guide to further information. Under normal conditions, excursions into the backcountry require attention to traffic, road and trail conditions, weather, terrain, the capabilities of your party, and other factors. Keeping informed on current conditions and exercising common sense are the keys to a safe, enjoyable outing.

The Mountaineers Books

Mountain Weather 101

It was calm with that absolute silence which can be so soothing or
so terrible as circumstances dictate. Then there came a sob of wind
and all was still again. Ten minutes and it was blowing as though
the world was having a fit of hysterics. The earth was torn in pieces;
the indescribable fury and roar of it all that cannot be imagined.
Apsley Cherry-Garrard,
The Worst Journey in the World

Feathery streaks of cirrus clouds reached toward the eastern horizon,
their roots beyond the western horizon. The last rays of the setting sun
bathed the undersides of these quill-like patterns with molten hues of
copper and gold. As the color faded and night fell, my attention returned to filling stuff sacks, lots of them, with sleeping bags, tent, food,
clothing—all the gear needed for a three-day trip and, I admit, some
that was not. The significance of those passing clouds did not register,
at least not yet. After all, this was not to be much more than car camping in Washington's North Cascades National Park, interspersed with
day hikes up some of the serrated granite peaks that have earned this
area the nickname "America's Switzerland."

It was obvious the next morning that the cirrus clouds had been
the vanguard of an approaching weather system; the sky was an almost featureless gray, with only a pale hint of the late summer sun
somewhere above the steadily lowering and thickening clouds. The
fickle but mostly northerly winds of the evening before were now
freshening from the southeast. Still, not so much as a hint of a

sprinkle was evident as we backed out of our driveway. Optimism overcame caution and experience, aided by the lack of any encounters with rain on the drive up the busy northbound interstate. Traffic was sparse as we gained elevation, and my wife and I were focused more on the prospect of a few days away from work than on the potential impact of these now sullen clouds.

Vine maple and aspen leaves rattled as we unrolled our tent. Even the larger limbs began to sway in the rising wind. Just as I staked one corner of the tent, an occasional gust lifted another, making the whole process a decidedly two-person effort, and a third would have been helpful. No sooner was the rainfly attached than the odd sprinkle was abruptly transformed into a pelting downpour. Dashing from car to tent and back again, we threw needed supplies and gear into our now trembling shelter. Although I tried to keep as much of my body inside the tent as possible, safe operation of our little camping stove required exposure from my armpits up, which meant an opening big enough to allow windborne blasts of rain inside. Once dinner was cooked and eaten and utensils quickly stowed (with the hope that the weather was too foul even for bears and other four-legged marauders), we tossed our wet clothing in one corner of our tent and faced the challenge of forcing our clammy limbs downward into our sleeping bags. Crescendos of rain interspersed with snapping, rattling tent fabric made it difficult to sleep. Each time exhaustion overcame those distractions, downpours of renewed vigor reawakened us.

I awoke to a dark tent with the distinct sensation of floating. Initial serene confusion over where the waterbed had come from was quickly replaced with the rude recognition that our tent was afloat— not just wet but afloat. Although absent the butcher, the baker, and the candlestick maker, there was no denying this now sodden crew was essentially rub-a-dub-dub a couple in a tub. Now cold and awake, we hoisted anchor (or tent pegs), stowed gear hastily in our small car, and grimly set sail for home.

Either a little attention to the thickening, lowering clouds moving in from the southwest, or to the shifting, freshening winds, or a respectful look at the forecast could have spared us the unanticipated discomforts and hasty retreat. Whatever other challenges we faced, our ability to respond to this experience at first with resolution and eventually with humor was, perhaps, the best predictor that our marriage would span decades. As any wise husband or wife knows, though, it is best not to press your luck unnecessarily—something also true of those who venture into the mountains. At times, weather systems cover an entire mountain range and the choice posed to skiers, boarders, climbers, and hikers is a simple one: stay home or go home. At others, weather patterns in and near the mountains are subtle, localized, and temporary. While deciphering such clues takes both knowledge and practice, these patterns offer more options than a simple go or no-go. The basics in the following pages offer first steps toward understanding patterns that are either large or localized and then acquiring the ability to make decisions that will maximize both time and safety in the mountains.

A LITTLE BASIC METEOROLOGY

The sun is the engine that drives our atmosphere. It provides the heating that, together with several other factors, creates the temperature variations that are ultimately responsible for wind, rain, and snow.

Earth's location—93 million miles or almost 149 million kilometers from its sun—is what makes life as we know it possible. Venus, with an orbit just 25 million miles closer to the sun, experiences average surface temperatures of roughly 800°F, (426°C), while more distant Mars averages –81°F (–63°C). That may be hospitable enough for certain forms of bacteria, but it is a little tough on humans.

Proximity to the sun is only one factor. The intensity of the sun's heating, or *radiation,* varies across Earth's surface. Given a choice for an October backpacking trip between the Brooks Range in northern Alaska and the Wasatch Mountains in Utah, a hiker with limited tolerance for the cold will likely opt for an outing in the Wasatch. Utah is closer to the equator, and thus the sun will be more directly overhead at noon and, therefore, the heating from the sun will be more intense.

This relationship between heating from the sun and the angle of the sun above the horizon also explains why summer, when the sun is more directly overhead, is warmer than winter. You can see how this works by shining a flashlight on this page, first from directly overhead, then at an angle. The beam of light shining from directly above the page creates a brighter reflection than the beam striking the surface at an angle. Not only does the sun provide more light when it is most directly overhead, but it also provides more heating.

Given more intense sunlight at the equator than at the poles, the temperature differences come as little surprise. Extremes in temperature, large as they may be, however, are controlled by the movement of air. Differences in air temperature cause air movement, which prevents runaway heating or cooling.

Temperature and Air Pressure

Anyone who has had to chase a tent in a windstorm knows that air moves sideways. It also rises and descends, which can generate or dissipate clouds.

Air tends to expand and rise when it is heated. Rising air reduces the downward pressure on the surface below as the atmosphere above us is, effectively, losing weight. Just as the reading on our bathroom scale drops when we lose weight, the reading on a barometer falls when some of the air moves up and away. A barometer is nothing more than a scale that measures the weight of the air above, but it expresses that weight as *pressure,* usually in inches of mercury or in millibars. Standard pressure at sea level is 29.92 inches of mercury, or 1013.2 millibars. One inch of mercury is equivalent to approximately 34 millibars.

Just as heating air makes it rise, cooling air makes it sink. Because cold air is more dense than warm air, it tends to find its way to the bottom of the atmosphere: to the ground. Cold air tends to collect in low places such as valleys and canyons, making them chilly campsites on cold, windless nights.

To summarize, the sinking of cool air increases air pressure, while the rising of warm air decreases air pressure. These pressure differences, which are the result of temperature differences, produce moving air,

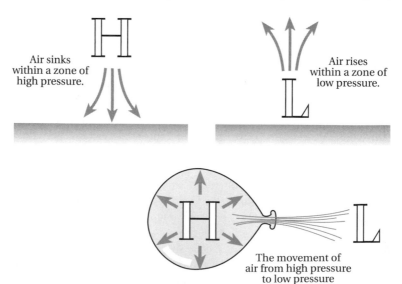

Air sinks within a zone of high pressure.

Air rises within a zone of low pressure.

The movement of air from high pressure to low pressure

High and low pressure influence the movement of air.

which we refer to as wind. Air will tend to move from an area of high pressure to one of low pressure, just as it would flow from a balloon if you stop pinching the neck closed. This movement of air from high to low pressure is what meteorologists call the *pressure gradient force*. Moving air eventually leads to a collision between *air masses,* which are bodies of air with different temperatures and sometimes different amounts of moisture.

Air Pressure and Fronts

Because polar and Arctic air is colder and, therefore, more dense than air farther south, it sinks and tends to spread away from the poles. The zone where it sinks and "piles up" is a region of *high pressure.* As the air sinks and the pressure increases, the temperature also increases. The effect is similar to what happens to football or rugby players caught at the bottom of a pile. The players on the bottom get squeezed the most, and their temperatures (and possibly their temperaments!) heat up. In the atmosphere, this warming within a high tends to evaporate the

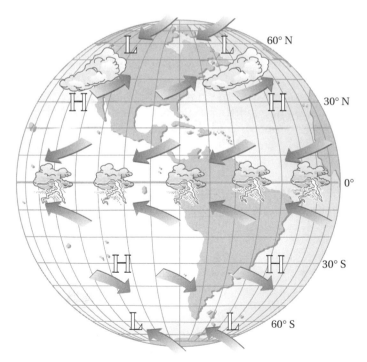

Large-scale circulation of air over the earth

little moisture present in cold polar and Arctic air, which is why the Arctic is classified as a desert, receiving very little precipitation: Not all deserts are covered by sand.

Barrow, for example, on the north slope of Alaska, receives an average of only 28 inches (71 centimeters) of snow each year, in contrast to Fairbanks, which receives 66 inches (167 centimeters), and Juneau, which averages 105 inches (256 centimeters). Each town is progressively farther south.

If Earth did not rotate, this cold air would just continue to slide southward to the equator. Intense solar heating near the equator forces the air there to rise, creating a region of *low pressure* that rings the globe. The air sinking and moving south from the pole and the air rising from the equator do not form a simple loop moving from north to south and back again. The rotation of Earth deflects this air, creating a considerably more complicated circulation of air over our planet.

Some of the air rising from the equator descends over the subtropics. This sinking air creates a region of high pressure. As it sinks within this high, Earth's rotation produces a force known as the *Coriolis force*, named after the nineteenth-century French mathematician Gustave-Gaspard Coriolis. The combination of the Coriolis force and the effect of friction from air moving over land and the water (the *friction force*) causes the air sinking within the high-pressure system to rotate in a clockwise direction in the Northern Hemisphere and counterclockwise in the Southern Hemisphere. The air rising up and away from a low-pressure system behaves exactly the opposite: It rotates counterclockwise around the low in the Northern Hemisphere and clockwise around the low in the Southern Hemisphere.

That behavior typically brings warmer air from the south toward the north ahead of a low or behind a high, and it usually brings cooler air from the north toward the south behind a low or ahead of a high. That is why air masses move and collide and form *fronts*. A front is nothing more than a boundary between two different air masses.

There are four types of fronts. A *warm front* is a boundary where warm air is replacing colder air. A *cold front* is a boundary where cold air is replacing warmer air. A *stationary front* marks a boundary between warm and cold air that is not moving much. An *occluded front* combines the qualities of warm and cold fronts and forces warm air up when two colder air masses collide.

Fronts do not exist only at Earth's surface. They also extend up into the atmosphere. When cool air meets warmer air, the warmer air

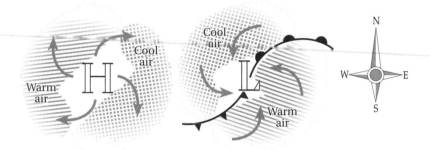

The circulation of air around high and low pressure systems generates warm and cold air masses.

rises because it is less dense and lighter. That warm air carries the moisture needed to create clouds and rain and sometimes thunderstorms.

Winds Aloft and the Movement of a Surface Weather System

The fronts, along with the high- and low-pressure systems at the surface, are steered by winds higher up in the atmosphere. That is why these winds are often referred to as *steering currents;* their impact on weather systems is similar to that of a river's current on a canoe. Where winds at the surface are the result of balancing pressure and Coriolis and friction forces, the direction of winds high up in the atmosphere is influenced only by pressure and Coriolis force. Friction from mountains, hills, and other features on the ground is not a significant factor at high altitudes. Look at a weather map depicting patterns in the upper atmosphere, and you will notice winds snake between the major areas of

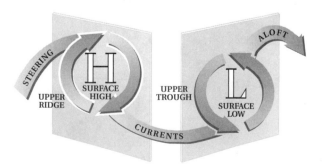

Where surface high and low pressure systems are found relative to upper air troughs and ridges

high and low pressure, instead of spiraling from high to low pressure.

The *jet stream* marks zones of the fastest-moving winds aloft; the greater the temperature difference from north to south, the stronger the jet stream will be. Therefore, the jet stream reaches its maximum strength during winter months and pushes farther south. Less difference in temperature occurs during the summer, which is why the jet stream weakens and recedes to the north. Finding the location and direction of the jet stream will yield important clues as to where fronts will move. That information is available via the Internet (see Chapters 5 and Chapters 7)—and in the sky. The jet stream is often marked by the thin, feathery clouds meteorologists call *cirrus clouds*. Thus, understanding and watching clouds can offer valuable information that will help keep you safe outdoors.

> Watch the direction cirrus clouds are moving, and you will have an important clue as to where the jet stream is moving and where it will direct fronts.

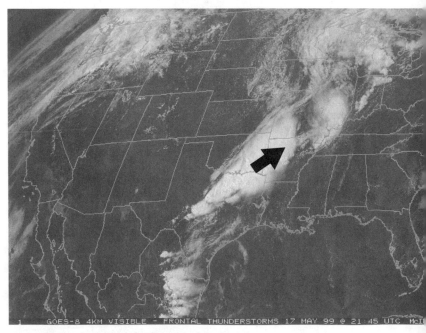

Cirrus clouds can indicate the direction of winds aloft.

Moisture, Fronts, Clouds, and Precipitation

We see the effect that results from warm air rising over colder air along a front when we breathe out on a cold day. The air inside our body is both moist and warm—fairly close to our normal body temperature of 98.6°F (37°C). As we breathe out into colder air, the moisture in our breath condenses—that is, it changes from water vapor (a gas) into a small cloud of liquid water droplets. When water vapor cools and condenses into liquid water droplets, it gives off heat; thus condensation actually adds heat to air. That is one reason that cloudy nights tend to be warmer than clear nights—the other is that clouds act as an airborne blanket, reducing the loss of heat into space.

Although we expect to be able to "see our breath" when the temperature drops to 32°F or 0°C, the transformation of the air's water vapor from a gas to a liquid does not always happen at the same temperature. Rather, that depends upon how much water vapor is already mixed with the other gases that make up the air. The temperature at which water vapor will begin condensing into liquid water is called the *dew point*. If the dew point of the air is 54°F (about 12°C), water vapor will condense into liquid water droplets when the actual air temperature cools to 54°F. We say the air is *saturated* when it cools to the dew point.

If a lot of water vapor is mixed in with the air, the dew point will be relatively high; dew points in the 70s are not unusual in the tropics. If the amount of water vapor in the air is a bit less, the dew point will be lower, perhaps in the 40s or 50s. This is common in the Rockies during the

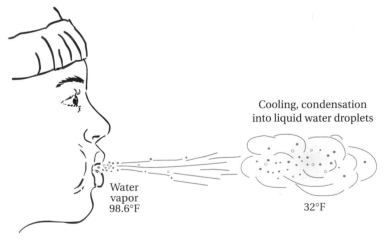

Cooling, condensation
into liquid water droplets

Water
vapor
98.6°F

32°F

We *"make a cloud"* by breathing out on a cold day, condensing water vapor into liquid water droplets.

summer. Desert regions can have dew points in single digits, and they can be below zero in the Arctic or Antarctic—that is, the temperature would have to cool to below zero for condensation to occur. Whatever the dew point, unless the air temperature cools to that temperature,

Relative humidity
25 percent

Relative humidity
75 percent

Relative humidity
100 percent

Relative humidity is a measure of air's changing capacity to hold moisture.

Typical variation of dew points in different geographic areas on a single day

condensation will not occur and clouds will not form. As you may suspect by now, warmer air has a greater capacity to hold moisture.

Relative humidity is a term commonly used on broadcast weather reports and forecasts. It is a comparison of how much water vapor the air is holding (measured by the dew point) and what it is capable of holding (measured by the actual air temperature). Relative humidity is reported as a percentage: the water vapor the air is holding as a percentage of what it is capable of holding. Keep in mind that although Mount Victoria in Alberta and Blood Mountain in Georgia may both be reporting relative humidities of 90 percent, the hikers on Blood Mountain will feel soggier: With dew points of, say, 45 on Mount Victoria and 65 on Blood Mountain, the air surrounding the friendly troop in Georgia will be holding perhaps twice as much water vapor as the air surrounding the intrepid climbers in the Canadian Rockies.

If rising air does cool to the dew point, and relative humidity reaches 100 percent, the water vapor will condense into microscopic cloud droplets thinner in diameter than a human hair.

Warm Fronts, Clouds, and Precipitation

Along a warm front, the warm air gradually slides up and over the cold air it is replacing. This is a stable situation that produces flat stratus clouds with widespread precipitation—typically along, and especially ahead of, a warm front. *Rain bands*—areas of more intense precipitation—can occur, and under special circumstances so can a thunderstorm. However, a warm front is not a particularly common place to find thunderstorms.

Different types of clouds develop along warm fronts than along cold fronts, and the differences in their shapes can provide the field forecaster with valuable clues to coming changes in the weather. These variations in cloud shapes actually mirror differences in the physical processes that are taking place along or near those fronts.

If a low-pressure system is approaching, the first clouds visible are typically those associated with the warm front. Because the approaching warmer air is less dense than the cooler air it is replacing, it is lifted, gradually sliding up and over the cooler air at Earth's surface. As that warm, moist air rises, it cools. If this rising air cools to its dew point, the water vapor in the air mass will either condense into water droplets or *sublime* into ice crystals.

Sublimation is the atmosphere's shortcut, transforming water vapor directly into ice crystals without it first condensing into liquid water. The result is determined by the temperatures aloft. Because the

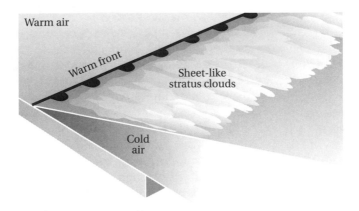

Warm air

Warm front

Sheet-like
stratus clouds

Cold
air

Warmer air rises over cooler air along and ahead of a warm front, generating clouds at different altitudes.

advancing warm air usually rises very high, 20,000 feet (approximately 6000 meters) or more, the temperatures are well below freezing, usually cold enough to sublime the water vapor into ice crystals.

Cirrus Clouds and Warm Fronts

The first clouds we see as the warm front advances are the fibrous high clouds called *cirrus*. They are thin, often less than 1000 feet (300 meters) thick. The ice crystals or water droplets in cirrus clouds act as miniature prisms, bending and splitting sunlight or moonlight into its component colors. The result is the halo often seen ringing the sun or moon as cirrus clouds move in with an approaching warm front. Such halos are very wide and change in color from red at their inner ring to yellow to green to blue; they usually precede precipitation by 24 to 48 hours.

> A ring around the sun or moon suggests approaching rain or snow, especially if followed by thickening, lowering clouds.

Lenticular Clouds and Warm Fronts

Some reports of UFOs, though certainly not all, have actually been inspired by the type of cloud created by mountains (please do not contact the author with arguments supporting extraterrestrials). These *lenticular* clouds, so named because they are shaped like a lens, form when moist air moves up and over a mountain peak. Such lenticular clouds

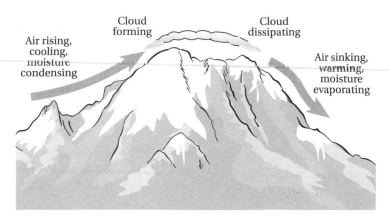

Cloud forming

Cloud dissipating

Air rising, cooling, moisture condensing

Air sinking, warming, moisture evaporating

The formation and dissipation of lenticular, or cap clouds, over mountain peaks

are particularly common over the largest peaks, especially over volcanic peaks such as Mount Rainier and Mount Hood in the Pacific Northwest, Mount Shasta in California, and Mount McKinley in Alaska. Such clouds are often hints that a weather disturbance is nearby and that a warm front may be approaching.

Lenticular clouds form when moisture high in the atmosphere runs into a major peak and is deflected upward. As that moist air rises, it cools sufficiently to condense into a cloud. As it passes over the peak and begins descending, it warms and the water droplets or ice crystals that make up the lenticular cloud evaporate. Although lenticulars ap pear to be stationary, they are continually dissipating on the leeward edge. If followed by cirrus and eventually stratus clouds, lenticulars often give mountain travelers 24 to 48 hours notice of precipitation. Native Americans in the Pacific Northwest used to say "When Mount Rainier wears a hat, rain is likely to soon follow."

Lee-Wave Clouds

Mountain travelers occasionally see what looks like a corduroy sky: stripes of clouds running parallel to and beyond a mountain range. The up and down motion of air traveling over a mountain peak or range occasionally continues well downwind of the range, much like the ripples produced by a rock thrown into a pond. This results in a series of clouds forming and dissipating as the air rises and falls in a wavelike fashion.

Such clouds are called *lee-wave clouds* and can stretch for hundreds of miles downwind of the mountain barrier. Because these clouds form to the lee side of mountain ranges, and prevailing winds aloft in the

The formation of lee-wave clouds downwind of a peak or ridge

mid-latitudes typically move from west to east, they are most frequently found to the east of the Vancouver Island, Cascade, and Coast Ranges in the Pacific Northwest, the Sierras in California, the Rockies in both western Canada and the United States, and the Appalachians in the eastern United States. If the alignment of the cloud and the sun is oriented in a certain way, wave clouds are often tinted in beautiful, iridescent colors.

Stratus Clouds and Warm Fronts

As a warm front advances, the boundary between the warm air and the cooler air below gradually lowers closer to the ground. More moisture is available at the warmer temperatures closer to sea level and thicker clouds form: sheetlike *altostratus clouds* ranging in altitude from 20,000 to as little as 6000 feet (6100 to 1800 meters) above sea level and, eventually, thick blanketlike layers of *stratus clouds* ranging in thickness from a few hundred feet to several thousand feet.

A circular "rainbow," similar to the halo seen as cirrus clouds approach, often rings the sun or moon through altostratus clouds. This is called a *corona*, and it hugs the sun or moon much more closely than a halo. For that reason, while halos tend to indicate that precipitation is at least 24 hours distant, coronas usually suggest imminent precipitation: Begin seeking shelter now!

The flatness of these stratiform clouds is a consequence of what meteorologists call *stability:* the resistance of air to some force that is attempting to push it upward. Stable air tends to spread out in a flat layer; unstable air tends to balloon upward, like the bubbles in a pot of boiling water. When air cools very slowly with increasing altitude, or when warm air actually overlies cooler air near the surface, as in a warm front, the air mass is very stable. The result is often a thick, flat sheet of stratus clouds that may stretch from hundreds of miles offshore over the Pacific Ocean to well inland over the Rockies, to give just one example.

Under these circumstances expect steady, widespread precipitation. (Mountain travelers must remember these are general guidelines and, depending upon the orientation of the mountains, may not always hold true. However, if most of the above clues are present, the conditions certainly favor the arrival of a warm front.)

CLUES THAT A WARM FRONT IS APPROACHING

- Look for approaching high clouds (cirrus), typically from the southwest, west or northwest.
- Look for flat, sheetlike clouds (stratus).
- Look for thickening, lowering clouds.
- Look for surface winds from the east to southeast.
- Look for a decrease in air pressure.
- Look for an increase in air temperature.

Warm Fronts and Precipitation

There are no absolute rules for determining whether a warm front will produce rain or snow. For one thing, snow is hardly limited to winter months. Snow can fall any month of the year in the mountains, depending upon elevation.

As a rule of thumb, assume precipitation will fall and remain as snow (even though it may not stick to the ground) down to approximately 1000 feet (about 300 meters) below the *freezing level*—the elevation or altitude at which the air temperature drops to or below freezing. Current and forecast freezing levels can be obtained from National Oceanic and Atmospheric Administration (NOAA) Weather Radio and websites, avalanche hotlines, and web pages, as well as some television and radio broadcasts and newspapers. The Meteorological Service of Canada provides similar information, as do the meteorological services of other countries. Chapter 7 presents additional sources of weather information and pre-trip weather briefings.

It is important to remember that the freezing level reported or forecast is usually the free-air freezing level—that is, the level at which air temperatures drop to or below freezing if not influenced by terrain effects. Examples of terrain effects that can affect freezing level include trapped cold air in valleys and heating of slopes by sunshine.

For example, suppose that NOAA Weather Radio (NWR) reports the freezing level is at 4000 feet (roughly 1500 meters). You are camped at 3000 feet on Oregon's Mount Hood under a sky of dense, gray clouds that have moved in recently. In this case, the precipitation is likely to begin as snow. (As mentioned, this is a rough rule of thumb that can be affected by a variety of local factors.) A locally heavy shower, for example, can lower the snow level as much as 1500 to 2000 feet (roughly 490 to 610 meters) below the free-air freezing level, because moderate to heavy precipitation can drag cold air farther from the base of the cloud. Such showers are more likely near cold fronts than warm fronts (see Cold Fronts, Clouds, and Precipitation).

A second point is that although precipitation associated with approaching warm fronts tends to be widespread, its distribution is uneven. University of Washington researchers have determined that precipitation tends to be clumped in cigar-shaped bands parallel to a warm front. These bands tend to range in width from 5 to 20 miles (8 to 32 kilometers). Therefore, the precipitation from a warm front will vary with time. Even a slow-moving, wet warm front will be marked by occasional decreases in precipitation, if not outright breaks.

Rain and snow are not the only forms of precipitation produced

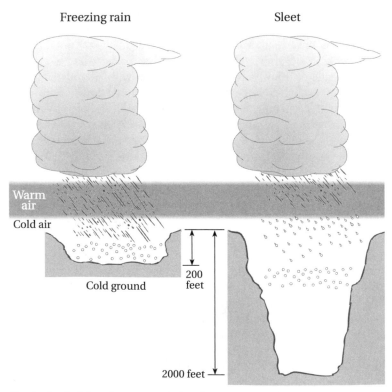

The depth of cold air determines whether freezing rain or sleet occurs.

by warm fronts, especially in the mountains. If the air beneath is below freezing and the overlying air is warm enough to produce rain, the warm front can produce either freezing rain or sleet. If the layer of cold air is shallow, freezing rain is most likely because the precipitation will tend to freeze on contact with the ground. A thicker cold air layer is more likely to produce sleet, because the precipitation will be more likely to freeze before it nears the ground.

If, for example, you are snowshoeing in a valley with below-freezing temperatures and the forecast freezing level is not much more than 2000 feet (about 600 meters) above your elevation, then freezing rain is most likely to glaze over everything exposed to the elements. However, if the valley and nearby passes are all below freezing, the cold air layer will probably be thick enough that rain falling from the warmer air aloft will probably freeze long before it hits the ground (and you). The result will be an uncomfortable pelting with sleet.

The Never-Never Land between Warm and Cold Fronts

Perhaps you have spent a morning (or longer) trapped in a tent by precipitation from a passing warm front. Eventually, the precipitation tapers off and the clouds thin, possibly revealing streaks of blue sky. The air still feels relatively warm and moist. You are in the never-never land between warm and cold fronts, an area called the *warm sector.* Despite the clearing (what pilots occasionally refer to as "sucker holes"), the potential for rain remains great, along with the possibility of thunderstorms.

Inland mountain ranges, such as the Rockies or Appalachians, often see more massive cloud buildups, a more definite break in precipitation, and some clearing (albeit hazy) between warm and cold front passage, or at times only high clouds. Coastal ranges—such as the Cascades and Sierras in the United States and the Vancouver Island and Coast Ranges in Canada—usually experience a fairly brief interval between warm and cold fronts, often marked by an accelerated drop in pressure and renewed precipitation.

Whatever your location, this is a time to be especially observant. Watch for a "mackerel sky," so-called because it resembles the scales on a fish. These high-based cumulus clouds suggest the potential for rain shower or thundershower development. If they begin to expand, look for cover. The same is true if lower cumulus clouds appear. Squall lines typically move out from cold fronts in the warm sector, producing very gusty winds. Look for a solid line of very dark clouds with gusty winds often kicking up dust in advance of them. These thunderstorms can be intense and dangerous.

Cold Fronts, Clouds, and Precipitation

As a cold front approaches, cold air streaming down the backside of an approaching low collides with the warm, moist air, abruptly thrusting it upward. If warm fronts are the turtles of the meteorological world, moving slowly but steadily, cold fronts are the jackrabbits.

Cumulus Clouds and Cold Fronts

The approaching cold air behind the front is much more dense than the warmer air ahead, so the push upward can be very strong and fast, exceeding 20 miles per hour (32 kilometers/hour). The result is not layered clouds but a line of towering cumulus clouds.

When such clouds produce precipitation or thunder and lightning, we call them *cumulo-nimbus clouds*. These can extend as much as 50,000 feet (15,240 meters) above Earth's surface. However, along the Pacific coast of both the United States and Canada, where approaching cold air has usually been warmed by its passage over the Pacific Ocean, the temperature contrast between the approaching cold air and the warm air already in place is not as great. As a result, the cumulo-nimbus clouds do not grow quite as tall. A more common maximum height along the Pacific coast is 20,000 to 30,000 feet (6100 to 9100 meters), particularly to the west of the Coast Mountains of Canada and the Cascades and Sierras of the United States.

The exceptions to the rule of quick cold-front passage tend to occur when the cold front is sliding parallel to a mountain range, typically with south to southwesterly winds in the upper atmosphere. Again, this tends to be most frequent along or near the Pacific coast.

CLUES THAT A COLD FRONT IS APPROACHING

- A warm front is followed by brief clearing, or a decrease or end to precipitation.
- Clouds thicken, lower, merge, and darken.
- Winds increase, usually from the east or southeast, depending upon mountain orientation.
- Air pressure begins to drop, usually rapidly.

Under these circumstances, expect intensified precipitation with the front, colder temperatures after it moves through, and a wind shift to the southwest or west—again depending upon mountain orientation.

Cold Fronts and Precipitation

As the University of Washington research team had found along warm fronts, precipitation ahead of and along cold fronts also tends to be organized in cigar-shaped bands parallel to the front. This precipitation tends to be more intense because of the rapid upward movement of the moist air ahead of and along the cold front.

The upward movement is usually ten to a hundred times more rapid than along a warm front. Whereas warm-front precipitation tends to be prolonged, however, often lasting as long as a day, cold-front precipitation is much more brief, due to the front's more rapid movement. Precipitation associated with a cold front generally lasts only an hour or two.

Although the snow level usually extends only 1000 feet (approximately 300 meters) below the freezing level when stratus clouds are producing the precipitation, cumulus clouds may drive the snow level as far as 2000 feet (approximately 600 meters) below the freezing level in heavy showers, especially after the cold front has passed.

Serious to severe thunderstorms are sometimes associated with the approach and arrival of cold fronts. This is especially true of inland ranges such as the Rockies, where very cold, dry air from the Arctic or sub-Arctic regions slides southward through Canada and into the United States. Along and near the Pacific Coast ranges, the proximity of the Pacific Ocean moderates temperature contrasts; that is why thunderstorms tend to follow cold fronts, instead of preceding or accompanying them. Such coastal areas tend to receive their heaviest precipitation after cold front passage. The areas that receive precipitation can be widespread

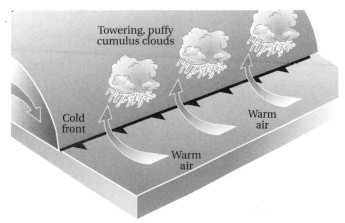

Air moves along a cold front, resulting in thick cumulus clouds and more intense precipitation.

or very localized, depending on the delicate interplay of terrain features and wind. The following chapters on thunderstorms and regional weather patterns present this in greater detail.

Occluded Fronts and Precipitation

An important variation on warm and cold fronts is the *occluded front*. Because of the sandwiching of cold and warm air, an occluded front

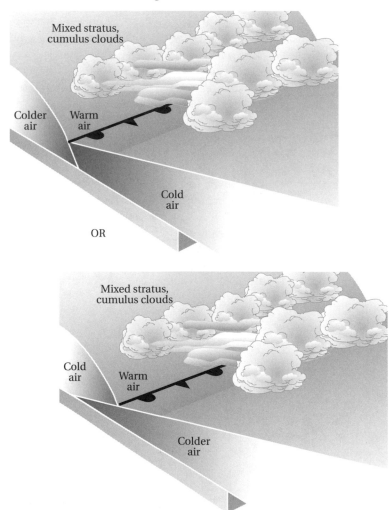

The structure of two different types of occluded fronts: one in which the coldest air is in the back and one in which the coldest air is in front

combines the precipitation characteristics of both warm and cold fronts.

If you are experiencing prolonged rain or snowfall with occasional strong bursts and, possibly, thunder and lightning, an occluded front is the most likely culprit. Depending upon the direction of movement of the overall weather system, the passage of occluded fronts, like that of cold fronts, is usually much more rapid than that of warm fronts.

Stationary Fronts and Precipitation

Stationary fronts are exactly what their name implies: stationary. The boundary between cold air and warm air is not moving much, if at all, and the result is prolonged precipitation. If it is good weather you are after, avoid areas where stationary fronts exist or are forecast. Chapters 3 and 5 explore this topic further.

Fog

Route finding is rarely easy in the mountains, and fog can make it next to impossible. The potential for danger rises sharply for mountain travelers navigating rugged trails or glaciers seamed with crevasses, where the boundary between sky and snow is indistinct. As temperatures dip below freezing, rock wrapped in fog's silent embrace can ice up with astonishing speed.

Fog takes five primary forms: radiation, advection, warm frontal, upslope, and ice fog. Before exploring the subtleties of each, it makes good sense to understand the fundamentals common to all.

The example of seeing your breath on a cold day is again useful. To review: As we inhale air, it warms close to our body's normal temperature of 98.6°F (37°C) and is moistened by the water that pervades our body. As we exhale, that warm, moist air is rapidly cooled to the environmental temperature and may condense from water vapor (a gas) to water droplets (a liquid) just as steam from the shower condenses on a cold bathroom mirror. The result is a cloud in front of your face—or, when water vapor condenses from cooling at ground level in the atmosphere, fog.

Radiation Fog

Radiation fog is most common during the autumn and winter months and usually follows wet weather.

Perhaps rain fell during your drive to the trailhead, followed by nighttime clearing that revealed a dazzling, star-filled sky. You are surprised to awaken to dense fog the next morning, possibly with light drizzle beading on your tent fly or on your forehead as you look outside.

Then, after breaking camp and climbing to a peak overlooking your campsite, you notice the gray fog gradually brightens, the sun first appearing as a fuzzy disk of light, then a dazzling yellow as you emerge from the fog layer. In the mountains, 500 to 1000 feet (150 to 300 meters) down the trail or up a ridge can produce dramatically different weather.

Radiation fog is produced when damp ground (often saturated by rain or melting snow) loses some of its moisture through evaporation to the lowest layer of the atmosphere. As the disturbance that produced at least some of that moisture passes, the clouds clear. Overnight, considerable heat is lost by the ground to the cooler atmosphere above. The moist air close to the wet ground cools and condenses into a layer of fog. Because the cooling and condensation that produce this fog occurs when heat rises, or radiates, from the surface, it is called radiation fog.

Rain falls, saturates ground

Radiation fog is especially common in valleys and cirques, because cold air tends to drain downslope, hastening the cooling and condensation of the moist air below. It is occasionally rather thin, often only several hundred feet (perhaps 100 meters or so) deep. Even when radiation fog is thicker than that, it typically burns off by midafternoon, then progressively earlier each day. However, if a trail is shaded by tall trees or steep slopes, the evaporation of the fog will be slowed or prevented.

Warm air rises, radiates away from ground at night with clearing

The same is true if the moist air is trapped beneath a layer of warmer air. Meteorologists call this situation an *inversion* because

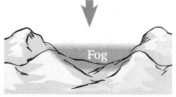

Moist air near ground cools, condenses into fog

The typical formation of radiation fog

the normal pattern of cooler air aloft is reversed, or inverted. This typically occurs when high pressure settles over an area; the sinking air within the high results in a warmer layer just above the cool, moist air near the ground.

CLUES FOR RADIATION FOG

- The ground is moist from rain or melting snow.
- Skies clear, allowing extensive cooling overnight, especially in late autumn to early spring, when nights are long.
- Winds are light, generally 5 knots or less.

Advection Fog
While radiation fog is most common during the months when nights are long, *advection fog* is most common during the summer months, particularly along the mountains of the west coast of the United States and Canada. Rare is the person who has not seen photographs of the Golden Gate Bridge extending above a fog bank obscuring San Francisco Bay.

Advection fog typically forms as moist ocean air moves from an area with warmer water temperatures to an area with cooler water

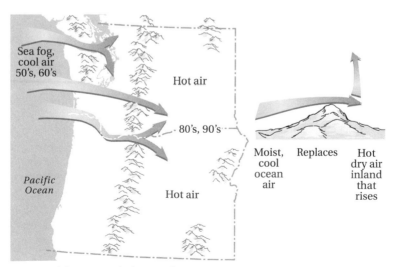

The typical formation of advection fog

temperatures. This horizontal movement is referred to as *advection*. Such fog banks are commonly seen on certain daytime satellite photographs taken along the West Coast. During the summer, daytime air temperatures are considerably warmer over land than are ocean water temperatures just offshore, often by 30°F (15°C) or more. As the air over land is warmed by the sun and rises, the fog bank along the coast moves inland. If fog has not already formed, the cooler, more moist ocean air moves inland to replace the rising air warmed by the ground. As the air temperature drops at night, the moist ocean air condenses into fog or a low layer of flat stratus clouds over land.

Such advection fog typically develops shortly before sunrise, moving inland as the land heats up, blanketing the western slopes of coastal ranges such as Canada's Coast Mountains, the Cascades of Washington and Oregon, and California's Sierra Nevada. Such advection fog can be as thick as 5000 to 6000 feet (approximately 1500 to 1800 meters), but it is often thinner. Such fog, or stratus, rarely crosses the crests of these ranges, so knowledgeable sunseekers often choose destinations along the east slopes.

Advection fog, like other weather phenomena, rarely moves in without warning, although the clues can be subtle. The indications to watch for are shown in chronological order in Clues for Advection Fog.

CLUES FOR ADVECTION FOG

- Hot weather is present in the interior valleys just west of the major West Coast ranges.
- Fog becomes evident along the coast or just offshore on satellite images.
- The direction of surface winds shifts onshore.

Marine advisories or warnings can be valuable aids in gauging how thick the fog or low stratus layer is likely to be in the mountains, since such alerts reflect the expected strength of the push of ocean air into the interior. Remember, wind speeds are given in knots (1 knot = 1.15 statute miles per hour = 1.85 kilometers per hour), and the wind direction must be onshore to drive the moist ocean air inland.

MARINE ADVISORIES/ADVECTION FOG GUIDELINES

Advisory Type	Fog/Stratus Depth	Precipitation	Likely Burnoff Time
None (10–25 knots)	1000–2000 feet/ 300–600 meters	Less Likely	Afternoon
Small Craft	2000–4000 feet/ 600–1200 meters	Drizzle Possible	Late Afternoon
Gale Warning	4000+ feet/ 1200+ meters	Drizzle/Rain	Next Day

The thickness of the advection fog or stratus layer, as the preceding table illustrates, offers clues as to how soon it may burn off. If the layer is more than 2000 feet thick (600 meters), it may not clear at all the first day, perhaps not until midafternoon on the second day, and then progressively earlier after that. Incidentally, southwesterly winds along the West Coast will tend to thicken fog layers while northwesterly winds will tend to thin them.

Warm Frontal or Precipitation Fog

Radiation fog and advection fog offer hikers, climbers, skiers, snowboarders, and the like some definite options. Head to the eastern slopes of the West Coast ranges to escape advection fog; move higher to escape radiation fog and, occasionally, advection fog. The third type of fog offers no such option, short of heading for another part of the country. *Warm frontal fog* covers a large geographic area and is produced when precipitation falls from warm air aloft into cooler air near the surface. The precipitation saturates the cool air, which then condenses into a thick layer of fog.

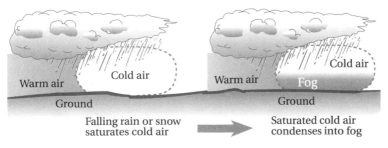

The formation of warm frontal fog

Unlike other varieties, warm frontal fog is unlikely to burn off during the day. It disappears only after the warm front shifts through, bringing an end to the contrast between the warm, moist air aloft, the colder air near the ground, and the precipitation formed by this process. Along the Rockies and the Appalachians, such fogs can persist for days during winter, often followed by freezing rain or drizzle as the layer of cold air near the ground thins. Along the West Coast, the duration of warm frontal fog is much shorter, simply because warm fronts tend to move through more quickly and because the contrast between the warm air aloft and the cooler air near the surface is not as great.

CLUES SUGGESTING WARM FRONTAL FOG

- Flat stratus clouds arrive, gradually lowering and thickening.
- Surface winds shift to the east or southeast.
- Precipitation develops and becomes steady.
- Small clouds develop close to the ground with a shredded or torn appearance.

Upslope Fog

The difference between the impact of fog and low clouds can be an important one in the mountains. Wind speed is usually the determining factor, as wind mixes some of the moist air near the ground with cooler, drier air aloft. That "lifts" the fog into a layer of flat stratus clouds, or evaporates it altogether. Wind speeds of 5 knots or less are most conducive to fog formation; wind speeds greater than 5 knots usually lead to the formation of stratus clouds. However, moisture

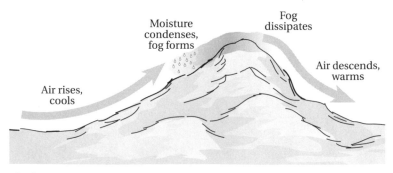

The formation of upslope fog on windward slopes and ridge crests

moving upslope can develop thick fog with wind speeds of up to 10 knots (11.5 miles per hour or 18.5 kilometers per hour). Such fogs develop because the moist air cools and condenses as it ascends a slope. Look for such *upslope fog* to develop along the western slopes of a mountain range with a moist west wind, or along the eastern slopes with a warm easterly wind, particularly during winter after a thaw has melted snow, saturating the air with moisture. Such upslope winds can also thicken advection fog that has moved inland to mountain ranges.

Ice Fog

The fifth type of fog is less common than the four already discussed. *Ice fog* is chiefly found in Canada and Alaska, though it can certainly develop in or near the northern Rockies and also in Maine, Vermont, and New Hampshire following the arrival of frigid Arctic air. Composed of suspended ice crystals, ice fog is rare at temperatures warmer than −20°F (−29°C). However, it becomes progressively more common at colder temperatures near a source of fast-moving unfrozen water or a herd of animals such as elk or caribou supplying moisture as they exhale. Ice fog is usually very localized but can be very dense. I saw spectacular examples of ice fog in the Yukon one February—spectacular but best enjoyed from indoors with a warm beverage since the outside air temperature was pushing −40°F!

One weather hazard deserves a chapter—or two—of its own. That hazard is thunderstorms, and it is explored in depth in the following chapter.

Mountain Thunderstorms 101

It turned out badly. From an inky sky heavy rain pelted down upon us. Between repeated thunderclaps lightning struck very close, blinding us with its dazzling, dread glare and hurting our eyes. We were drenched to the skin, cold to the marrow. Bernard looked at his watch: it was six o'clock. Another bivouac on the face!

Gaston Rebuffat, *Starlight and Storm*

Clear skies and light winds are almost guaranteed to bring rainbow-hued hot air balloons to the Sammamish River Valley east of Seattle. Each crew first stretches out its brightly colored fabric balloon on the grassy field, then directs a fan into the balloon opening to inflate it. Only after the caramel-colored wicker basket is securely tethered to the ground do the crews light the burners. The air inside the balloon warms and expands, its buoyancy gently lifting the basket as far as the tethers allow. Once the passengers and pilot are safely inside, the straining ground tethers are released and the now stately balloon soars upward. The pilot fires the burner periodically to keep the air inside the balloon warmer and less dense than the air outside. As long as the air inside is warmer than the air outside, the balloon remains buoyant and keeps rising. Once the air inside the balloon cools, it stops rising and will eventually descend. In practice, the pilot can also make the balloon descend by releasing some of the air through vents in the top.

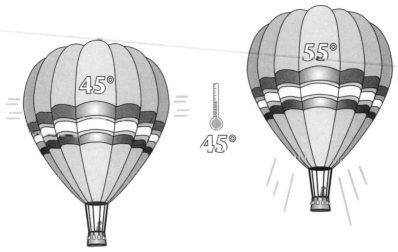

Air temperature inside balloon equals outside air temperature—balloon stops rising

Air temperature inside balloon warmer than outside air temperature—balloon keeps rising

Differences in air temperatures inside and outside of a hot air balloon determine whether it rises or remains at the same altitude.

The principle behind the operation of hot air balloons is also at work in the atmosphere, particularly in the most common type of thunderstorm found in the mountains: the *air mass* or *"popcorn" thunderstorm*. Thunderstorms develop when moist air is lifted, which happens when a large change in temperature occurs with height. Heating the air near the ground is one way to make that moist air rise; cooling the air higher up in the atmosphere is another. When you understand how air mass thunderstorms develop, you have the foundation for understanding the range of thunderstorm types and hazards.

If the air near the ground is heated enough, it will begin to rise. If an air mass thunderstorm is the atmosphere's equivalent of a hot air balloon, the sun's heating of the ground, along with the return of some of that heat to the air above, is equivalent to turning up the burner. Open fields heat up more rapidly than forest or water, and rocky slopes heat up faster than ground covered by vegetation. We know from experience that walking barefoot on grass on a hot day is far more comfortable than walking barefoot on stone or pavement. Hot air balloon pilots know that too; if they drift over bare pavement, they will get a little boost upward, but if they drift over water or forest, they will likely descend. We see this process of lifting and sinking, called *convection*,

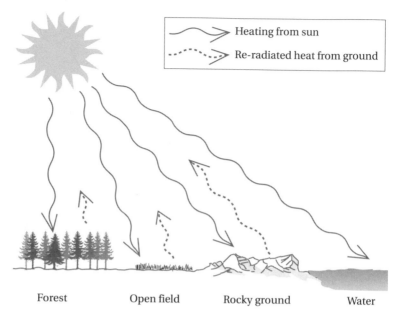

Forest　　　　Open field　　　Rocky ground　　　　Water

Various ground surfaces absorb heat, warming at different rates. This results in different rates of warming of the air above those surfaces.

whenever we heat soup in a pot. The soup over the burner heats first and rises to the top of the pot. As it spreads out toward the cooler sides, it descends toward the bottom.

Convection is the process that fuels thunderstorms, but with air and water vapor instead of broth and noodles. You may not see the water vapor, but it is there. Calling to mind an imaginary flight in a hot air balloon, if you soared high enough and the surrounding air became cool enough, you would see your breath when you exhaled. The water vapor in your breath would cool and change into liquid water droplets, a process called *condensation* (see the illustration on page 29). Whenever we find that it is cold enough to see our breath, we are actually seeing water vapor condense into a small cloud of water droplets. When water vapor cools and condenses into liquid water droplets, it gives off heat; thus condensation actually adds heat to air, which helps it rise. The process is akin to opening the burner a little more in a hot air balloon.

The transformation of the air's water vapor from a gas to a liquid does not always happen at the same temperature. Rather, that depends upon how much water vapor is already mixed in with the other gases that make up the air. As previously noted, the temperature at which water vapor will begin condensing into liquid water is called the *dew point*. If the dew point of the air is 55°F (approximately 12°C), water vapor will condense into liquid water droplets when the actual air temperature cools to 55°F. We say the air is *saturated* when it cools to the dew point.

If a lot of water vapor is mixed into the air, the dew point will be relatively high; dew points in the 70s are not unusual in the tropics. If the amount of water vapor in the air is a bit less, the dew point will be lower, perhaps in the 40s or 50s. This is common in the Rockies during the summer. Desert regions (such as Death Valley, California) can have dew points in single digits, and dew points are commonly below zero in the Arctic or Antarctic—that is, the temperature would have to cool to below zero for condensation to occur. Whatever the dew point, unless the air temperature cools to that temperature, condensation will not occur and clouds will not form. As you may suspect, warmer air has a greater capacity to hold moisture.

Relative humidity, as noted in Chapter 2 (see the illustration on page 30), is a term commonly used on broadcast weather reports and forecasts. It is a comparison of how much water vapor the air is holding (measured by the dew point) and what it is capable of holding (indicated by the actual air temperature). Relative humidity is reported as a percentage: the water vapor the air is holding as a percentage of what it is capable of holding.

If rising air does cool to the dew point, and relative humidity reaches 100 percent, the water vapor will condense into microscopic liquid water cloud droplets, thinner in diameter than a human hair. The rising air, or thermal, carries these miniscule cloud droplets until its temperature cools to that of the air around it and stops rising. Sometimes that happens in less than 1000 feet, and the result is called *fair-weather cumulus:* pretty to look at, but no rain falls from them. The droplets never grow large enough and heavy enough to fall through the rising updrafts of the thermal. Such cumulus clouds are fleecy with flat bottoms and gently mounded tops. Their bottoms are flat because the water vapor in the rising air begins to condense at the very elevation where the air temperature cools to the dew point. Meteorologists call this level the *lifting condensation level:* It is where water vapor in the air lifted by heating or other methods will begin to condense into liquid water droplets.

However, if the rising air remains warmer than what surrounds it and continues to rise, a sort of aerial game of pinball begins: The cloud droplets move up, down, and sideways in a turbulent movement of air within the growing cumulus cloud—just like the little

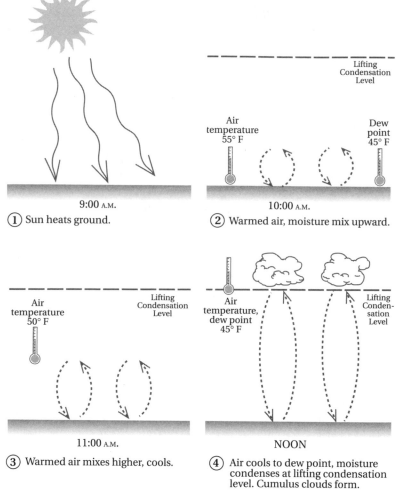

9:00 A.M.
① Sun heats ground.

10:00 A.M.
② Warmed air, moisture mix upward.

Air temperature 55° F

Dew point 45° F

Lifting Condensation Level

11:00 A.M.
③ Warmed air mixes higher, cools.

Air temperature 50° F

Lifting Condensation Level

NOON
④ Air cools to dew point, moisture condenses at lifting condensation level. Cumulus clouds form.

Air temperature, dew point 45° F

Lifting Condensation Level

The formation of fair weather cumulus clouds

balls in an arcade pinball game—which is why flying through such clouds can be so uncomfortable. The little droplets bounce off other droplets and occasionally stick to make bigger droplets, or they fall into drier air and evaporate. The cloud begins to resemble an oversized head of cauliflower, but such growing cumulus clouds are not made up entirely of water droplets. Because not all of the water vapor condenses right away, some is carried high enough and cools enough that it freezes. Some of the water vapor condenses into tiny water droplets, and then it freezes. It may come as a surprise that does not automatically happen when the water cools to freezing. In fact, water will not freeze on its own until it cools to roughly −40°F (also −40°C). That may seem difficult to believe because we all have seen frost form shortly after the air temperature drops to freezing. However, when water freezes at these "warmer" temperatures, it has the assistance of grit or particles called *ice nuclei*.

Ice nuclei can be thought of as helpers in the freezing process. They can be made of dust, volcanic ash, clay, or any number of other substances. They are all around us in the air, as well as high in the atmosphere. The more closely one of these particles mimics a real ice crystal, the faster an ice crystal will form on it. Sometimes a droplet wraps around such a particle like a slush ball, which helps jump-start freezing. At other times, ice crystals form shortly after a water droplet touches an ice nuclei. This is called *deposition*. Whichever process takes place, it requires both the time and the opportunity for either water vapor or droplets to meet up with one of these ice nuclei. That is why you do not automatically find ice crystals in the cloud where the air temperature is 32°F (0°C). Water droplets that exist at temperatures below freezing are called *super-cooled droplets*. Eventually ice crystals will form if the cumulus cloud keeps growing upward. As that happens, the cloud eventually meets a stable layer of air called the *tropopause*, which suppresses the rising motion. Then the powerful winds aloft will begin blowing some of the airy ice crystals ahead of the cloud, forming a distinctive flat-topped *anvil*.

The pinball motion of cloud droplets and ice crystals produces bigger and bigger raindrops and snowflakes. Eventually the droplets and crystals grow large enough to fall through or around the rising air of updrafts. However, it is not a steady process. Often a snowflake falls and melts, only to get caught up in another updraft and refreeze. This process can continue several times, with frozen water droplets picking up moisture on the way up and freezing again on the way down. The result is an *ice pellet* or *hailstone*, layered with growth rings, similar in form to those found in trees. Officially, the result is called an *ice pellet* until it reaches the size of a pea, about 0.25 inches or 5 millimeters; after that, it is called a *hailstone*, which can get as big as a softball (and sometimes bigger!). The biggest hailstone found in the United States as of this writing fell in Potter, Nebraska, in 1928: It measured 17.5 inches in circumference (44.5 centimeters) and weighed 1.5 pounds (0.7 kilograms)!

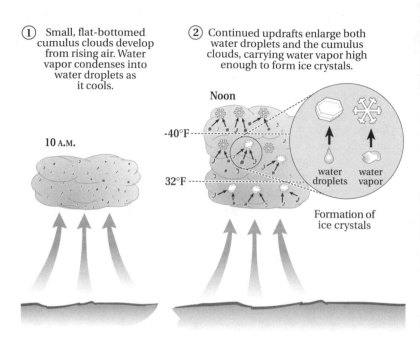

① Small, flat-bottomed cumulus clouds develop from rising air. Water vapor condenses into water droplets as it cools.

② Continued updrafts enlarge both water droplets and the cumulus clouds, carrying water vapor high enough to form ice crystals.

Noon

10 A.M.

-40°F

32°F

water droplets   water vapor

Formation of ice crystals

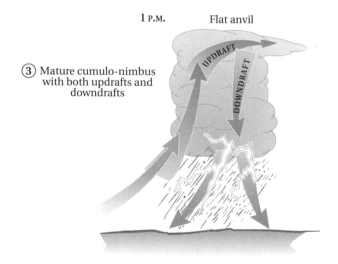

1 P.M.   Flat anvil

③ Mature cumulo-nimbus with both updrafts and downdrafts

UPDRAFT

DOWNDRAFT

The development of cumulus clouds into cumulo-nimbus clouds may produce thunder and lightning

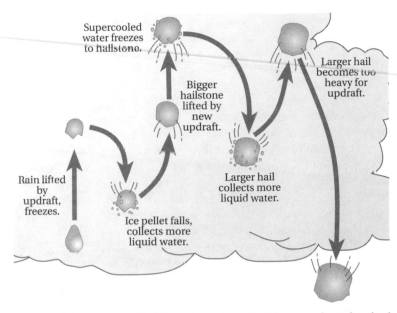

Supercooled water freezes to hailstone.

Bigger hailstone lifted by new updraft.

Larger hail becomes too heavy for updraft.

Rain lifted by updraft, freezes.

Ice pellet falls, collects more liquid water.

Larger hail collects more liquid water.

The up-and-down journey of hail formation and growth within a cumulo-nimbus cloud

Hail on the ground following a thunderstorm (photo courtesy of NOAA)

The same pinball motion that builds bigger raindrops, ice pellets, and hailstones can also create lightning. Think back to a cold, dry day. As you walked across a carpet, perhaps you scuffed your feet a little. You reached for the doorknob, but before you could even touch it—zap!— an electric charge sparked across the gap and gave you a painful shock. Some children even make a game of scuffing their feet, trying to give each other shocks. Outside of the pain (and perhaps some fiendish delight), what is going on?

As you scuff your feet along the floor, you are separating the electrical charges. Each quarter-inch of spark that jumps from the doorknob to your finger produces a 10,000-volt difference in charge, which is what scientists call *electrical potential*. The turbulence within the cloud also helps separate electrical charges, but on a much bigger scale.

The updrafts and downdrafts within a building thunderstorm may vary in speed from a few feet per second to as much as 100 miles per hour. The vast scale of the pinball game within the cloud sorts out different-sized particles that carry different electrical charges. The heavier particles carry negative charges toward the base of the cloud, while the updrafts carry the smaller, lighter particles with positive charges to the upper part of the cloud. That is how one popular theory explains why much of the upper part of a thunderstorm becomes positively charged and much of the base becomes negatively charged. Earth's surface also tends to be negatively charged. Because like charges repel each other (think of trying to put the negative ends of two magnets together), the negative charges near the base of the cloud tend to push away the negative charges on the ground, leaving a positive charge. Some of that positive charge flows up large objects, such as mountain peaks and towers—even people. That is why your hair can stand on end if you are close to a thunderstorm. Those positive charges are blocked from continuing to flow up into the thunderstorm because the air tends to hinder, not help, the flow of electricity. That tendency is called *resistance*.

Consider the buildup of negative charges within the lower part of the cloud to be like water collecting behind a dam. As the pressure builds (in this case, the electrical potential, or voltage), eventually the dam (the natural resistance of the air) cannot hold back all the negative charges, so some flow toward the ground. They do not move in one vast flood: If they did, it would eclipse any special effect ever conceived in Hollywood.

The negative charges move haltingly downward in what is called a *stepped leader,* typically about as thick as a pencil. As the stepped leader

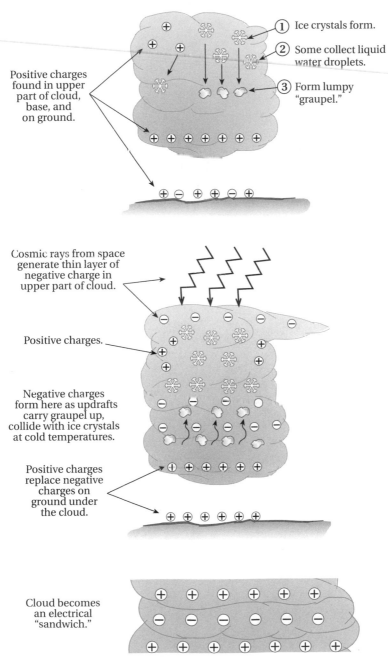

The separation of electrical charges within a growing cumulus cloud

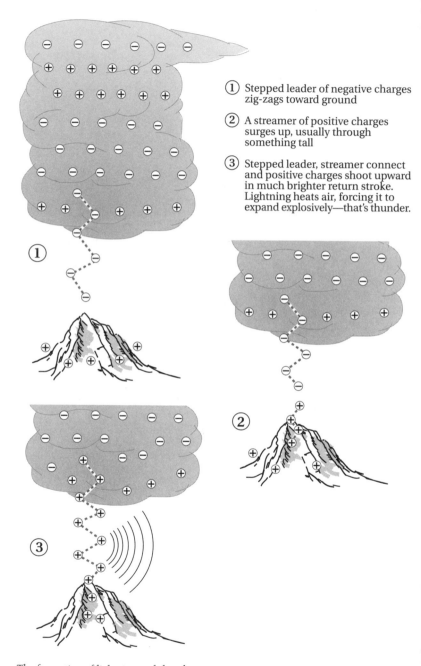

① Stepped leader of negative charges zig-zags toward ground

② A streamer of positive charges surges up, usually through something tall

③ Stepped leader, streamer connect and positive charges shoot upward in much brighter return stroke. Lightning heats air, forcing it to expand explosively—that's thunder.

The formation of lightning and thunder

approaches the ground, it attracts the positive charges, which typically move up something tall, like a tree or rocky pinnacle, in what is called a *streamer*. As the leader connects to the streamer, a flood of positive charges surges back up into the cloud at about one-third the speed of light, in a much bigger and brighter return stroke. That is the actual lightning bolt we see. The immense flow of electricity superheats the surrounding air to as much as 50,000°F, far hotter than the surface of the sun. This heating sets off a shock wave that exceeds the speed of sound. The resulting sonic boom is *thunder*.

Once the stepped leader and streamer connect, several pulses of electricity can surge through the channel, producing repeated flashes. A single lightning bolt does not flicker: That comes from repeated flows in the same channel. Because the near speed-of-light movement of lightning is much faster than the speed of sound, we see the lightning first and then hear the thunder. That difference can be used to estimate the distance of the thunderstorm, and even its direction of movement (see Chapter 4).

The life cycle of one of these thunderstorms is typically less than an hour. Lightning can be a danger during the *developing stage* as the cloud builds upward. Very little rain falls then: Almost microscopic cloud droplets are being carried upward, colliding and enlarging, and ice crystals are beginning to form. Lightning is a major hazard during the *mature stage*, marked by both updrafts and downdrafts within the cloud. This stage produces heavy rain, hail, gusty winds, and lightning. However, even after the downdrafts choke out the updrafts and the storm enters the *dissipating stage* and begins to die, lightning remains a danger. What, you say, of the old story about a bolt out of nowhere? It is true. Lightning can strike objects as much as 10 miles (6+ kilometers) from the side of a massive thunderhead. Although these air mass thunderstorms typically last only 30 to 50 minutes, other thunderstorms do last much longer and move farther.

Air mass thunderstorms have a fairly predictable pattern: Puffy cumulus clouds develop in the morning, swell into towering cumulonimbus during the afternoon, then dissipate as the sun sets. That is the reason behind the climber's adage:

Move high in the morning, get low in the afternoon.

That is a good general principle. Such clouds are relatively easy to see, but anyone who has spent much time outdoors knows that many thunderstorms do not follow that pattern. No thunderstorm is to be taken lightly, especially in high country.

MOUNTAIN THUNDERSTORMS

Spend much time in the mountains, and you will become convinced that peaks and ridges can generate their own weather. It is true. The higher the peak, the more sparse the vegetation. As you now know, less vegetation

Some moist air carried upward by sun heating slopes, some by wind hitting windward slopes or ridges—develops into thunderstorm.

Moist air flows around isolated peak or local range, converges downwind, develops into thunderstorm.

Mountains influence where thunderstorms develop.

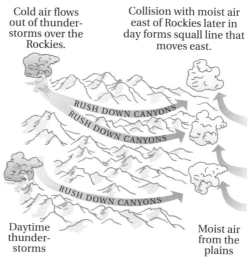

Thunderstorms over the Rockies can produce squall lines moving over the plains.

means more exposed soil and rock, and rock and gravelly soil heat up much more rapidly than ground covered with trees and plants. That heating generates thermals, which carry moisture upward and jump-start thunderstorms faster than would happen over less rugged and barren terrain.

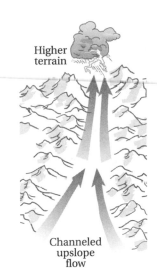

Thus the tendency is for such thunderstorms to develop during the afternoon hours, after the ground has been heating for a number of hours, causing moist air to rise; or because of cooling aloft. That certainly happens in the mountains, but that source of lifting can be amplified or replaced by another source: wind flowing against, up, and over either an iso-

Daytime heating and resulting up-valley winds can produce localized thunderstorms.

lated peak or an entire ridge. Along with the upslope flow already discussed, this is an *orographic effect.*

When such prevailing winds move against a mountain peak or ridge, they boost the natural tendency of thermals to carry moist air aloft, and can set off the convection that triggers thunderstorms. This influence also allows the thunderstorms to persist much longer, occasionally well after dark. The downslope winds on the leeward side tend to suppress thunderstorms. This might suggest that if you know the general direction of winds aloft, you can better anticipate on which side of a mountain ridge thunderstorms will tend to develop, but it is important to recognize that does not mean you will be safe from thunderstorms along the lee or downwind side of a peak or ridge. Winds can shift the thunderstorms farther downwind. Planning your climb or hike for the leeward side of a peak or ridge may improve your margin of safety, but you had better keep an eye out for evidence of thunderstorms drifting downwind. (See Chapter 5 for more information about such winds, whether you are at home or in the field.)

Winds moving around a peak or ridge can also converge on the downwind side. As those winds converge, the moist air often has no other direction to go than up, which can set off thundershowers. Such showers typically do not occur directly over the downwind slopes but rather at a distance downwind. This is called a *convergence zone.*

A SUMMARY OF MOUNTAIN THUNDERSTORMS

- Mountain thunderstorms are most frequent during the afternoon.
- Mountain thunderstorms are most frequent along the windward slopes, especially if cooler air has moved in and the sun is warming the slopes.
- Mountain thunderstorms may form downwind of individual peaks or small ranges in a convergence zone.

THUNDERSTORMS AND FRONTS

In summary, thunderstorms need moisture, something to lift that moisture, and air that cools enough with altitude so the moist air can keep rising. That tendency is called *instability*, a condition that usually exists when much cooler air lies on top of warmer air. That is what helps hot air balloons rise.

In air mass thunderstorms, either the heating of moist air near the ground or the cooling of air higher up provides that initial boost. *Orographic thunderstorms* happen either with the heating of moist air near the ground that then rises as thermals develop along hills or mountains, or with the forced lifting of moist air by wind moving against and up a mountain. Still another way to force moist air to rise enough to produce a thunderstorm occurs when two different types of air masses collide, such as along a front.

Let's review the four types of fronts discussed in Chapter 2. A *warm front* is a boundary where warm air is replacing colder air. A *cold front* is a boundary where cold air is replacing warmer air. A *stationary front* is a boundary between warm and cold air that is not moving much at all. An *occluded front* combines the qualities of warm and cold fronts and forces warm air up when two colder air masses collide. Remember that fronts do not exist only at Earth's surface: They also extend up into the atmosphere. When cool air meets warmer air, the warmer air rises because it is less dense and lighter. That warm air carries the moisture needed to create clouds and sometimes thunderstorms.

Along a warm front, the warm air gradually slides up and over the colder air that it is replacing. This is a stable situation that rarely leads to the rapid and sustained lifting needed to produce a thunderstorm. That is why flat, stratus clouds with widespread precipitation are typically found along and especially ahead of a warm front. Once a warm front moves through, though, thunderstorms are a distinct possibility.

A cold front, on the other hand, behaves like a snowplow: It rapidly boosts upward the warmer and often moist air ahead of it. This kind of lifting can easily produce thunderstorms and often does, and it is why towering cumulus clouds are typically found along a cold front. Although fronts can be difficult to track through mountainous regions—as air that is already converging and rising along a front is further boosted upward by mountains—some impressive thunderstorms can develop.

An occluded front typically occurs when cold air pushes through

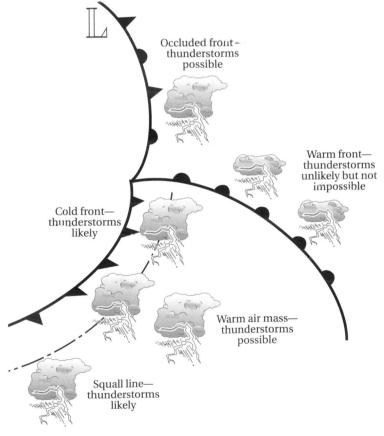

Where thunderstorms are most likely to be found in relation to different types of fronts

warmer air and runs into another cold air mass. Sometimes it shoves under the cold air ahead and sometimes it pushes over it, depending upon which of those two air masses are colder. Because warm air is abruptly forced upward, occluded fronts are another common place for thundershower formation.

A stationary front occurs when the boundary between the cold and warm air masses is not moving. Typically this produces widespread clouds. Occasionally this can also produce thunderstorms.

Because the upward motion of warm, moist air is controlled by the movement of a front instead of heating from the sun, frontal thunderstorms can occur anytime during the day. When a forecast tells you a front is approaching the area of your planned outing, it is time to ask two important questions: Are thunderstorms forecast, and how exposed would I be to thunderstorms given the location and type of activity planned? (See Chapter 4 for more important information about these questions.) In any case, always remember the following:

- Thunderstorms occasionally form along warm fronts and stationary fronts.
- Thunderstorms frequently form along cold or occluded fronts.
- Thunderstorms frequently form in the warm air between warm and cold fronts.

Take every opportunity during cloud breaks or clearing to look for signs of upward-building clouds or anvils spreading from the top of such clouds.

POST-FRONTAL THUNDERSTORMS

The danger of thunderstorms may persist after a cold front has passed. This may happen with the passage of an *upper trough,* an area of low pressure high in the atmosphere. True to its name, a trough is a place where water (and air) collect, leading to the lifting motion that can set off thunderstorms. Along the Pacific coast of the United States and Canada, thunderstorms can also be triggered when the cooler, drier air following a cold front moves over the warmer ocean water of the Pacific. Just as air being heated by the ground will rise, so will air heated by warmer water. Post-frontal thunderstorms gain strength as they collide with the coastal mountain ranges that boost the warm air near the surface even higher. The following are the most important to remember:

- If an upper trough is forecast to follow a cold front, thunderstorms may develop, especially along the west slopes of mountains.
- Such post-frontal thunderstorms are most common along the

coastal ranges of the western United States and Canada, including of course, Alaska.

Thunderstorms are a bit like fingerprints: No two are exactly alike. Knowing their different forms and behaviors and the words used to describe them will help you make more intelligent decisions based on forecasts before you leave home or on what you see in the field. Chapter 4 offers specific strategies to help you avoid or survive thunderstorms in the field, using the Four A's of Thunderstorm Safety. Chapter 4 also explains the forecasts and information that can help you make effective go–no go decisions.

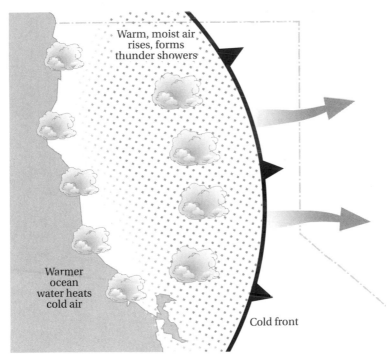

Warm, moist air rises, forms thunder showers

Warmer ocean water heats cold air

Cold front

The development of coastal thunder or rain showers after a cold front moves through

Strategies for Safety and Survival

Not a cloud. The blue sky glittered like a new-honed knife. . . . the purity of the sky upset me. Give me a good black storm in which the enemy is plainly visible. I can measure its extent and prepare myself for its attack.

Antoine de Saint-Exupery,
Wind, Sand and Stars

Few mountains dominate a city as thoroughly as Mount Rundle dominates Banff in the Canadian Rockies. A massive ramp of layered shale and limestone, Rundle is not really a single peak but an entire range. It stretches southeast from Banff to the town of Canmore, with seven distinct peaks: The highest reaches 9335 feet (2846 meters). We had pitched our tent on a ridgeline directly across the Bow River Valley. Just the sight of its sheer northeastern face is enough to inspire vertigo. It is like camping beneath the crest of a tsunami frozen in time. As night fell, a large wedge-shaped void in a sky otherwise filled with stars marked the presence of this looming peak. Our eyes grew weary, new constellations rose as others set, but the void remained stationary.

Perhaps two hours later, I was awakened by the slow, deliberate roll of thunder. It was so close that I could feel the shock waves. I listened for the rain, expecting heavy drops to pelt our tent, but none fell. There was little wind. Fitful flashes of lightning illuminated our tent. My watch showed it was a little after midnight. Surprisingly, my wife and son continued to sleep through the atmospheric bombardment. Still, given our exposed position, I began to wonder whether I should rouse them, break camp, and seek a more sheltered location. I began to time the interval between the lightning and the thunder that followed. It did not change, which suggested the storm would keep its distance. I snuggled back into my sleeping bag, enjoying the sound and light show for perhaps another hour, then slowly drifted back to sleep. Our campsite was untouched by the thunderstorm.

Why did I decide to stay where I was? Pure laziness, dumb luck, or perhaps because my technique of timing the interval between the lightning and thunder really indicated the storm would not pose any threat? If it was a matter or laziness or dumb luck, rest assured I would not document it in this book. It was because using this *flash-to-bang principle* offered strong evidence that the thunderstorm would not move toward our campsite. This chapter offers techniques like this which you can use to maximize your safety. Those techniques will be easiest to remember and most effective if you make them part of a plan.

THE FOUR A'S OF THUNDERSTORM SAFETY

Success is more likely in any outdoor activity if you have a plan and follow it That is true in general about dealing with mountain weather, and it is certainly true when dealing with thunderstorms. I have developed a simple strategy that has helped me avoid weather accidents, especially from thunderstorms, over the course of countless outings throughout the United States, Canada, and Europe. It has four elements, which I call the Four A's of Thunderstorm Safety.

1. Anticipate
2. Assess
3. Act
4. Aid

1. Anticipate

The best strategy, of course, is to avoid being near thunderstorms in the first place. This means *anticipating* the risk. If you have read Chapter 3, you know how thunderstorms behave and that it is next to impossible to accurately predict where a bolt of lightning will strike next. *There is simply no defense for lightning.* Since so many variables are at play, it is foolish to consciously go out or stay out in a lightning storm if there is any alternative. While it is true that 80 percent of all victims of lightning strikes survive, one in four survivors suffer major aftereffects.

The best solution, therefore, is to anticipate the hazard before you are dangerously exposed. That is not always possible, but it is an important habit to develop before every outing. You anticipate by gathering information before you hit the trail or climbing route.

First, recognize what information is available. Formal weather watches, warnings, and forecasts are issued by the National Weather Service in the United States and its counterparts in other countries. Those official alerts and forecasts will be all you will need sometimes to make an informed decision. Your search for guidance does not have to (and usually should not) end there. The following table presents the types of information available and where you can find them. Chapter 7 focuses on effective pre-trip weather briefings, but this information is worth covering twice.

WHERE TO OBTAIN WEATHER INFORMATION

Information Type	Source	Availability
Severe weather watches, warnings	National Weather Service	NOAA Weather Radio, TV and radio newscasts, websites
Zone and state forecasts	National Weather Service, broadcast meteorologists	NOAA Weather Radio, TV and radio newscasts, websites, newspapers
Extended outlook	National Weather Service, broadcast meteorologists	NOAA Weather Radio, TV and radio newscasts, websites, newspapers
Satellite photos	National Weather Service	TV newscasts, websites, and newspapers
Weather radar	National Weather Service, broadcast meteorologists	TV newscasts, websites
Current weather Observations	National Weather Service, private observers	NOAA Weather Radio, TV and radio newscasts, websites
Private observations	State patrols, sheriff and police departments, park rangers	Telephone or personal visits

If a watch or warning is posted for your destination, delay the trip or choose a different destination. Granted, the weather may appear fine when you depart: Without direct knowledge of thunderstorm watches or warnings in the field, different strategies will be needed to assess the potential for thunderstorm formation (see the following section). However, if warnings or watches already exist for your intended destination, either delay your departure until the hazard has passed or choose a different destination for which no watches or warnings are in effect. Even in the absence of any official watches or warnings, a forecast that mentions any of the following suggests the possibility of thundershowers:

- Cold fronts
- Troughs
- Squall lines
- Dry lines

2. Assess

If anticipating the risk of thunderstorms before leaving home is the first step toward backcountry safety, assessing the threat while in the backcountry is the second step. This involves assessing the threat from the sky and assessing elements of the environment around you that may add to or subtract from that threat.

No academic degree in meteorology is needed to realize that seeing lightning and hearing thunder means you are in danger. The goal is to recognize clues that will give you a little more time to react. If thunder and lightning are already present, though, ask these two questions right away: How far away is the thunderstorm? Where is it headed?

If you can see lightning or hear thunder, seek shelter immediately. Do not wait for the rain. If you can hear thunder, the storm is probably within 6 to 10 miles (10 to 16 kilometers), and you should take prompt action to protect yourself and others. However, the absence of thunder is not a guarantee that the storm is more than 6 miles away. Noise or intervening ridges may prevent you from hearing thunder until the storm is within 2 or 3 miles (3 to 5 kilometers). If you can see the lightning bolt, the storm is typically within 15 miles (24 kilometers), but this depends upon your vantage point, visibility, and other factors specific to your locale. The distance between successive strokes can be 3 to 5 miles or more (5 to 8 kilometers): Lightning has struck as far as 10 miles (16 kilometers) away from rainfall. That means that although it may not be raining at your campsite, you could still be struck by lightning. Remember this, too: A thunderstorm can easily cover a lot of ground between lightning strikes.

The Flash-to-Bang Principle

If you can see lightning and hear thunder, assess the threat by utilizing the following information and the flash-to-bang principle:

1. Once you see the flash, start timing.
2. Stop timing when you hear the bang.
3. Divide that number by 5.

A count of 15, for example, means the thunderstorm is 3 miles away, a count of 10 means it is 2 miles away, and a count of 5 means you are in big trouble. The reason the flash-to-bang principle works is that lightning moves almost at the speed of light (186,000 miles per second), essentially instantaneously. The speed of sound is much slower, at 1129 feet per second, or approximately 770 miles per hour. The exact speed varies with temperature. The speed given here is for 68°F (20°C). In 5 seconds, the sound would have traveled 5 x 1129 feet or 5645 feet, which is very close to 1 mile (5280 feet).

In the metric system, the speed of sound works out to approximately 340 meters per second. Dividing 1 kilometer (1000 meters) by that number yields, more or less, 3. Climbers and hikers who are more familiar with this system of measurement can start timing at the flash, stop timing at the bang, and divide by 3. The result will be the approximate distance in kilometers from the thunderstorm.

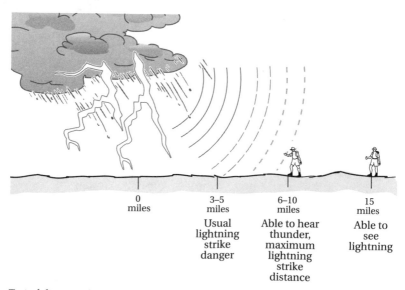

0 miles	3–5 miles	6–10 miles	15 miles
	Usual lightning strike danger	Able to hear thunder, maximum lightning strike distance	Able to see lightning

Typical distances from a thunderstorm at which you can hear thunder, and see or be hit by lightning

FLASH-TO-BANG PRINCIPLE

If thunder and lightning are present, use the flash-to-bang principle to estimate the distance of the storm. Divide the interval between the lightning and thunder by 5 to obtain the approximate distance of the storm in miles, or divide the interval by 3 to obtain the approximate distance of the storm in kilometers. Continue to calculate the distances over time: If the interval is shrinking, the thunderstorm is moving toward you. If the interval is increasing, it is moving away from you.

The sky offers clues long before the boom of thunder and the flash of lightning, often before thunderstorms even begin to develop. Since moisture is a prime ingredient of thunderstorms, increasing humidity indicates an increasing chance of thunderstorm formation, particularly with the expected approach of a front or trough, or with heating from the sun. If the air feels more humid or if you notice you cannot see as far as you could (decreasing visibility), be on the lookout for developing thunderstorms. Increasing moisture in the air decreases visibility.

> If the air feels more humid or you cannot see as far, moisture in the air is increasing, which increases the potential for thundershowers.

The photographs on page 72 were taken in Montana's Glacier National Park and show a common sequence in the development of thundershowers in the mountains. First, small and fluffy cumulus clouds appear. Next, the small cumulus clouds expand into much larger clouds that resemble heads of cauliflower. In less than an hour, these clouds may develop into full-blown cumulo-nimbus, producing heavy rain or snow showers and gusty winds at the least, and possibly thunder and lightning. Watch also for the hard-edged cauliflowerlike shape of growing cumulus to give way to a softer, fuzzy outline higher up. That signals the development of ice crystals that precede thunder and lightning. The second photograph was taken only a half hour after the first: Fifteen minutes later thunder, lightning, hail, and snow chased me down the trail—the possibility of an encounter with a grizzly bear became secondary.

If a thunderstorm is being produced by the movement of a cold

Young cumulus clouds over Glacier National Park, Montana

The same cumulus clouds thirty minutes later, now developed into cumulo-nimbus clouds (photos by author)

front or squall line, the first clue may be a dark line of clouds on the horizon, the telltale anvil cloud or clouds up high, followed by a sudden gust of wind as the storm's gust front spreads out ahead of it. It is important to remember that with this type of thunderstorm or line of thunderstorms, you have no time to lose in seeking shelter. However, if the thunderstorm is embedded near a warm or occluded front, other clouds may make it difficult to see the storm coming. Then it is back to using the flash-to-bang principle.

If clouds are growing upward, if the edges of the upper part of the cloud become fuzzy instead of hard edged, and a flat anvil sprouts from the top, thunder and lightning are likely soon to follow.

After assessing the clues based on what you can see in the sky, it is time to assess your environment in terms of the ground and water. What you are standing on or near, even what you are wearing, will determine how likely you are to be struck, and if you are struck, what your chance of survival will be. Your next step is to assess your environment with a few simple questions.

QUESTIONS FOR ASSESSING LIGHTNING RISK

- Am I in the open?
- Am I on or near isolated, tall objects?
- Am I on or near water?
- Am I near, wearing, or holding metal objects?
- Am I feeling a tingling sensation or hearing a buzzing noise?

3. Act
Once you have assessed your risk, it is time to act—quickly!

Am I in the open?
If you are in the open, seek a more sheltered location. If a car or metal shed is available, get in: Lightning travels along the outside of metal objects. Be certain not to touch metal handles and such until the thunderstorm and risk of lightning strikes are definitely over. A cave offers protection only if it is deep. Ground currents can jump from the roof of a shallow cave to you and then to the floor. Wait at least 30 minutes after the last thunder or lightning to resume activity. If shelter is not available, get low. If you cannot move, crouch down, with feet close

together, and put your hands over your ears for protection from close thunder, which can damage hearing. No evidence suggests that standing on your pack, clothing, or sleeping pad will protect you from ground currents. Do not lie down, and do not stand close to others: If you are in a group, spread out and remain a minimum of 15 feet away from each other. It is not true that standing near a taller person will reduce your danger of being struck.

Am I near isolated, tall objects?

Don't seek refuge under isolated trees. The highest object will tend to attract the stroke of lightning. If possible, seek groups of trees or shrubs of similar height. If the lone tree is the only choice of refuge, move away from it and seek the lowest ground available, following the tips for safety in open locations. If you're on a high, exposed ridge or peak, try to climb down as quickly as is safely possible. If low, rolling hills are nearby, seek refuge in a low spot. Such terrain is especially common on golf courses or along shorelines.

Am I on or near water?

If you are near water, move away. If you are in the water, get out. It is that simple and that important. Not only is the lightning a hazard, but gusty winds could churn up the water and swamp your canoe or small boat. Even wet, marshy ground can increase your risk of being hit by lightning.

Am I near, wearing, or holding metal objects?

Metal objects are like miniature lightning rods: They draw the stroke. If you are near, wearing, or holding something made of metal, you are part of that lightning rod. If a thunderstorm approaches, you want to get as far away as possible from metal objects. If you are a climber, this means ditching your pack (it may have a metal frame, either external or internal), dropping your ice ax, and removing your crampons. If you are carrying slinged protection (camming devices, chocks, carabiners, and the like), take off that sling if at all possible and move away. If your tent is staked with metal pegs, move away since a tent offers no protection from lightning. This also applies to graphite objects such as fishing rods. Do not hold onto a metal-tipped umbrella either: It is better to get soaked than struck!

Am I feeling a tingling sensation or hearing a buzzing noise?

A tingling sensation, particularly on your scalp or the hair on your arms indicates movement of electricity, probably from the ground up toward the descending leader that will become the visible lightning bolt. A loud buzzing noise or the smell of ozone are also danger signs, as is a bluish glow around rocks or a companion. Move immediately! If you see a friend's hair sticking out or up, get them to move, too!

4. Aid

What if a companion is hit by lightning? Can you safely help him or her? What should you do? This section is not intended as a first-aid primer (and is no substitute for formal first-aid training), but it will touch on some key principles that relate to lightning injuries.

Make no more casualties.

If one injury has already occurred, do not add another by putting yourself at risk if the storm is still raging. If you are within 3 to 5 miles of the storm, you are still within the prime lightning danger zone. Before attempting to help a victim, plan how you can minimize your exposure before you move.

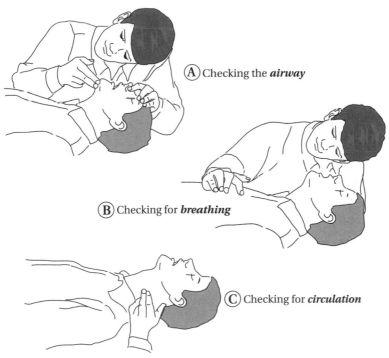

(A) Checking the *airway*

(B) Checking for *breathing*

(C) Checking for *circulation*

The ABCs of First Aid

Remember that the victim cannot hurt you.
Once you have decided to provide aid, recognize that the victim does not carry a charge. The only way you can get hurt is by another lightning strike.

If possible, send for assistance.
Seeking assistance obviously depends upon your location and circumstances. If you are deep in the wilderness, you are on your own. If you are not alone and within a mile or two of assistance, send one person to seek help. Are you carrying a cell phone? If so, call 911. If you have a radio, use it to summon help.

First treat those who appear to be dead.
Remember the ABCs of first aid: Check for an open *airway,* check to see whether or not the victim is *breathing,* and then check for evidence of *circulation* (a pulse). Be patient in checking for evidence of breathing and circulation for at least 20 to 30 seconds. If you cannot detect breathing or circulation, begin CPR. If you have not completed CPR training or it has been a while since you have practiced, sign up now for a new or refresher course. It takes so little time to learn, and it can make a big difference later.

Move the victim if lightning is still a threat.
If your position (or that of the victim) is still dangerous, look for a less exposed position and move. In most lightning strikes, fractures or major bleeding are unlikely unless the victim suffered a fall or was thrown a distance. With no evidence of breathing or circulation, administer two quick breaths, then move the victim to reduce the threat of another lightning strike.

Treat for hypothermia.
Odds are that if the victim was struck by lightning, he or she is also wet from rain. Put a protective layer between victims and the ground to diminish the chance of hypothermia and cover them with any extra clothing to keep them warm.

OTHER THUNDERSTORM THREATS

Lightning is a thunderstorm's biggest threat to your safety, but it is not the only threat. Thunderstorms can also produce dangerous winds, flash flooding, and fires. Chapter 5 explores thunderstorm winds and provides details about mountain winds and safety strategies, but it is worthwhile to examine the threat of flash floods and lightning-triggered fires now.

THUNDERSTORMS AND FLASH FLOODS

Sunday, July 31, 1976, was an oppressively hot day in the Colorado Rockies. Campers probably welcomed the sight that afternoon of billowing cumulus clouds, which offered the promise of rain and relief from the heat. As light easterly winds continued to lift moist air over the Front Range, the cumulus swelled into mature thunderstorms. The rumble of thunder was soon followed by cooling downpours early that evening. Typically, winds near the crest of the Rockies soon push such thunderstorms back over the plains to the east. Refreshing rain and blustery winds give way to clearing skies and more comfortable temperatures. This evening, though, winds aloft were very weak: The thunderstorms were not going anywhere.

Eight inches of rain fell in just one hour in the Big Thompson River basin in north central Colorado. The Big Thompson plunges through sheer canyon walls, dropping more than 2000 vertical feet from its origin near Estes Park to its exit in the rolling plains near Loveland. The near-vertical canyon walls support little vegetation to absorb storm runoff. The stationary thunderstorms transformed the Big Thompson from a lazy 2-foot-deep meandering stream to a massive wall of water 19 feet high. Boulders 10 feet high were thrown like driftwood. There was little warning. The flash flood swept away everything in its path: trees, cars, entire buildings. One hundred and forty-five people died—some within the river—but many were caught in homes and even motels adjoining the river that were obliterated by the massive wall of water and debris.

This disaster led to the creation of early warning systems throughout the country to protect mountain communities, resorts, and campgrounds from flash floods. However, the lead time for such warnings is short, and they seldom offer much help to anyone in the backcountry. The growing popularity of hiking in slot canyons or rappelling down their walls expands that threat. Flash flooding poses a risk to any canyon in a thunderstorm, and you should always be alert before entering one. Know that you will not be able to swim out of such a flood: Even a sudden flow of just 500 cubic feet per minute will hit with a force of more than 30,000 pounds. That is like being struck by a fully loaded semitrailer truck: If the impact alone does not kill you or knock you senseless, being flushed against the canyon walls or floating debris will. Your safety is your responsibility, and anytime you enter a narrow canyon, you are assuming a risk. Obtaining the current forecast is critical.

Thus it is essential to follow the important safety guidelines established by the National Park Service. I present them again in the context of the Four A's of Thunderstorm Safety:

1. Anticipate

- Check weather and flood forecasts before leaving home.
- Check for updated weather forecasts, flash flood forecasts, and canyon closures before leaving a trailhead.
- Remember that thundershowers, and therefore flash floods, tend to be most common from late June through August in the canyons of the western United States.

Keep in mind that the percentage chance of precipitation does not suggest how intense the precipitation will be. A forecast calling for a 20 percent chance of showers or thundershowers does not mean they will be light showers. It means there is a 20 percent chance that measurable rain will fall at any given location, *but it does not have to be raining above you for a flash flood to occur.* Rain miles away may drain into a canyon and cause a flood.

Before entering a canyon, check with rangers, land management personnel, or whoever else might be knowledgeable about updated forecasts and closures. If a canyon is closed, it is for your safety. The

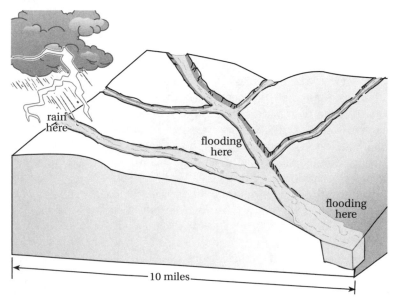

rain
here

flooding
here

flooding
here

10 miles

Distant thunderstorms still pose a threat of flash flooding in the mountains.

canyon will always be there another day, but hikers ignoring such a closure may not.

2. Assess

Even the best prepared, most conscientious hiker or canyoneer may be caught by deteriorating conditions several days into a trip, so it is important to know the warning signs of a possible flash flood:

- Clouds building up or darkening above
- Sounds of thunder or flashes of lightning

① Darkening sky

② Presence of thunder, lightning

③ Water becomes muddy or less clear

④ Floating debris appears

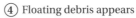

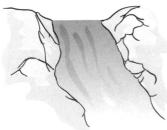

⑥ Sound of roaring water upcanyon

⑤ Water level rises or current increases

Signs of possible flash flooding

- Sudden changes in water clarity from clear to muddy
- Sudden appearance of floating debris in water
- Rising water levels or stronger currents
- An increasing roar of water upcanyon
- Sudden appearances of waterfalls on canyon walls

3. Act

If you see or hear any of the signs pointing toward a flash flood, you do not have long to take the following actions:

- Seek higher ground immediately: Even climbing a few feet may make the difference between life and death.
- If no higher ground is available, take shelter behind a rock jutting from the canyon wall. That may break some of the impact of the floodwater.
- If possible, wedge yourself into a crack above water level.
- Remain on high ground until water levels drop and water clarity improves.

4. Aid

The possibility of being stranded, together with the potential for injury and hypothermia, are good reasons to always carry the Ten Essentials.

TEN ESSENTIALS: A SYSTEMS APPROACH

1. Navigation (map and compass)
2. Sun protection (sunglasses and sunscreen)
3. Insulation (extra clothing)
4. Illumination (headlamp or flashlight)
5. First-aid supplies
6. Fire (firestarter and matches/lighter)
7. Repair kit and tools (including knife)
8. Nutrition (extra food)
9. Hydration (extra water)
10. Emergency shelter

Keep in mind that even the most agile hiker can slip into the water, and that can give important equipment a thorough dunking. Consider carrying plastic trash bags and zip-type bags to waterproof your gear inside your pack. The possibility of a dunking in cool water is why hypothermia is a big risk in canyon country.

Hypothermia Signs and Treatment

If you or a partner take a dunking or get soaked by rain and then chilled, be on the lookout for hypothermia. Following are the warning signs:

- Complaints of feeling cold
- Violent shivering
- Stumbling, poor coordination, falling
- Slurred speech
- Irrational behavior

If you are unsure if it is hypothermia, have the person in question (including yourself, if you are feeling ill or odd) try to walk a straight line for 25 to 30 feet; if the result resembles a snake dance, treat for hypothermia as follows:

- *First and foremost,* exchange wet clothes for dry clothes and get the victim out of the elements and into a shelter.
- Wrap the victim in a space blanket or a dry, prewarmed sleeping bag.
- Sharing body warmth is an option.
- Insulate from the ground.
- Cover the head.
- Feed warm drinks (non-alcoholic!) and sweets.
- Evacuate as soon as possible and seek professional medical care.

A sleeping bag can be prewarmed by having someone who is not chilled crawl into the bag first. Having that person share the bag with the hypothermia victim is an excellent method of rewarming. If the victim has a bad case of hypothermia, medical experts emphasize that it is important to handle him or her gently, as any jarring can trigger a fatal arrhythmia (an alteration of the rhythm or force of the heartbeat).

THUNDERSTORMS AND WILDFIRES

Of the forest fires in the United States alone, 70 percent are set off by lightning strikes. Wilderness and wildfire are inseparable: Spend much time in the wilderness, and you will probably encounter wildfire. It is an awe-inspiring and frightening experience, even at a distance. A little thought can keep it from being dangerous or deadly.

1. Anticipate

Backpackers, climbers, fly fishers, and kayakers can avoid most wildfire situations by seeking the answer to a simple question: What is the fire danger level? It is typically given as one of four levels: low, medium, high, or extreme. Any time the level is given as high or extreme, you should proceed very carefully. This information is usually given on billboards outside major national, state, or provincial parks or forests, but it can also be obtained in advance by calling park rangers or other personnel, who can also alert you to area closures or recent lightning activity. The National Weather Service websites also offer excellent fire and weather summaries, combining the relevant weather and fire hazard information into a couple of pages. The U.S. Forest Service offers extensive fire information on its websites, exploring past and present fires in addition to projected fire threats. Such information is as important as a current weather forecast if an outing is planned during the dry season or a drought.

2. Assess

Assessing the potential for lightning-caused (or human-caused) wildfires in the field should begin upon your arrival at the trailhead. As noted, fire-danger signs will be posted at the entrances of most national parks and forests. Your vigilance must match the danger level. Check with rangers or other personnel for area closures or other advice. In my backcountry travels throughout North America, I have found rangers unfailingly helpful. In addition to supplying information I have requested, they usually offer helpful tips that make a trek more enjoyable. When a closure is posted, resist the all-too-human temptation to ignore

① Is vegetation dry and crumbly?

② Are there crunchy piles of dead leaves or needles?

③ Are cumulus clouds growing?

④ Are cumulus bases high?

Key fire danger signs in the backcountry

it. Once you have shouldered your pack, check for clues both in the sky and on the ground:

- Is the vegetation green and pliable or bone dry, brown, and crumbly?
- Are piles of crunchy dead leaves or pine needles lying under trees?
- Are cumulus clouds forming or growing?
- Are the bases of the cumulus clouds low—that is, just above or near ridgelines—or are they high?

If the vegetation is dry and crumbly, it will make excellent fuel for fires. Growing cumulus clouds signal the potential for thunderstorms. Low-based cumulo-nimbus can actually be helpful: They are more likely to produce needed rain. Lightning strikes can certainly occur, but the rain is likely to prevent such strikes from igniting fires. Caution is always important, especially if high-based cumulo-nimbus form because they are unlikely to produce rain and very likely to set off lightning. If you observe thunderstorms forming with the bases substantially above ridgelines, be very alert, especially if they follow a string of sunny days. On clear days, ground temperatures may reach 160°F (71°C). The highest temperatures will be found on southwestern slopes during afternoon hours.

After checking for signs that might lead to a fire, look for signs that one might already be smoldering. One telltale sign might seem obvious: smoke. A *sleeper* is a fire that may remain hidden underground for days or a week or longer, typically smoldering in dried roots, waiting for above-ground conditions to dry out enough for it to flare up and ignite vegetation above ground. One of the best clues that a sleeper may be smoldering underfoot is the presence on the ground of splintered pieces of tree or the shattered and blackened remains of a tree trunk. A lightning strike superheats sap and water within a tree, forcing rapid expansion that literally blows apart a tree. In some cases, a tree may not heat up enough to explode, but it will typically show a spiral pattern of cracks down the tree trunk. Near such trees, odds are high there may be a sleeper fire underground.

Of course, more obvious signs of fire include the smell of smoke or clouds that are growing without a flat bottom. Flat-bottomed clouds are typically cumulus or cumulo-nimbus; those with round bottoms are generated by fire. You can be certain fire is present if the cloud has a boiling appearance or is tinted with shades of orange or brown: The latter are reflections of flames beneath and smoke carried upward. Leave the area immediately, and report your observations to park, forest, or law enforcement agencies as soon as possible.

Splintered pieces of tree on the ground

Freshly shattered, and/or blackened tree trunk

Smell of smoke

Round-bottomed "boiling" clouds

Orange- or brown-tinted clouds

Key signs of possible or actual wildfires

SIGNS OF AN ACTIVE FIRE

- Splintered pieces of tree on the ground
- A shattered tree trunk, especially if it is blackened
- Smell of smoke
- Round-bottomed clouds that appear to boil
- Clouds tinted brown or orange

3. Act

If smoke or actual flames are spotted, wildfire experts emphasize the safest action is to move downhill and away from the flames. If you are downwind, the fire will tend to move toward you. Ridgelines are popular places to hike—travel is easier and views more spectacular, but they are the worst place to be during a wildfire. Because heat rises, flames tend to be drawn upslope. Such upslope winds tend to be strongest on the south or southwestern slopes, which receive more direct sunlight

Daytime heating generates upslope or upvalley winds, which can direct fire upslope.

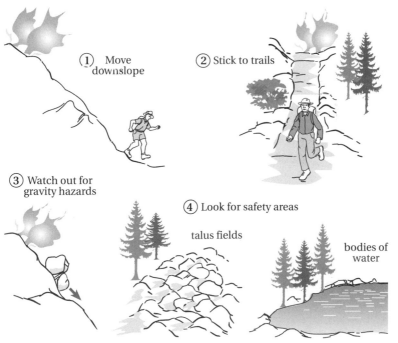

① Move downslope

② Stick to trails

③ Watch out for gravity hazards

④ Look for safety areas

talus fields

bodies of water

Safe ways to evade wildfires

during the warmer afternoon hours. The worst place to be is at the head of a fire, the leading edge of advancing flames. Fire can move much faster than any two-legged human.

While moving away, it is important to watch out for what are called *gravity hazards:* falling snags and rolling debris that are aflame. *Firewhirls* are another example of this threat. The heat generated by fires creates extreme instability in the air near the ground. The resulting violent corkscrew of wind can twist off tree trunks larger than 3 feet in diameter and can pick up and shoot out large embers, setting off entirely new fires.

Even the coolest thinker will find it difficult to resist plunging over logs and rocks to escape a raging wildfire, but it is best to stay on the trail. Stress and haste can rob even the most agile of coordination. The possibility of injury is too great to risk bushwhacking your way out of a fire zone.

Experienced firefighters recommend looking for what they call safety areas: places that are unlikely to catch fire. Those would include rock slides, wet meadows, lakes, ponds, rivers, and streams. When conditions make a blaze possible, scout out such safety areas and the best evacuation routes.

To summarize, take the following actions when confronted by a fire:

- Move downslope and downwind of the fire.
- Stick to trails if at all possible.
- Watch out for gravity hazards: debris rolling downhill.
- Scout out safety areas and evacuation routes.

4. Aid

The best way to help others in a wildfire is to help yourself: Evacuate the fire zone promptly but carefully. Firefighters will have enough of a battle on their hands without having to search for and evacuate injured hikers. Warn others who you may encounter, then contact local authorities as soon as possible to report the fire.

Wildfires, like lightning and the flash floods triggered by thunderstorms, demand respect. The best course is to anticipate or assess conditions well enough that action or aid is not necessary. Thunderstorm winds—for that matter, any of the variety of wind phenomena found in or near the mountains—also demand careful consideration. At their best, winds can lead to an unpleasant, sleepless night. At their worst, winds can present an epic battle that is impossible to win—you can only survive. That is the subject of the next chapter.

Chapter 5

Mountain Winds

The men were done—incapable of any work. The mountain above, whenever parting clouds revealed her, was smoking angrily with driven mist and snow. The gale was tearing over her ridges a hundred miles an hour, flinging the snow a thousand feet into the air.
Edward Felix Norton, *Field Notes from the 1924 British Everest expedition*

The last of the Boy Scouts had turned into their tents an hour ago. Only a few embers remained from the once-blazing campfire that had offered such welcome warmth on this chilly April evening. Snow still covered much of the ground, making it unlikely that the older scouts would venture out to pull pranks on their younger neighbors. Adults think about things like that. The only sound was that of quiet conversation from a young couple camping nearby. Confident that our young charges were peacefully asleep, we fathers who had remained awake wished each other a good night and zipped our tents shut. The rapidly vanishing warmth of the now extinguished campfire made our sleeping bags feel especially snug.

Deep sleep can confuse one's sense of time, particularly on a pitch-black night high in the mountains. It was impossible to guess how long after we turned in that an abrupt roar rent the quiet of the wilderness. Believing at first that the noise came from military jets on a night-time training mission, I simply rolled over. We were camped near a lake on a favorite low-level training route. But the roar did not stop. It grew in pitch and volume, and just as the noise seemed to reach a crescendo, my own tent began to flap wildly in the sudden wind. It seemed ready to take flight, though the pegs held fast. Small evergreen boughs, pine cones, and other debris began to pelt the rainfly. Exclamations issued from one tent after another. A sleeping bag is not made for speedy exits, and my well-named mummy-style bag was no exception. Once free, I cautiously exited my tent to check on the scouts. Although alarmed, all were fine, their tents securely staked.

As other fathers emerged to help reassure the boys, we heard new shouting: It came from more mature voices expressing just as much fright as our youngest tenderfoot. Judging the direction of the shouts was not easy in the howling wind, but we saw flashlights illuminating what seemed to be a writhing blob of protoplasm just through the trees. It was the young couple's tent. Either they were in the throes of sublime delight or in serious trouble. As some of our older scouts emerged, their confidence restored and curious to see the source of the continued screaming, it was with some relief that a few seconds of observation showed the latter was true. Either they had not staked their tent to the ground, or they had done a very poor job of it. Whatever the case, their tent seemed determined to take flight, with the couple as very reluctant passengers. First the corners would lift, a gust would shoot under the base, the whole works would tremble and flap, and the unfortunate couple would shriek anew. Momentarily forgetting our maxim to do a good turn daily, two other fathers and I were shaking with laughter. Fortunately, the wind was loud enough to mask our regrettable lack of compassion.

The young man attempted to emerge from the tent, valiantly seeking to save the situation. No sooner had he partially unzipped the entry than the wind seized on that opening as an opportunity to send the tent into orbit. It reminded me of my first model rocket's unsuccessful attempt to lift off, the tiny tent simultaneously rotating around all three axes of movement, trying to jettison the hapless young fellow, his white knuckles almost luminous in the moonlight. Our sense of duty finally exceeded the entertainment value of the scene, and we rushed to aid the reluctant tent jockey. Minutes later, we had lashed the writhing beast (the tent, that is) into submission, retrieved a few spare pegs to complete the process, and left the couple to regain their composure.

Some readers might suspect I made up this story. Anyone who has spent much time in the mountains will know better. Almost every camper (including me) has been caught at least once with an inadequately staked tent on a windy night and learned the value firsthand of properly anchoring one's shelter. That is only partial insurance against a UFO (unanticipated flying opportunity). At the very least, understanding wind and the way it behaves in the mountains can save you embarrassment and inconvenience. At best, it can save your life. On high peaks, winds can easily exceed 100 miles per hour (160 kilometers per hour). The highest wind speed recorded in North America is 231 miles per hour, reported by the Mount Washington Observatory in New Hampshire. Climbers have literally been peeled from high peaks and blown to their death.

MOUNTAIN WINDS: THE BIG PICTURE

Wind is nothing more than moving air, which tends to flow from regions of high pressure to regions of low pressure. The greater the difference in pressure between two locations, the greater the pressure *gradient* and the faster the air will tend to move. However, wind behaves vastly different at varying elevations or altitudes above the ground, especially in the rugged terrain of mountains. Anyone who has chased a tent that has been transformed into a kite knows mountain winds can develop suddenly, shift abruptly, and vary over extremely short distances. Mountain winds are either caused or influenced by passing weather systems, by the interaction of wind with mountain ridges, peaks, and valleys, and as part of daily cycles. This chapter explores the variety of mountain winds and examines strategies to either anticipate and avoid such winds or to safely cope with them.

WINDS IN THE UPPER ATMOSPHERE

Winds aloft set the agenda for what happens in the mountains. For the purpose of this book, we can consider those winds to be at and above 18,000 feet (5486 meters)—that is above the elevations of Mount Rainier in Washington State, Mount Whitney in California, and Pike's Peak in Colorado. Even though such winds typically are higher than most peaks, they also influence winds that move through the mountains. So it is worthwhile to spend a few moments to understand these winds.

In the upper atmosphere, the tendency for air to move from high to low pressure, the pressure gradient force, is balanced by the *Coriolis force,* which results from Earth's rotation. The force of *friction* (discussed later) is largely absent, and that leads to wind flows that are very different from those close to the ground.

The Coriolis force deflects the wind to the right (clockwise) of its original path (to the left—counter-clockwise—in the Southern Hemisphere) and offsets the pressure gradient force. Thus, instead of flowing from high to low pressure, wind tends to snake between the major high-

and low-pressure systems in the upper atmosphere, undulating from west to east. The bigger the difference between those pressure systems, the stronger the winds.

The highest-speed winds flow in a river of air meteorologists call the *jet stream.* A more general term is "steering currents"—an apt term because the winds aloft do just that: They steer the weather disturbances at the surface. Different storm tracks bring different precipitation patterns (see trail notes for different regions in Chapter 8).

The bigger the difference in temperatures between the Arctic and the mid-latitudes (that part of the planet between 30° to 60°

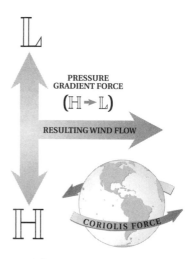

Wind flow in the upper atmosphere; a balance between the pressure gradient and Coriolis forces

north latitude), the stronger the winds will be in the upper atmosphere. Because that difference in temperature is greatest from late autumn to early spring, that is when the winds aloft tend to be the strongest. The stronger the jet stream or steering currents, the stronger the weather disturbances at Earth's surface, and the more likely they are to intensify.

Think of surface weather systems as riding on the steering currents of the atmosphere somewhat like a boat on a moving river. Some television weather presentations show, at least in a general sense, the directions of the winds aloft.

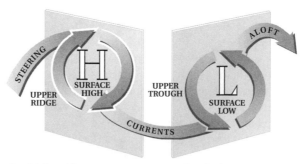

Where surface high and low pressure systems are found relative to upper air troughs and ridges

Surface weather disturbances tend to develop in specific locations relative to ridges and troughs in the upper atmosphere: High-pressure systems tend to be downwind of an upper ridge of high pressure (to the right on weather maps) and surface low-pressure systems tend to be downwind of an upper trough of low pressure. Even if an upper trough has not produced a surface low-pressure system, one can develop (see the illustration on page 90). This is information you can obtain on the Internet, and Chapter 2 also explores the subject in greater detail. Seeing such an upper trough just to the west in the Northern Hemisphere on a weather map (and to the east in the Southern Hemisphere) should lead to caution in selecting a recreation site. You may still choose to set out on your trip, but you should be more conservative in selecting routes or campsites.

Fast winds high up in the atmosphere tend to produce fast winds at the surface. In the mountains, when formal information is scarce, watch the cirrus clouds that arrive in advance of an approaching weather disturbance. If you can see those clouds moving, the winds aloft are probably blowing in excess of 100 miles per hour (160 kilometers per hour). Expect strong, gusty winds in and near the mountains soon.

WINDS IN THE UPPER ATMOSPHERE

- The movement of high clouds offers clues to wind speed and direction. Comparing the orientation of a strand of cirrus clouds to a compass will yield wind direction aloft.
- If the cirrus clouds are visibly moving, expect wind speeds aloft to be strong (in excess of 100 miles per hour) and know that surface winds will probably increase, too. Streamers of snow blowing off summits are another good sign of increasing wind aloft and wind direction.

Climbers, hikers, skiers, and snowshoers can obtain information on the winds aloft before setting out. (See Chapter 7 for additional sources.) However, lacking such information, doubling the surface wind speed at sea level as observed over open water or land can offer at least a workable estimate of wind speeds between 5000 and 10,000 feet (approximately 1500 and 3000 meters). If surface winds are forecast to be 20 miles per hour, expect winds between 5000 and 10,000 feet to reach 40 miles per hour (or more).

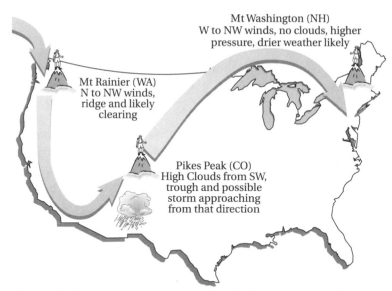

Using winds aloft as a guide to anticipating possible changes in the weather

HIGH-ELEVATION WINDS GUIDELINES

- The higher you go, the more the wind speeds will increase.
- Winds between 5000 and 10,000 feet will typically be twice the speed of surface winds.
- Trees on ridge tops will typically show prevailing wind direction, leaning away from the prevailing wind direction with more foliage on the protected downwind side.

Another clue pointing to moderately strong winds aloft and possibly gusty winds in the mountains comes from lee waves.

WINDS THAT MOVE OVER MOUNTAINS

So far, we have discussed the behavior of winds in the upper atmosphere without considering the impact of mountains. Obviously terrain has a major effect on winds. It is now time to consider that.

Lee Waves

Whitewater kayakers and fly fishers are skilled at observing the flow of water and using those observations to "read" a river. Kayakers use that knowledge to select a safe yet sporting line down a river, fly fishers try to discern possible hiding places for unseen trout. Water rises over submerged boulders, drops over the backside, sometimes curling in an eddy, then rises and falls over subsequent boulders downstream. Exchange mountains for boulders, and the same effect occurs in the atmosphere. We call this motion lee waves or mountain waves. Unlike water, air is invisible, but because air is cooled as it rises over the up-wind face of a peak or ridge, it often condenses into uniquely shaped clouds that help us detect such waves in the atmosphere. Flying-saucer–shaped lenticular clouds or cap clouds form over individual peaks and are curved to reflect the up and down motion of air. When conditions are right for lee waves, a series of such clouds will appear over or just downwind of individual peaks or ridges as the airflow repeatedly rises and falls (see the illustration on page 28).

Because wind speeds of 30 miles per hour are generally the bare minimum to form such lee waves, such clouds offer an excellent clue to at least moderately strong winds at altitude. If the actual clouds look ragged or torn, that is a sign that winds are very strong. Winds aloft need to be perpendicular to a ridge, or close to perpendicular, to produce such waves, which is another reason for caution: Such conditions are ripe for strong gap winds. That leads us nicely into the next type of mountain winds.

River rocks can produce waves similar to the lee waves generated by mountains. (Photo by author.)

MOUNTAIN WAVE GUIDELINES

- If wave clouds are present aloft, anticipate moderate to strong winds at altitude.
- If wave clouds look ragged instead of smooth, anticipate very strong winds.
- The presence of wave clouds suggests strong gap winds in passes or channels that cut through ridges.

Foehn, Chinook, and Bora Winds

When winds descend a slope, air temperatures can increase dramatically in what is called a *foehn wind* or, in the western United States, a *chinook wind*. These winds are significant because of their potential speed, the rapid rise in air temperature associated with them, and the potential they create for rapid melting of snow and flooding.

Chinooks are especially strong over the eastern slopes of the Rockies in Canada and the United States, the Cascades in Oregon and Washington State, and the Coast Mountains of British Columbia. The warming is caused by warmer air moving in from the Pacific, rising up the western slopes, crossing the mountain crest, and then sliding down the eastern slopes of the mountains. This air heats as it sinks and compresses on the east side of a crest. Chinooks also destroy the temperature inversion that normally precedes them, which traps cold air near the surface. Temperatures can easily rise 30°F (approximately 15°C) in minutes, melting as much as a foot of snow in a few hours.

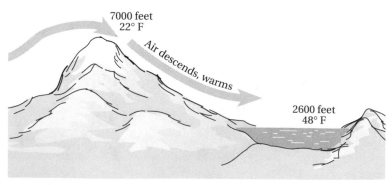

7000 feet
22° F

Air descends, warms

2600 feet
48° F

The development of chinook or chinook-type winds

Expect a chinook with warming of as much as 6°F per 1000 feet of descent (3.5°C per 300 meters) under the following conditions:

* You are downwind of a major ridge or crest (primarily to the east of the mountains).
* Wind speeds across the crest or ridge exceed 30 miles per hour (48 kilometers per hour).
* Precipitation is observed over the crest.

For example, the Absarokas in Montana exceed 12,000 feet in elevation. Given an air temperature of 22°F (–5°C), by the time that air reaches Absarokee, northeast of the range at an elevation of slightly more than 4000 feet, the temperature of the air may have warmed to 70°F (21°C). That is why Native Americans have long referred to chinooks as "Snow Eaters."

The opposite of a chinook is a *bora,* or, as it is called in Alaska, a *taku.* A bora is simply a *glacier wind* bringing air so cold that it is sinking, but the compressing motion as it flows dowslope fails to warm it significantly. Such winds are most common downslope of large glaciers. At times, the air cooled by ice and snow builds up and releases repeatedly, resulting in violent pulses of wind. Speeds can easily exceed 50 miles per hour (80 kilometers per hour), especially in Alaska where the glaciers are huge: Wind speeds exceeding 100 miles per hour (160 kilometers per hour) are not unheard of there.

The high wind speeds of both chinooks and boras can be at best inconveniences to hikers, climbers, snowshoers, and skiers—and at worst life-threatening. Chinooks present additional risks: The rapid warming of snow can increase the risk of avalanches, weaken snow bridges, and lead to sudden flooding from rises in stream levels. When conditions are ripe for a chinook, avoid the downwind slopes.

WINDS IN AND THROUGH THE MOUNTAINS

The direction of surface winds will be very different from the direction of winds aloft. Near the surface, the movement of air is somewhat more complicated than high up in the atmosphere. The pressure gradient and Coriolis forces are still present, but now friction comes into play.

The movement of air over water or land is not smooth: The rougher the surface, the greater the friction and the more turbulent the air flow over it. This upsets the balance between the pressure gradient and Coriolis forces. Air no longer flows parallel to high- and low-pressure systems as it does in the upper atmosphere: It now moves from high to low pressure, though indirectly. The rougher the terrain, the more the wind

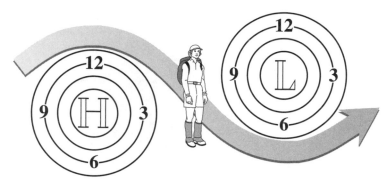

Using surface winds to find the position of a surface low pressure system

will tend to move from high to low pressure. In mountain passes, wind often flows directly from high to low pressure. Remember that air travels clockwise out of and around a surface high and counterclockwise and into a surface low. This tendency is reflected in a simple rule for locating high- and low-pressure systems when still in open terrain: If you stand with your back to the wind, low pressure will be to your left. (See the illustration on this page.)

Once you have used this technique to determine the relative position of a surface low, you can use a compass to find its magnetic direction—that is, whether the low is to the west, the northwest, or the north of your position. If the winds aloft are moving from the same direction, it will probably steer that low toward you. Using your compass to determine wind direction both at the surface and aloft is an excellent habit to develop. As you orient yourself along your route, note the direction of the wind. Make a mental note or jot it down in a small notebook or on the margin of your topographical map, along with the time of your observation.

For example, using the technique just described, you determine a low is to the southwest. Seeing cirrus clouds moving from the southwest to the northeast, you recognize the winds aloft will probably steer that low toward your location. If winds aloft are moving from the northwest to the southeast, that low will probably track to the south.

This technique obviously works in the lowlands and on peaks, but it does not work quite as well on lower slopes. Variations in wind direction caused by friction at elevations near or especially below surrounding terrain make this guideline unreliable. Use the technique only on exposed positions at elevations higher than surrounding terrain.

Beaufort Scale No.	Wind (mph)	Wind (kph)	Common Name	Clues on Land	Clues on Water
0	<1	<1	Calm	None	Mirrorlike
1	1–3	1–5	Light air	Smoke drifts	Scale-like ripples
2	4–7	6–12	Light breeze	Wind felt on face, leaves rustle	Small wavelets, glassy crests
3	8–11	13–18	Gentle breeze	Leaves, small flags in motion	Few crests begin to break
4	12–18	19–30	Moderate breeze	Dust swirls, small branches sway	Wave rows lengthen, half of crests break into spilling white wave crests
5	19–24	31–40	Fresh breeze	Small trees begin to sway	Most waves marked by white horses, some spray
6	25–31	41–52	Strong breeze	Large branches sway, whistling heard in trees	Extensive white horses, spray common
7	32–38	53–63	Moderate gale	Whole trees sway, walking against wind unpleasant	Extensive spray, streaks blown parallel to wind
8	39–46	64–77	Fresh gale	Small branches break, walking against wind difficult	Waves break away from shore, extensive streaks
9	47–54	78–90	Strong gale	Some damage to trees, permanent structures	Whole surface rolls, covered by extensive foam
10	55+	91+	Storm	Large trees fall	Poor visibility, waves have overhanging crests

The changes in wind direction that you observe may be due simply to variations in terrain, or they may be due to changes in weather systems. Look for other confirmations, such as changes in wind speed. For example, are the leaves or boughs of trees being rustled more forcefully along a wooded trail, or is more dust or snow being picked up along a trail in the open? An increase in the ripples or waves on a lake or stream may be another sign. Learning to match such clues to wind speeds can be very helpful. Commercial floatplane pilot candidates are required to learn this skill, and it was one this author found very useful when flying into remote areas. The preceding table, utilizing the Beaufort Scale—a method for ranking wind speeds, summarizes these clues. You will acquire amazing skill with a little practice. The wind speed ranges in this table are different from those in nautical tables because the wind speeds here have been converted to statute miles per hour and kilometers per hour, instead of the knots typically used by mariners. Clues observed both on land and water are given, as either or both may be available during your travels.

Three-hour Pressure Decrease	Altimeter Increase	Recommended Action
.02–.04 inches (in.). 6–1.2 mb.(millibars)	20–40 feet (ft.) 6–12 meters (m.)	None except for normal monitoring of sky
.04–.06 in. 1.2–1.8 mb.	40–60 ft. 12–18 m.	Watch sky carefully for thickening, lowering clouds. See if wind is increasing, shifting to east or southeast.
.06–.08 in. 1.8–2.4 mb.	60–80 ft. 18–24 m.	Watch sky, wind carefully as above. Consider terminating the outing due to the possibility of high winds or seek safer alternatives.
.08 in. or more 2.4 mb. or more	80 ft. or more 24 m. or more	Terminate the outing, or seek the safest alternative available.

Although the chart on page 97 helps you to assess current wind speeds, it does not allow you to anticipate changes in wind speed. An *altimeter,* which is frequently used as a route finding and navigation tool by mountaineers, is essentially nothing more than a specially calibrated barometer. Because changes in air pressure lead to changes in wind speed, careful attention to such changes can provide early warning of high winds. Watch for a continuous drop in air pressure: It will register on an altimeter as a continuous increase in altitude, even if you are walking along a level trail or actually descending. Preceding are some guidelines that have proven useful in my experience both in the forecast office and in the mountains.

Channeled and Gap Winds

Large-scale wind patterns are important, both at the surface and in the upper atmosphere. They have a big impact on our activities in the backcountry and demand close attention, but such winds are only part of the picture. By their very nature, mountains alter wind considerably over very short distances. Often, wind is channeled through such gaps in the terrain as major passes or between two peaks. In the story that opened this chapter, it was such a gap wind that disrupted our sleep. We were camped on the downwind shore of a long mountain lake sandwiched between two ridges. Wind speeds can easily double moving through such constrictions in the terrain, which also can change the direction of the wind to match that of the channel. A 30-miles-per-hour wind on the upwind side of a steep-sided pass may accelerate to a 60-miles-per-hour (100 kilometers-per-hour) wind through the downwind side of that same pass. Less rugged terrain may produce a 50 percent increase in wind speed, typical in the Appalachians. The effect is similar to pinching a water hose to increase the speed of the water that comes out.

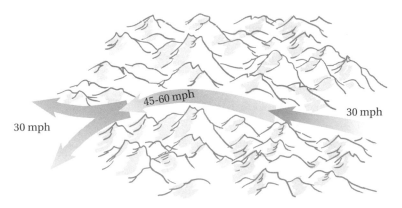

Wind accelerates while moving through a gap or pass.

The key lesson to be learned is to carefully examine current or forecast winds upwind of a gap or pass and, in the case of a trip planned in the vicinity of such terrain features, to expect wind speeds possibly as much as double those upwind. Such winds can be especially strong through gaps that drain dense, cold air from the interior toward less dense, warmer air near a coast. Examples include the ranges along the Alaska, Canada, and Pacific and Atlantic coasts of the mainland United States.

Converging and Diverging Winds

At times the arrangement of mountain ridges, peaks, and valleys does more than simply channel the wind in a new direction. It may split the wind flow, diverting it in two or more new directions: The effect is similar to a fork in a river. As the original flow of air splits and diverges, the wind speed decreases. A hike or campsite along one of the forks downwind of the split will offer lighter winds and more protection than one along the main valley.

Reverse the prevailing wind direction, and the opposite will occur. Instead of air splitting and moving out through the forks (splitting valleys), air will enter through the forks and converge in the main valley. The result will be wind speeds that will be stronger in the main channel or valley than in either of the converging

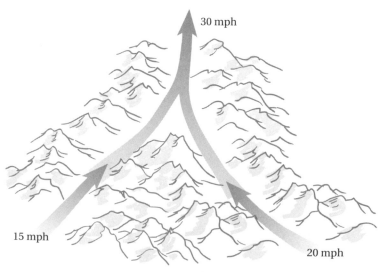

30 mph

15 mph

20 mph

Converging winds can result in increased wind speeds.

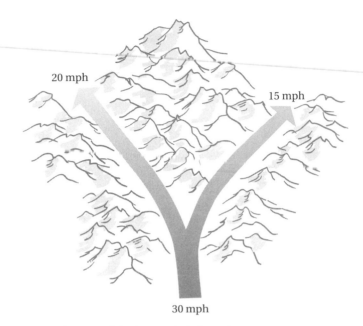

20 mph

15 mph

30 mph

Diverging winds can result in decreased wind speeds.

valleys. Again, if winds are likely to be strong and you have a choice, choosing one of the forks will offer more protection and lighter wind.

Corner Winds

When winds encounter a peak or the beginning of a ridgeline, they tend to curve around that feature. The faster the wind and the more abrupt the change in direction, the gustier the winds will tend to be.

Terrain Blocking

Just as mountains can channel and accelerate wind, they can also provide protection from it. Climbing, skiing, or hiking on the downwind or leeward side of a peak or ridge will offer considerable protection from the wind. However, a major peak will also offer some limited protection to other peaks just

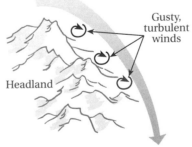

Gusty, turbulent winds

Headland

"Corner" winds can generate locally gusty winds.

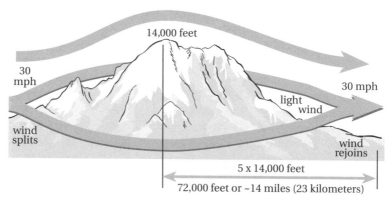

14,000 feet

30 mph

30 mph

light wind

wind splits

wind rejoins

5 x 14,000 feet

72,000 feet or ~14 miles (23 kilometers)

Terrain can "block" wind, resulting in light winds to the lee of that peak or ridge.

downwind. A little knowledge of terrain blocking may provide more comfortable options for an outing.

The flow of wind around a cone-shaped peak, such as Washington's Mount Rainier, will be split for some distance downwind. That separation zone (see illustration above) generally extends to five times the height of the mountain, as measured from the summit of the mountain downwind. Given Mount Rainier's height of 14,410 feet (4392 meters), the air flow around the mountain would be divided for a horizontal distance of 72,050 feet, or approximately 13.5 miles (21.6 kilometers). When searching for a smaller peak that might enjoy some sheltering, be certain to measure that distance from the summit, not the base of the mountain on the leeward side.

Use this guideline conservatively. Gusty winds or irregular peak shapes can shrink the separation zone, and changing wind directions can shift the zone elsewhere. An excellent technique to aid in visualizing the flow of wind around mountains is to slide your topographical relief map into a waterproof cover and use a grease pencil or water-soluble marker to draw arrows depicting wind directions reported or forecast before departure or the wind directions observed on wind-exposed sites. This practice will help you determine what areas are likely to be sheltered from the wind, how wind will tend to follow the shape of the land, and where gaps will tend to accelerate wind.

WINDS THAT CHANGE FROM DAY TO NIGHT

Just as changes in terrain can influence both wind speed and direction, so can the time of day. Specifically, the presence or absence of the sun can cause some winds to vary considerably from day to night.

Valley Winds and Gravity Winds

Differences in the heating of bare ground or rock, as opposed to ground covered by vegetation or trees, can produce *mountain winds* or *valley winds*. As the ground warms during the day, the air close to it also warms and rises, moving up both sides of a valley and spilling over the adjoining ridge tops. Such uphill breezes can reach 10 to 15 miles per hour (16 to 24 kilometers per hour), attaining peak speed during the early afternoon hours and dying out shortly before sunset. The strongest valley winds will be in wider, gently sloped valleys: The sun's rays are better able to warm the opposing slopes there than in a narrow, sheer gorge. Winds will also be strongest up western slopes in the morning, because those are the first to be exposed to the sun.

At night the land cools, and that cooler, more dense air flows downslope in what is called a *gravity wind.* Such downslope breezes reach their maximum after midnight, dying out just before sunrise. Speeds are similar to those of the uphill breezes but can easily be stronger at the base of a snowfield or steep slope or cliff—good reason to follow our safety guidelines at the end of this chapter before setting up camp. Briefly, the steeper the slope and the greater the elevation gain, the stronger the nighttime breezes. Gravity winds are stronger when the slopes above are bare rock or snow, and weaker when those slopes are covered by vegetation, especially trees. The vegetation slows the overnight cooling that produces gravity winds, and trees deflect and slow such winds. If you are camping at the base of a cliff or in a valley, try to put some trees or other obstacles between your tent and the slope above. The formal names for these two types of wind are *anabatic* (the daytime, upslope-moving valley winds) and *katabatic* (the nighttime, downslope-moving gravity winds). The nighttime gravity winds tend to be stronger than the daytime valley winds.

To summarize, gravity winds are strengthened by the following:
- Clear skies
- Prevailing winds of less than 10 miles per hour (16 kilometers per hour)
- Steep slopes of bare rock or snow

Sea and Land Breezes

Although mountains might seem to be exempt from what is called a *sea breeze,* this phenomenon can play a major role both in producing thunderstorms and in altering temperatures. The sea breeze is another consequence of different substances heating up at different rates. Because land heats up more rapidly than water, as the inland air rises, the air over water tends to flow inland during the day. As colder ocean or

Daytime upslope winds

Nighttime downslope winds

Daytime upvalley winds

Nighttime downvalley winds

Cross-slope winds toward
sun-warmed slopes

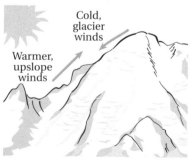

Glacier winds

Valley and gravity winds change with the time of day.

lake air moves inland, the boundary between that air and the warmer air inland effectively forms a front, which is simply a boundary between two different air masses. (Recall that an air mass is simply a body of air that is fairly uniform in temperature and moisture.) Although called "sea" breezes, such winds can also develop over inlets and lakes. Sea breezes typically develop during the late morning and early afternoon, though the exact timing can vary from place to place. Such a sea breeze commonly triggers thundershowers along the Atlantic and Gulf coast regions of the United States, resulting in a barrage of thunder, lightning, and rain in and near the Appalachians. Sea breezes are much less likely to generate thundershowers along the Pacific coast of the United States and Canada, as the onshore flow is likely to be stable, with high pressure tending to suppress the development of showers or thundershowers. Wherever they form, sea breezes are most likely in the absence of fronts or other significant weather systems.

Land breezes are essentially the reverse of sea breezes. Because land also cools much more rapidly than water, the air over land slides downslope in the evening, replacing the air over water that is now by comparison warmer and less dense.

The following are also true of sea breezes:

- Sea breezes are strongest when other weather systems are absent.
- Disturbances producing significant clouds or winds can prevent sea breezes from developing.
- Sea breezes typically develop late in the morning and peak during the afternoon.
- Sea breeze thunderstorms usually die out as the flow reverses late in the day, moving from land toward water.

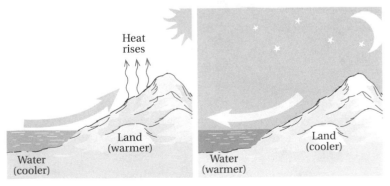

Daytime sea breeze vs. evening land breeze

THUNDERSTORM WINDS

Clusters and lines of thunderstorms developed during the early evening over western New York, and pushed into the Finger Lakes and then through the western Catskills during the mid to late evening hours. These thunderstorms packed strong wind gusts in excess of 60 mph as they raced across the area uprooting trees. Several boats were overturned in Owasco Lake, and at approximately 8:30 p.m. a four-year-old girl drowned underneath a capsized pontoon boat.

National Weather Service Summary,
July 3, 1999

To understand why thunderstorms produce strong winds, consider their size: A small to average thunderstorm is bigger than Mount Everest, which at 29,029 feet is no minor bump in the landscape. Some of the very biggest thunderstorms could practically hold two Mount Everests stacked top to bottom. If a climber standing on the summit could throw a snowball all the way to the Rongbuk base camp, it would be flying at terminal velocity by the time it hit the ground. That is a difference of 12,000 vertical feet. A hailstone flung from a thunderstorm may have fallen several times that distance!

Also, a thunderstorm does not drop just one hailstone. During its mature and dissipating stages, it may dump more than a hundred million gallons of rain and hail. As those hailstones and raindrops fall, they move through air, which resists the falling precipitation. The hail

Thunderstorm wall cloud (photo courtesy of NOAA)

and rain in turn pull some of the air along for the ride: That air is typically very cold—possibly well below zero.

That cold, dense air descends much faster than the surrounding air can warm it. The evaporation of rain cools it even more. The downrushing air, or *downdraft*, continues to accelerate as it falls, hitting the ground with a resounding smack. This rain-cooled air plows ahead of the storm, often kicking up dust in a *gust front*. These gust fronts, like the squall lines that often precede them, may span a dozen miles or more and are certainly strong enough to knock over mature trees and well-staked tents and can also swamp boats. They are typically marked by a long, horizontal, tube-shaped *roll cloud*. If you see such a roll cloud, or if a rotating, cylinder-shaped *wall cloud* extends vertically from the base of the thunderstorm, hit the deck! Both promise strong winds: Wall clouds often precede a tornado.

These signs have been known for decades. However, in the 1970s, meteorologists studying unexplained air crashes found evidence of highly concentrated downdrafts. The ground damage where these extreme downdrafts struck was far more severe than could be explained by an ordinary thunderstorm downdraft or gust front, but the pattern did not suggest a tornado. Rather, it looked like a waterfall of air had hit the ground. Researcher Ted Fujita was intrigued when he flew over impact zones that showed a starburst pattern of downed trees. He devised the term *downburst* to distinguish such events from the less destructive downdrafts. Downbursts tend to have both sharp boundaries and a short lifetime. While maximum winds may reach or exceed 60

Dust stirred up by a descending microburst (photo courtesy of NOAA)

miles per hour within the downburst, winds outside the impact zone may not reach even 10 miles per hour: From start to finish, the downburst may last only 3 minutes.

Fujita also discovered downbursts that occurred over extremely short distances, approximately 2.5 miles (4 kilometers) or less. He called these *microbursts*. Both downbursts and microbursts can plunge out of thunderstorms—producing precipitation—or out of thunderstorms in which the rainfall evaporates before it hits the ground. These dry thunderstorms are especially common in the arid parts of the western United States and northern Mexico. The evaporation of the falling rain cools the cascading air, strengthening the intensity of the downburst or microburst.

Whatever the source, you can anticipate the following about dangerous thunderstorm winds:

- They can occur beneath a thunderstorm whether rain is reaching the ground or not.
- They can occur well ahead of the thunderstorm in gust fronts.
- They can spread out from beneath the thunderstorm in downdrafts, downbursts, or microbursts.
- Wind speeds can easily reach or exceed hurricane force.
- They can last just seconds or persist much longer.

Anticipating Thunderstorm Winds

The best way to avoid dangerous thunderstorm winds is to keep some distance between yourself and the thunderstorm. Both checking forecasts before leaving home or interpreting changes in the sky can achieve that goal.

It is important to get your forecasts from agencies or sources familiar with your local area. Forecasts issued by the National Weather Service come from such local offices, as do forecasts issued by qualified meteorologists working for local television or radio stations. Each of these sources also usually posts its forecasts on websites. Commercial forecast services working out of a single national office simply cannot appreciate the local factors that can make a big difference. If NOAA Weather Radio broadcasts are available and transmit to your destination, by all means take along a weather radio and know the frequencies for your destination. Such radios have an alarm function that can save your life. If you have the opportunity, check the forecast when you arrive at the trailhead or campsite—typically, that means talking with a park ranger. If weather forecasts mention potential thundershowers, anticipate the possibility of dangerous thunderstorm winds.

The next step is to watch the sky for clues suggesting thunderstorm development or dangerous winds:

- Warm, humid air: Low visibility and unseasonably warm temperatures when coupled with high humidity are explicit danger signs.
- The bases of growing cumulus clouds change from white to dark gray or black.
- Lightning flashes, hail begins to fall, or you hear thunder.
- Dust begins to blow.
- Wind whips trees or other vegetation.
- Wave height on water increases suddenly.
- You observe either a roll cloud in advance of a thunderstorm or a wall cloud rotating from its base.

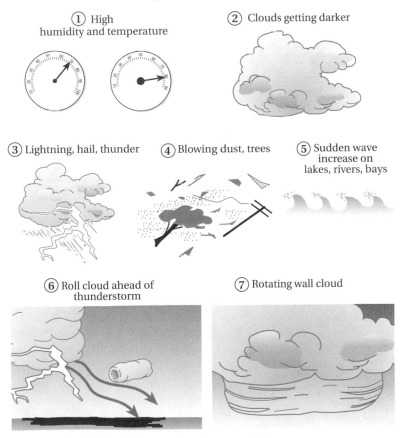

① High humidity and temperature

② Clouds getting darker

③ Lightning, hail, thunder

④ Blowing dust, trees

⑤ Sudden wave increase on lakes, rivers, bays

⑥ Roll cloud ahead of thunderstorm

⑦ Rotating wall cloud

Warning signals of possible strong thunderstorm winds

ASSESSING YOUR EXPOSURE TO WIND

Once you are in the backcountry, safety comes not only from anticipating high winds but also from choosing a campsite or refuge with
care. When winds howl, it is no longer important whether the source
is a thunderstorm, an approaching low, or gap winds accelerating
through a pass. What matters is whether your surroundings will enhance or reduce your exposure to wind-borne debris.

- Are the trees around you uniform in size, or are there some
  much taller trees that stick up above the canopy?

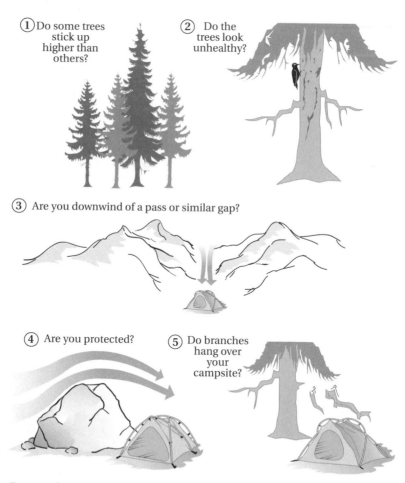

① Do some trees stick up higher than others?

② Do the trees look unhealthy?

③ Are you downwind of a pass or similar gap?

④ Are you protected?

⑤ Do branches hang over your campsite?

*Features that may increase or decrease your exposure to damage or injury from
strong thunderstorm winds*

- Are nearby trees healthy, or do they appear diseased or weakened by insects?
- Is your location downwind of a gap, pass, channel, or canyon?
- Is there a hill, bluff, or large boulder upwind?
- Do branches hang over your campsite?

An isolated tree, or trees significantly taller than the surrounding stand, will act as sails and catch more wind, and thus they are more likely to topple. Camp at a safe distance from them, as well as from trees that appear diseased or infested by insects. Caution signs include branches devoid of leaves, needles, or bark; trunks punctuated by woodpecker or flicker borings; and a coating of running sap or pitch. Such weakened trees will be among the first to drop in a strong wind. It is best to avoid camping under overhanging branches if at all possible.

Narrow openings in the terrain such as gaps, passes, channels, or canyons focus and accelerate the wind. If any winds come blasting through such an opening, your tent (and possibly you) may go airborne. Upwind bluffs, hills, or even large boulders or hedges upwind can serve as windbreaks.

Once you have selected a campsite, erect your tent into the wind. Use solid tent stakes and guylines. Without guylines, even a moderately strong wind can snap tent poles. Experienced campers have found the best anchor comes from attaching such lines about one-third to one-half of the way up a tent.

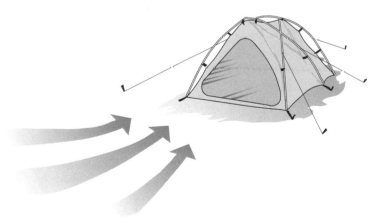

A tent properly pitched, facing into the wind with guylines secured for maximum strength

ACTING SAFELY IN A WINDSTORM

Actions can be either reactive or preventive, positive or negative. Negative actions increase risk, while positive actions decrease it. "Just Do It" may be a catchy advertising slogan, but it is not good

① Get out of your tent

② Seek a stand of similar-sized trees

③ Stay near a clearing

④ Crouch behind a rock, bluff, or hill

⑤ Crawl if the wind makes it difficult to walk

⑥ Seek refuge beneath a fallen tree

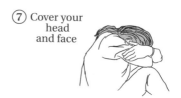

⑦ Cover your head and face

advice in the wilderness. The guidelines in the preceding sections suggest positive, preventive actions to take before a storm hits. Equally important, potentially life-saving actions should be taken when high winds hit:

- Get out of your tent. A tent offers little protection and will prevent you from seeing falling trees or large branches.
- If you are in the woods, seek a stand of even-sized trees. Avoid larger trees or trees that look sick or dead. Move toward a clearing or shoreline if possible.
- If you are in a clearing or on a shoreline, stay there: Do not run into the woods.
- Crouch behind the side of a hill, bluff, or rock that is sheltered from the wind.
- If large trees are already downed to the ground, seek refuge beneath one.
- Crawl if the wind makes it too difficult to walk.
- Cover your head and face.

AIDING OTHERS IN A WINDSTORM

Should an injury occur, the first step is to minimize the problem. Do not add another injury by putting yourself unnecessarily at high risk while the storm is still raging. Before moving or attempting to help a victim, plan how you can minimize your exposure. A tree limb blowing at 60 miles per hour can kill. An unconscious or dead rescuer will not be of much use to someone needing help.

If possible, call for assistance.
Seeking assistance obviously depends upon your location and circumstances. If you are deep in the wilderness, you are on your own. If you are not alone or are within a couple miles of assistance, by all means seek help. Are you carrying a cell phone? If so, try 911 or the emergency number used wherever you are. However, remember that not all backcountry areas have emergency service, and signals may not reach that far. Still, it is not a bad idea to carry the telephone number of the park headquarters or local fire or police agency. If you have a radio, use it to summon help. If it is not possible to communicate from your location and someone is injured, have someone remain with the injured person and send someone else for assistance. If your group is large enough, send two people. In all cases, make certain the storm is over before you move.

Personal locator beacons (PLB's) now offer backcountry travelers a much better chance of being found and rescued should they get into trouble. Similar to devices used by pilots and sailors for years, PLB's transmit a distress signal and a location to satellites. They are expensive and certainly no substitute for good judgment, but they can mean the difference between rescuers finding a victim alive or dead. They may make the most sense for small parties operating in remote areas.

Signal for help.

Severe windstorms can leave you isolated and possibly unable to move. That will force you to catch the attention of searchers by signaling. If at all possible, move out into the open. Unless the fire danger dictates otherwise, build a smoky signal fire. Whistles, signaling mirrors, and flashlights can also be effective ways to get attention.

Carry a first-aid kit, know how to use it, and first treat those who appear to be dead.

Remember the ABC's of first aid: Check for an open *airway,* check to see whether the injured person is *breathing,* and then check for evidence of *circulation:* a pulse. Check for evidence of breathing and circulation for at least 20 to 30 seconds. If you cannot detect breathing or circulation, begin CPR. (If you have not completed CPR training or if it has been a while since you have practiced, sign up for and complete a new course now. It takes so little time to learn and can make a big difference.) If anyone is wet, treat for hypothermia. Put a protective layer between the victim and the ground to diminish the chance of hypothermia, and keep him or her warm by covering the victim with any available clothing, blankets, or sleeping bags.

Set survival priorities.

If immediate rescue or evacuation is not possible or likely, set priorities:

- Keep a positive mental attitude—expect to survive.
- Administer first aid.
- Seek or build a shelter.
- Build a fire for warmth and signaling.
- Prepare rescue signals.
- Find water and purify it if at all possible by boiling, filtering, or using purification drops or tablets.
- Gather food. This ranks last in importance, but it can be a huge morale builder.

LIGHT WINDS

Much of this chapter has focused on dangerous wind situations. It is also nice to know which conditions are conducive to light winds. It can make for more comfortable camping (sometimes both for you and the mosquitos that come to visit). Expect winds to be less than 10 miles per hour (12 kilometers per hour) when you are not at the base of a snowfield, cliff, or mountain; when high pressure has moved into the area; or when pressure changes are less than 1 millibar or .04 inch over a 3-hour period; when your altimeter, while remaining at the same elevation, shows a fluctuation of less than 40 feet (12 meters) in a 3-hour period; and when skies are covered by flat, stratus clouds.

One parting bit of advice that may lead to a toastier evening: When winds are light and skies are clear, do not camp at the bottom of a valley. Remember that cold air drains downslope, making campsites upslope actually warmer overnight than those at the base of a mountain or in a valley.

Sometimes warmth is not your objective but rather the bracing cold that is needed for snow. The next chapter investigates snow and avalanche conditions: how to find the best snow for skiing, snowboarding, and snowshoeing and how to recognize signals that a slope is an avalanche waiting to happen.

Mountain Snow

The bowl was completely filled with snow, blown level with drifting clouds of it. I was the only thing standing, or showing. The dogs were covered and totally gone. Except for little puffs of steam released up through melted exit holes over each dog's nose where their breath came out, there was no sign of the team, the sled, nothing.

Gary Paulsen, *Winterdance:*
The Fine Madness of Running the Iditarod

The first trek on snowshoes to Mount Baker's Artist Point two winters earlier had been magical: clear skies, sparkling fresh snow, the joy of sharing the experience with friends. It brought the small group of college students back each year. The conditions on December 12 of 2003 were very different. Heavy, wet snow resulted in marginal visibility. Ten inches had fallen the night before. More sloppy snow was rapidly accumulating as the group set out from the parking lot. The avalanche forecast warned of "considerable" avalanche hazard, rapidly becoming "high." But this group had not checked the forecast. They had almost reached a saddle just short of their destination when a slab of snow released perhaps 50 feet above them. They had no time to react—in seconds they were encased in the soggy embrace of a slab that would hold them for 24 hours. Few people survive burial for more than 45 minutes—if they are very lucky. Two of the students defied the odds: They survived—barely. The third did not.

A few months later, an experienced group of mountain rescue climbers were inching their way up a frozen waterfall in Alberta. It looked like a perfect day for an ice climb. Skies were sunny, but temperatures at the base were cold—perfect for securely frozen ice. The rhythmic motion of swinging ice axes and front-pointing with crampons had quickly settled the climbers into a routine of assessing their line, the quality of the ice just above them, the progress of their partners. This group was disciplined, experienced, and thorough. Just one small detail had eluded them. A temperature inversion had formed, leading to much warmer conditions near the top of the waterfall than at the base. As the group progressed steadily upward, melting water percolated into fissures in the ice, weakening a massive chunk. When it gave way, the climbers could do absolutely nothing. They were literally sitting targets.

A third group of backcountry skiers pushed beyond the ski area boundary under the tutelage of their avalanche skills instructors. Moving carefully down a ridge, they eased out onto the slope: close to an escape path but on the same pitch they hoped to ski. Each had carefully analyzed the avalanche forecast, which was for a moderate hazard: Each now began to dig snow pits to analyze the stability of the slope. They performed a *Rutschblock test,* which involves isolating a block of snow and then testing its stability—by first stepping lightly and then progressively increasing the load—eventually jumping—to see whether the block will slide. All indications pointed to stable conditions. After reloading their packs, they skied down through knee-deep powder, with small crystals tickling their noses. Reassembling at the bottom, they wore the wide grins that follow the kind of perfect run you remember a long time.

Walk on snow, and you are essentially walking on water. From the preceding examples, it may seem as though you are walking on thin ice. Actually both impressions are incorrect. Walk on snow, and you are walking on air—with a little water mixed into it. That may sound even more implausible, but everyone who has attempted to break trail in fresh powder, who has sunk to their knees or hips with every laborious step, knows this by experience, if not by reason. That is why a cloud that would otherwise produce an inch of rain will produce an average of 10 inches of snow. You do not even have to open your eyes to know that it is snowing. You can sense it. Snow absorbs sound, resulting in unusual quiet. It covers and conceals, offering shelter and insulation to creatures snuggling beneath the blanket of white and a dazzling crystalline beauty to those above it.

Snow provides an almost irresistible excuse to play, but it can also be dangerous. That sparkling blanket of white conceals a complex, changing structure. Snow may be the solid form of water, but it is hardly a rigid shell covering the ground. It is plastic in many ways: It flows, and it compresses. In fact the very shape and character of snow are transformed by changes in temperature, moisture, wind, and time. Understanding a little about how snow forms and behaves can vastly improve your fun on skis, snowshoes, or a snowboard. If you choose to venture into the backcountry, that knowledge can be critical to your safety.

No single chapter is sufficient to adequately prepare you for the decision making needed in such an environment. Even an entire book devoted to snow and avalanche safety will provide you with only part of the foundation needed to safely navigate the snow-covered backcountry. The solution is to take an avalanche course from accredited professionals offering hands-on training in the snow. Contact the American Avalanche Association (*www.avalanche.org*) for a list of avalanche educators throughout the United States and Canada. This chapter explores the various stages of snow as it can impact our activities: as it falls from the sky, as it accumulates on the ground, and as the snowpack changes over time.

FROM SKY TO GROUND: UNDERSTANDING AND FINDING GOOD SNOW

Travel in the coastal ranges of the Cascades, the Olympics, the Coast Mountains, or the Sierra Nevada, and the snow will be heavier and wetter than in ranges farther inland. You will be more nearly walking on water. Move farther inland to the Wasatch or Tetons and the water content drops. You will be closer to walking on air. Available moisture and temperature make the difference. Air moving off the oceans is wetter, but the farther it moves inland, the less moisture remains in the clouds. Each time moist air is forced over a mountain range, some of that moisture falls out as either rain or snow. It is like passing a snack plate down a table: The person sitting at the end will find fewer snacks to sample. Snow also forms differently as temperatures change. Close to an ocean, temperatures are moderated by the relatively warm sea surface temperatures. Move inland and that moderating influence either disappears or is minimal, as mountain ranges block that ocean air. That is the difference between a maritime and a continental climate, and that difference requires vastly different strategies for anyone heading into the backcountry.

Snow forms very differently from rain, yet what begins as snow often ends up melting and falling as rain. Liquid precipitation—rain— is first the result of water vapor condensing. You see this happen every time you breathe out on a cold day. As you exhale, warm, moist air rapidly cools. That cooling slows what is called the *kinetic energy*, or movement of the water vapor molecules, and they essentially huddle closer together—not unlike people when it becomes chilly. As the temperature continues to cool, water vapor molecules continue to huddle more closely until the air temperature reaches the dew point (see Chapter 2) and the water vapor condenses into miniscule water droplets. This happens more quickly if dust or salt particles are suspended in the air. The air within a cloud moves, and that results in countless collisions between these invisibly tiny water droplets. Given the right circumstances, the droplets stick to each other, eventually growing large enough to fall as rain.

Air temperatures below freezing do not guarantee snow. Cloud droplets will not automatically freeze at 32°F (0°C) but can persist as liquid water at temperatures as cold as −38°F(−39°C). In an example of extreme understatement, such water droplets are called *supercooled*. If those droplets chill any further, they will freeze instantly, but the air temperature within the cloud does not have to get that cold to produce snow because clouds are not a pristine collection of just air and liquid water droplets or water vapor. All manner of atmospheric flotsam is

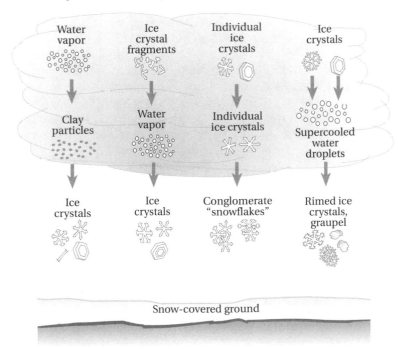

The various ways snow forms

present, including tiny particles of clay. The physical structure of clay and some other substances makes it very attractive to water vapor, essentially jump-starting the formation of ice crystals within the refrigerator-like environment of a cloud. Once this process begins, the conversion of water vapor and supercooled water droplets into ice crystals proceeds like a row of dominos toppling over each other. Ice crystals form and some break, transforming still more water vapor into ice crystals. At this point, the cloud is a stew of clay and ice particles, ice crystals, water vapor, and supercooled water droplets, all suspended in a broth of very cold air.

The temperature of the air surrounding this nursery of ice crystals determines their shape. Like children, they can develop in vastly different ways, depending upon the environment. Picture a snowflake or ice crystal, and you will probably visualize something like the lacy, star-shaped patterns you snipped from construction paper as a child. These are *stellar dendrites,* yet they are only one of a staggering variety of ice crystals. Ice crystals can be shaped like slender needles, stout columns, columns with caps on either end, and flat, six-sided plates. The temperature at which those ice crystals form and the amount of water vapor in the air determine their exact shape. Cool the air to −12°C to −16°C, add some air with water vapor, and you will get the classic, star-shaped dendrites. Warm it a few degrees, and you will get the flat, six-sided plates. Notice how the number six keeps popping up? The Mickey Mouse shape of a water molecule—the oxygen atom as the head with two hydrogen atom ears—and the way those molecules attach or bond to each other causes ice crystals to grow in six-sided or six-armed symmetry.

These growing crystals will continue to scavenge water vapor from the surface of supercooled water droplets, or tiny droplets will freeze right onto the crystal—a process called *riming.* Turbulent clouds with lots of water droplets will so coat the original crystal that it is unrecognizable. The result is called *graupel,* which typically falls along or near a cold front. Even less turbulent clouds will combine individual ice flakes into a larger conglomeration called a *snowflake.* In an atmospheric version of nature versus nurture, the end product can bear little resemblance to its original shape: It can become a sort of "Franken-flake." The turbulence, wind, temperature, and moisture encountered as an ice crystal descends to the ground can all lead to major transformations in shape or size.

For practical purposes, we want to know where we can expect to find snow on a mountain, preferably the best-quality snow. It is not that hard if we take it one step at a time. The first step is to determine

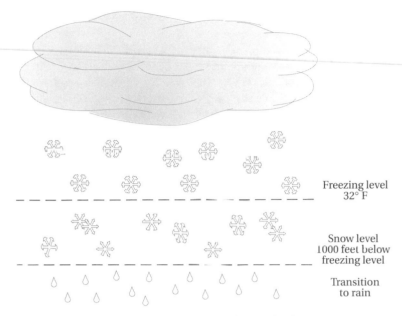

Freezing level
32° F

Snow level
1000 feet below
freezing level

Transition
to rain

The relationship between the freezing level and the snow level

the elevation where the air temperature is freezing. Once you do that, you can develop a reasonable estimate where the snow will stick. The altitude where the air temperature is freezing is called, not surprisingly, the *freezing level*. You will find snow falling there and at lower elevations. Typically, the snow level is 1000 feet below the freezing level because as snow hits warmer air or ground, it melts and evaporates. That lowers the temperature, just as surely as water evaporating from your skin can cool you on a hot day. In the atmosphere, that cooling will allow snow to begin accumulating on the ground, depending upon the temperature of the ground. If cumulus clouds are producing snow, cold downdrafts may lower the snow level as much as 2000 feet below the freezing level.

You can find the freezing level in some mountain forecasts or in the specific avalanche and mountain forecasts issued in many states and provinces. (See Appendix V for contact information.) If that is not available but you have a thermometer and an altimeter, you can make an estimate by using the temperature at your elevation and the "standard lapse rate," the average between what are called the *moist lapse rate* and the *dry lapse rate*—the rates at which air cools with increasing altitude above Earth's surface in saturated and unsaturated air. The standard lapse rate is 3.5°F per thousand feet of elevation (or 2°C per 304 meters).

The following example is figured in feet and °F. Camped at 3000 feet, you observe the air temperature to be 39°F. Subtract 32 (the freezing temperature) and multiply by 1000 (feet). The result is 7000. Divide this by the standard lapse rate of 3.5°. The dividend is 2000, indicating the freezing level should be 2000 feet above the campsite. Add that to your current elevation to get the estimated freezing level: 5000 feet. (I picked an easy example).

THE SNOW LEVEL WILL USUALLY BE 1000 FEET (300 METERS) BELOW THE FREEZING LEVEL

Specifically, to estimate the freezing level, perform this simple calculation:

$$\text{Your Elevation} + \frac{\text{Camp Temperature} - 32° \times 1000 \text{ feet}}{3.5° \text{ (standard lapse rate)}} = \text{Estimated Freezing Level}$$

$$3000 \text{ feet} + \frac{39° - 32° = 7 \times 1000 \text{ feet} = 7000 \text{ feet}}{3.5°} = 5000 \text{ feet}$$

The freezing level is 5000 feet, approximately 2000 feet higher than your campsite elevation. The same example, figured in meters and degrees Celsius, follows:

Camped at 910 meters (approximately 3000 feet), you observe the air temperature to be 3.9°C. There is no need to subtract the Celsius freezing temperature, because that is simply zero. Multiply by 304 meters. The product is 1182. Divide by the standard lapse rate of 2°C. The dividend is 591 meters above the campsite. Add that to your existing elevation of 910 meters to get the estimated freezing level of 1501 meters.

$$\text{Your Elevation} + \frac{\text{Camp Temperature} \times 304 \text{ meters}}{2° \text{ (standard lapse rate)}} = \text{Estimated freezing level in meters}$$

$$910 \text{ meters} + \frac{3.9° \times 304 \text{ meters}}{2°} = 1501 \text{ meters}$$

Now, a word of caution. Temperature inversions are common in the mountains (that is, the air temperature decreases more slowly than the standard lapse rate or actually increases with altitude). Therefore, the standard lapse rate may not reflect reality: Use it as an approximation. If winds have been light and skies clear or covered by stratus clouds, odds are an inversion exists. If winds have been brisk or a weather system is approaching, present, or departing, an inversion is less likely, and the result from the formula for estimating the freezing level will be more accurate.

These guidelines will help you find the best snow available (or at least to avoid the worst). However, too much of a good thing is possible: Heavy snowfall in avalanche terrain can quickly elevate the hazard of slides. Weather, past and present, is one of three essential elements to consider.

SNOW ON THE GROUND: WHEN IT'S RISKY, WHEN IT'S NOT

The Avalanche Assessment Triangle was constructed to help backcountry travelers accurately assess the likely hazard of slides by summarizing the major elements that contribute to avalanches: specifically, *weather, terrain,* and *snowpack.* The discussion that follows is intended only to be an introduction to each, and all should be explored in greater depth by taking an avalanche course from a qualified instructor. Such classes will expand upon the information given here and will show you how to apply that knowledge in the field. This will be fun, interesting, and—most importantly—will aid you in assessing whether or not a slope is safe.

Weather

In coastal ranges, direct-action avalanches are most common, generally occurring during or within 24 hours of *major precipitation.* The weight of snow alone can trigger an avalanche, as can the added weight from a skier or vibrations from someone crossing a snowfield. A general rule of thumb is that snow falling at or above a rate of an inch per hour (2.5 centimeters per hour) will boost the potential for direct-action avalanches.

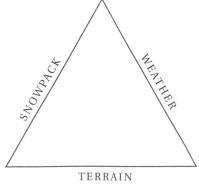

The Avalanche Assessment Triangle

Temperature not only determines the type of snow that will fall but also contributes to the stability or instability of the snow as it accumulates on a slope. If temperatures warm during a snowstorm, the avalanche hazard will increase. Wetter, heavier snow will rest on top of less dense snow, an unstable pattern that is essentially an avalanche waiting to happen. A good rule of thumb is to watch out when freezing or snow levels are forecast to rise. *The bigger the rise, the greater the risk.* Obviously rain falling on fresh snow is very dangerous. If high pressure builds over your area, check for evidence of a temperature inversion. For example, if temperatures reported by a ski area's upper lift stations are warmer than those at the base, expect unstable conditions on higher slopes in the backcountry. (See Chapter 7 for additional sources of information on this topic.)

Winds of 10 to 15 miles per hour (16 to 24 kilometers per hour) or more also elevate the avalanche hazard. These winds tend to pick up snow from windward slopes and deposit it on leeward slopes. This produces deeper snow or increased *wind loading.* In addition, such winds tend to break up ice crystals, allowing the snow to pack together more efficiently in a compressed layer called a *slab.* This is especially likely on lee slopes. See Chapter 8 for guidelines specific to your destination. Certain key indicators can help you determine recent wind direction, particularly cornices pointing away from the wind and plumes of snow blowing off ridge tops away from the wind. On the other hand, rime ice that grows on either trees or rocks will point into the wind.

The final element is the *sun,* particularly in spring. Avalanche fatalities often rise during spring, particularly in late March and early April. This spring increase is attributed to what avalanche forecaster Rich Marriott calls the "bluebird syndrome": the belief that if skies are blue, nothing bad can happen to you. Sunshine makes it pleasant to be

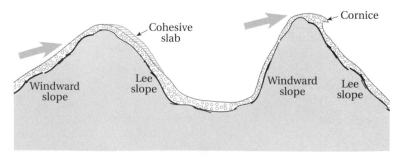

Wind direction influences key snowpack features.

outside, but it can also warm snow, loosening the bonds between snow-flakes or crystals and making the top layer heavier. This is why sun-warmed south-facing slopes tend to be more dangerous in late winter and early spring.

KEY AVALANCHE WEATHER RISKS

- Snow falling at a rate of 1 inch per hour (2.5 centimeters per hour)
- Wind speeds of 10 to 15 miles per hour or more (16 to 24 kilometers per hour or more)
- Rising freezing/snow levels

Terrain

After you check present, past, and forecast weather, it is time to focus on the *terrain*. The key question is "Is it steep enough to slide?" No matter how much it snows, it is not going to avalanche in the Plains states. The western United States and Canada and parts of the northern Appalachians present a very different situation. Most avalanches occur on slopes ranging from 25° to 45°. However loose, wet snow slides can occur on slopes as shallow as 15°, and slab avalanches can release on slopes as steep as 56° or greater. Loose snow normally sloughs off the steeper slopes, preventing much of a buildup, but wet snow can glue itself to the steepest slopes along ranges like the Cascades or Coast Mountains in the Pacific Northwest. Do not relax your guard when crossing a flat stretch below a steep slope: Such areas are called *runout zones* for good reason. A slab avalanche barreling down a slope does not magically stop at the bottom. Its inertia can carry the slide across the valley bottom, and if narrow enough, it even can continue up the adjoining valley wall. This is exactly what caught and killed a number of Canadian high school students on an outing in Alberta. A cornice collapsed on a ridge top, triggering a massive slab avalanche on the slope below. This huge slice of the snowpack ran across the valley floor, finally halting partially up the opposite slope, catching the students and their guides in what seemed to be a safe zone for travel. Anyone planning an outing in such a location must be willing to change their plans if the avalanche pattern increases.

Analyzing terrain does not end with the slope angle. An avalanche risk exists anytime objects that tend to anchor snow become buried. Examples include closely spaced boulders, old tree trunks, and small trees or shrubs. Some of these same objects can indicate slopes that avalanche frequently. In fairly dense timber, look for what is called the *trim pattern*. If lower limbs are missing on the uphill side, you are still within the runout zone—and at risk. A conservative guideline is that if you can ski through the trees you can have an avalanche, but if you have to hike through them an avalanche is unlikely because more closely spaced trees will more effectively anchor the snow in place.

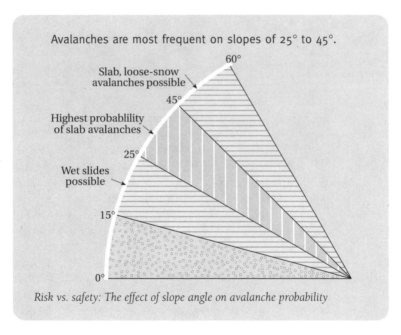

Risk vs. safety: The effect of slope angle on avalanche probability

Snowpack

The third element of the Avalanche Triangle is the *snowpack*. What appears to be a featureless blanket of white is actually a highly complex, evolving structure. Try this: Drive on a freshly plowed road on which the cleared snow was thrown far enough away from the edge that you can see the distinct layering that reveals the sequence of snowstorms, both great and small. Just as the sheer, layered walls of a mountain gorge reveal chapters of Earth's history to the trained eye of a geologist, so can the varied layers within a mountain snowpack reveal the story of each individual snowfall and the overall stability of the snowpack to an avalanche expert.

Understand first the two basic types of avalanches: slab and loose snowslides. Loose snow avalanches tend to be less dangerous, unless they sweep backcountry travelers toward what are called *terrain traps:* cliffs, trees, and the like. Slabs are heavy and cohesive: The impact alone can kill. It is easy to get a better understanding of the way these layers develop by digging a pit in the snow and spraying the exposed surface with a mix of water and food coloring. The distinct layers will stand out. The factors responsible are complex but include differences in the original types of ice crystals that fell, differences in wind speed and direction that compact the drifting snow into slabs, the settling caused by gravity, and the changes that occur over time due to variations in temperature.

If temperatures cool after a snowfall, water vapor will be deposited on the surface, resulting in the attractive sparkle of *surface hoar.* This can be fun to ski on but dangerous if it is buried beneath subsequent layers of snow because the feathers of hoarfrost do not bond well but rather provide a loose, sliding surface for the layers above. That can also happen when the upper layers of the snowpack become markedly colder than the snow beneath. The gradient, or difference in temperatures, can lead to recrystallization of the snow: Water vapor moves upward from warmer (and more moist) layers of snow to colder, drier layers. The *depth hoar* or *faceting* that may occur results in a loose layer that is similar to dominos arranged upright between two boards. A slight disturbance of either board will cause the dominos to collapse and the upper board to slide. In the case of snow, the dominos represent the unstable layer of depth hoar, and the upper board represents a slab. This arrangement is why skiers, climbers, and other backcountry travelers often report hearing a "hollow" sound in such cases, followed by a "whumping" sound as the hoar collapses and the slab settles and slides. A slower gradient, or change of temperature within the snowpack, leads to more stable conditions. Avalanche expert and educator Paul Baugher of the Northwest Avalanche Institute teaches students to think of the snowpack as a sandwich: "Peanut butter over jelly is unstable, jelly over peanut butter is not." That is, dense snow over a slippery, loose layer can slide easily with serious consequences, while lighter snow atop a heavier base is more stable.

Lighter snow on top of heavier snow tends to be *stable.*
Heavier snow on top of lighter snow tends to be *unstable.*

Backcountry skier analyzing snowpack (photo by author)

Over time, new snow settles and changes shape in a way that leads to stronger connections, or bonds, between individual snowflakes. Water molecules move from the outer part of the flake to the body, eventually becoming a round snow or ice grain. This practice is called *equilibrium metamorphism*. Assuming this process continues, these grains will become connected by thicker and thicker necks. This process varies from one region and season to another, but will continue if temperature differences through the layers of a snowpack are small. During spring, for example, longer days lead to increased melting. The water percolates down through the snowpack, and when it hits a layer of crust, it spreads out, acting as a lubricant for the slab above. However, when the meltwater refreezes, this process, called *melt-freeze metamorphism,* can also result in a stronger snowpack.

The trigger for spring avalanches comes from the daily cycle of melting and freezing. When clouds develop, leading to warmer nighttime temperatures, the crust does not redevelop on the surface of the snowpack. The next day, the sun will not have to melt off the surface crust and the density of this layer will increase with added snowmelt, so backcountry travelers should be prepared for a larger number of slides, especially from late morning to late afternoon. These seasonal changes also affect the stability of snow and ice bridges on climbing routes. (See Chapter 8 for more about local weather patterns.)

An example of why careful attention is so important comes from the experience of two avalanche experts. Late one warm, sunny April day, these two were playing a game of Frisbee on skis. No avalanches had occurred, and the pair did not want to lose any altitude, so they selected a long traverse across a relatively steep slope. Focusing on their Frisbee, they were surprised to suddenly hear "thunder" and were chilled to see an avalanche throwing up chunks of snow the size of compact cars and roaring down a section of the slope they had crossed less than 10 minutes earlier.

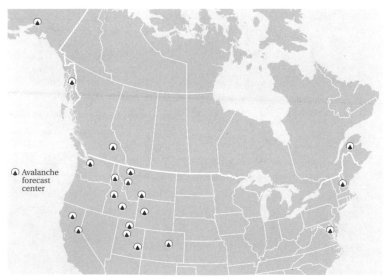

Map of avalanche forecast center locations

If all this sounds a bit complicated, it is, which is why taking an avalanche course is so important, as are checking avalanche forecasts before heading into the backcountry and possessing the proper equipment and attitude. Skiers, boarders, and climbers may have the proper training and equipment but can still get into trouble by not taking advantage of the avalanche forecasts specific to their intended destinations.

Avalanche forecasts use the hazard scale shown in the following table. Each hazard level corresponds to the probability and recommended action shown.

Avalanche Hazard	Probability	Recommended Action
Low	Natural/human avalanches unlikely.	Normal caution advised.
Moderate	Human triggered avalanches possible.	Use caution in steeper terrain on certain aspects.
Considerable	Natural avalanches possible, human avalanches probable.	Be increasingly cautious in steeper terrain.
High	Natural/human triggered avalanches likely.	Travel in avalanche terrain is not recommended.
Extreme	Widespread natural/human triggered avalanches certain.	Travel in avalanche terrain should be avoided, confine travel to low-angle terrain away from avalanche path runouts.

GLACIERS AND WEATHER

Glacier travel requires consideration of more than just avalanches. No matter how smooth the surface may appear, climbers can count on the presence of crevasses. Glaciers form when more snow falls than melts over the course of a year. That snow compacts over time, eventually forming ice. Gravity tugs this ice sheet downhill, where it begins to melt into runoff. Although a glacier is unquestionably hard, it varies from brittle on the surface to more plastic in its super-compressed base. As the glacier flows downslope, it adjusts to changes in the terrain. The brittle surface cracks during that process, especially as it accelerates onto a steeper slope or moves around obstacles. These cracks, or crevasses, range from the thickness of a finger to the width of a freeway. The principle of "see and avoid" does not work in navigating on a glacier. Falling or drifting snow can cover much if not all of a crevasse. The snow bridges that form can offer safe travel over a crevasse, speeding ascents or descents, but also can pose considerable risk.

Relatively wet winter zones, such as those experienced in the Cascade Mountains, the Coast Ranges, the Vancouver Island Range, and the Sierra Nevada, rarely experience extreme cold. Heavy snow in winter can hide crevasses, but such bridges are usually safe during mid- to late winter. By spring, longer days bring more direct sunlight and warmer temperatures: That begins to weaken snow bridges that may sag and even collapse. This typically begins in the lower reaches of the glacier, progressing farther upslope later in spring and summer. Travel is most risky during the afternoon or evening hours. Nighttime freezing makes such bridges safest overnight into the early morning hours. However, the presence of clouds may prevent such firming.

During summer, more snow bridges collapse and crevasses open. Danger increases when new snow falls, concealing the real margins of a crevasse with just a few inches of snow. This is also true into the midautumn months, when heavier snows and colder weather finally begin to rebuild and strengthen snow bridges.

Farther inland over the Canadian and U.S. Rockies, lighter and more limited winter snowfall does little to rebuild snow bridges, which typically remain suspect into early spring. Spring snowstorms help rebuild these bridges—occasionally. Temperatures may be cold enough to firm up these rebuilt snow bridges or warm enough to weaken them—especially with a mix of rain and snow.

Farther north in Alaska, the Yukon, and northern British Columbia, the spring thaw of April, May, and June allows meltwater to percolate deeply into the snow, making snow bridges treacherous for weeks. Wind-stiffened snow bridges may show little obvious sign of collapse, but they will do so abruptly, especially during the afternoon. By midsummer, crevasses open and bridges collapse. Firmer, more trustworthy bridges often will not develop until after the more frequent snowfalls of late summer into winter. Earlier snowfalls often just insulate suspect snow bridges from the cold and prolong instability.

Obtaining timely weather information and forecasts is critical to avoiding avalanches and anticipating glacier conditions. That is the subject of Chapter 7. As avalanche expert Andre Roch has said, "Be careful. The avalanche does not know you are an expert." To that I add, "But it will surely discover your ignorance." As the Northwest Weather and Avalanche Center in Seattle states on its website, "The more you know, the safer the snow—make every trip a round trip!"

Pre-Trip Weather Briefings

An expert is someone who knows some of the worst mistakes that can be made in his subject, and how to avoid them.
Werner Heisenberg, *Physics and Beyond*

In the mountains, an accident and a mistake are different. Both can kill, but an accident may have been difficult if not impossible to anticipate. A mistake should never have happened. The death of nine climbers high on the shoulders of Oregon's Mount Hood in May of 1985 was a mistake. It should never have happened. The seeds of the disaster were sewn long before the group from a Portland-area school shouldered their packs and trudged out of the parking lot at Timberline Lodge.

The first sign of trouble—the weather forecast—came before the group left Portland. An unseasonably strong storm was forecast, with heavy snow, lowering snow levels, and very strong winds. High clouds were already racing across the sky. By the time the climbers assembled in the inky darkness early on the twelfth of May, clouds blanketed the sky and the wind was rising. Still, the decision was made to depart. Post-holing at times up to their knees, progress came slow for the climbers. Exhausted less than 3 hours into the climb, five students and one adult headed back down the mountain. By 8:00 that morning, another adult and student were suffering badly from altitude sickness.

Temperatures were warming, strengthening winds buffeted the fatigued climbers, and the clouds continued to lower. A professional guide urged the school's climb leader to turn back. The leader refused. By midafternoon, visibility was down to 50 feet, then 30, then 10. Severe gusts made it difficult to stay upright, much less make any further progress toward the summit. Finally, the decision was made to descend. As light faded, the fatigued party, some already suffering from hypothermia, began to dig a snow cave. It was a night of fitful sleep, trying to keep warm, to warm those suffering from hypothermia, or just getting a lungful of air to breathe. Some crawled out of the hastily dug cave for fresh air. Clothing critical to survival was lost trying to maneuver in the rapidly accumulating snow. By daybreak on the thirteenth, there was no improvement in the weather—it was getting worse. Heavy snow, the kind locally known as "Cascade concrete," continued to fall. Winds howled. Visibility was nonexistent. Any body warmth gained from the night in the cave was lost in minutes. The leader was shivering violently, unable to form words. Others were only slightly better off.

Two climbers—a student and the professional guide—decided to seek help. Staggering through fierce winds and heavy snow, forced to navigate mostly by hunch, they eventually reached a nearby ski area. A search party was mobilized. The next morning, May 14, three students were found scattered on the snow. It is believed they decided to seek help for the other eight. All three would die from hypothermia, despite the best efforts of emergency room doctors. On May 15, searchers found the snow cave with the remaining climbers. Only two of the eight survived.

Mountaineering and medical experts compiled a report analyzing the disaster. Several issues were identified as contributing to the nine deaths. Most would be obvious to anyone with moderate experience in the mountains: The deteriorating weather. The division of the group when some chose to turn back. The small number of guides compared to the size of the climbing party. The decision to press on for the summit late in the day in the face of worsening weather. The inescapable truth, not directly stated, is that the deaths were the result of a mistake, not an accident. Not a single death was unavoidable. Given the explicit forecast, the climb should have been postponed.

The previous chapters contain guidelines to help you enjoy the mountains and wilderness safely. The best guidelines, however, are of little use without sound, current weather information and forecasts, as was made clear in the Mount Hood tragedy.

As a flight instructor, I taught my students both how to obtain thorough weather briefings and how to use that information to make good decisions: simply put, whether they should stay on the ground, depart as planned, or select an alternate route. This is no less important for someone heading into the backcountry on foot. If the weather deteriorates, a pilot can reverse course at speeds exceeding 100 miles per hour (160 kilometers per hour) or more. The speed of mountain travelers is a fraction of that, of course, increasing the hazard of exposure to hazardous weather (although you have the advantage of already being firmly attached to the ground!).

There have never been as many good sources of weather information as there are today. The maturing of the Internet offers data that previously would have been available only to professional meteorologists. It also offers a mishmash of misinformation guided in some cases by the desire to make fast money, in others by good intent but ignorance. The aim of this chapter, then is to help you navigate successfully through the occasional fog of weather information and forecasts, learning what to look for and what to avoid. The first topic presented is examining sources of information and forecasts, then how to put that information together to make good decisions. To paraphrase the old pilot's adage, "It is better to be at home wishing you were in the backcountry than to be in the backcountry desperately wishing you were at home!"

MOUNTAIN WEATHER SOURCES: THE GOOD, THE BAD, AND THE UGLY

Whether you are planning a picnic or a multiday summit attempt on a major peak, the sources most frequently used for gathering weather information are the same: television, radio, and newspapers. However, the most widely used sources are not necessarily the best.

Although newspapers offer you the option of digesting forecasts and weather data at your leisure, the information is dated and occasionally obsolete by the time it reaches your front doorstep or the newsstand. Many dailies rely on national forecasting firms to prepare their "local" forecasts, which results in a forecast prepared with little genuine knowledge of local weather patterns. Some newspapers utilize the forecasts of local meteorologists: They are worth seeking out. Look on the newspaper's weather page to see who prepares the forecast. If the source is the local office of the National Weather Service, or a local commercial or broadcast meteorologist, the information is probably worth reading. More on this topic follows.

Radio weathercasts can be aggravatingly brief, often pared to a bare minimum to fit in a format designed to appeal to ever-shortening attention spans. I have heard weather forecasts that bore little resemblance to the information or computer guidance at hand. A little detective work showed the forecast given was more than 24 hours old! Radio stations specializing in news and information tend to offer more reliable and up-to-date weather information: NOAA Weather Radio offers the best information. The NOAA (National Oceanic and Atmospheric Administration) is the parent organization of the National Weather Service. Commonly used by boat owners, good radios dedicated to the NOAA Weather Radio frequencies (no tuning is necessary) can be purchased for less than a hundred dollars and represent good insurance to keep track of overall trends, as well as short-term watches, warnings, and advisories. Overall, mountain weather forecasts and information offered on radio tend to be brief. Radio is best used as a source to alert you to impending severe weather, to expected changes best checked in greater detail elsewhere, or simply to confirm trends.

The quality of television weather broadcasts varies widely and often places more emphasis on cuteness than on content. Recreational and mountain weather is often glossed over or nonexistent. That said, many serious, highly trained television meteorologists offer excellent weather information and forecasts. Before relying on a television weather presentation, be certain the weathercaster is a meteorologist with a degree in the field and, even better, actually spends time in the mountains from time to time. Otherwise excellent meteorologists may still not understand the influence of mountains on weather. Personnel in recreational and outdoor shops are often good sources of recommendations. Television offers the benefits of immediacy and the ability to see current information: Its disadvantage in most cases is that once the weathercast is over, you cannot review the information.

The Internet has become a treasure chest of excellent weather information. The depth and breadth of weather observations and forecasts are unmatched. That actually can be a problem: Some of the information is designed for professional meteorologists and may be confusing. As is often the case, a little knowledge can be dangerous. And sometimes outright garbage is what is put out—some well-meaning, some not. I offer two brief examples.

One November afternoon I discovered my email inbox was overflowing, most focused on the same topic: a web-based pronouncement that the coming winter would be the snowiest in 50 years. Curious, I looked up the source of this excitement and discovered that a local public works official who fancied himself a weather sage was forecasting a winter of Old Testament proportions: He prophesied drifts that would loom overhead, together with snow-congested streets that would not clear until the next spring. I phoned a friend of mine on the faculty of the University of Washington who had been deluged with similar email. It took a news release from that university, the local office of the National Weather Service, and repeated broadcasts on our station to finally stem the furor. The source never was "available" for comment.

The second example deals with the phenomenon of "personalized" forecast services. Such firms offer what they claim are highly localized projections (sometimes referenced to a zip code) based on proprietary computer models. Intrigued, I signed up for one to check out its claims. The forecast quality was mediocre to poor, and even went so far one day as to alert me that the weather was perfect for big game hunting—in downtown Seattle! For obvious reasons I resisted the impulse to purchase an elephant gun and go searching for trophies lurking behind latté stands. Further investigation showed the quality of the computer model utilized was at best second rate and lacked elements offered by regional models. Do not bother with such "personalized" Internet forecasts, increasingly offered by cell phone and pager companies.

STRATEGIES FOR PRE-TRIP WEATHER BRIEFINGS

Assessing weather for a trip within an hour's drive from home can and should begin with a look out the window: Simple observations can offer much information of value. Just two simple and inexpensive home weather instruments can enhance the value of such observations: a barometer and a wind vane. There are essentially three observations to make: changes in the sky, changes in the wind, and changes in barometric pressure. These three elements are the foundation of getting good weather information from any source, whether inside or out.

Let's begin with changes in the sky. Approaching weather disturbances, as previously noted, are typically marked by lowering, thickening clouds. Before those appear, you may see lenticular clouds over mountain peaks or a halo around the sun or moon. Lenticular or mountain wave clouds offer evidence of strong winds at

Typical indoor barometer

Rooftop weather vane

altitude, as well as increasing moisture, possibly from an approaching low. Coronas or halos around the sun or moon can signify the approach of a disturbance within as few as 12 or as many as 36 hours, particularly if followed by lowering and thickening clouds. Look also for the appearance of small cumulus clouds: If such clouds appear, continue to watch them for evidence of upward growth. (See also Chapters 2 and 3.)

A wind vane on your roof or a mast in your yard can also enhance your weather sleuthing. If mounted on a mast, make certain the vane is higher than your roof (and if at all possible, higher than neighbors' roofs and trees). Because changes in wind direction typically are the result of shifts in high- and low-pressure systems and fronts, they can offer excellent clues to impending changes in the weather:

- A shift from *north or northeast to southeast winds* generally signals the approach of a low (in the northern hemisphere).
- A shift from *southeast to southwest winds* usually occurs with the passage of a cold front.
- A shift from *southwest to north winds* typically signifies the building of high pressure.

Consider such changes in wind direction together with changes in wind speed. Increasing winds can suggest an approaching front. Certainly an *anemometer* that precisely measures wind speeds can be useful, but you can also obtain helpful information from watching the environment around you, as discussed in Chapter 2.

Long before clouds appear or the wind shifts direction, a barometer can detect changes in air pressure that indicate significant, impending changes in the weather. Such a tool is an important addition to your home. It offers valuable guidance on the approach speed of weather disturbances, or the speed at which a high is building, or what winds are likely at home or in the mountains. Choose a barometer with a resettable guide, which will allow you to quickly see how much the pressure has risen or fallen since you last checked. Following are some guidelines to help you assess changes in pressure, with measurements in both inches of mercury and in millibars.

- *If* pressure changes are less than .04 inch/1.2 millibars in a 3-hour period, *then* monitor as usual.
- *If* pressure changes are .04 to .06 inch/1.2 to 1.8 millibars in a 3-hour period, *then* watch closely for changes in the sky and winds.
- *If* pressure changes are .06 to .08 inch/1.8 to 2.4 millibars in a 3-hour period, *then* monitor NOAA Weather Radio or other sources continuously and consider delaying a backcountry trip.
- *If* pressure changes exceed .08 inch/2.4 millibars in a 3-hour period, *then* delay departure.

Although most attention is focused on falling pressure, an increase in pressure is not an ironclad guarantee of wonderful weather. Rapidly building highs can also generate strong winds. Given the channeling effect of passes and gaps in the terrain, speeds of 60 miles per hour (100 kilometers per hour) can develop in the mountains. Consider waiting until the high has had an opportunity to build over your region. That typically will happen 12 to 24 hours after air pressure begins to skyrocket.

Using Newspaper Weather Information

Newspapers offer you the opportunity to review weather information at your convenience, but they lack currency. You will not be able to obtain current observations, much less severe weather watches, warnings, or advisories from newspapers. However, reviewing the weather page before heading out on a trip is worthwhile. Typically, the information you will obtain falls into the following categories:

- Past weather in the mountains or backcountry
- Satellite photos
- Jet stream or winds aloft
- Forecast mountain weather
- Longer-range forecasts for nearby cities

Past weather in the mountains may simply consist of the previous day's high and low temperatures and precipitation. Granted, weather observation stations in the backcountry tend to be few and far between, but any available information can provide you with a foundation of what the weather has been like. Satellite photos can show what type of clouds are over the area you plan to visit and just upwind. Some newspapers will offer a brief discussion of weather trends and will overlay the jet stream on a satellite photo like the one shown on page 153.

Widespread, flat, and relatively featureless clouds tend to suggest widespread precipitation, while what appears to resemble cottage cheese or polka dots points to cumulus clouds and their localized, but often intense, precipitation (more on this later in this chapter). If the jet stream is moving directly toward your destination, expect bad weather and plenty of it. If it is to the north of your location, expect relatively mild temperatures. If it is to the south of your location, cool temperatures are likely and the air mass could be unstable—that is, prone to showers and thundershowers. Also consider the movement of the jet stream relative to the mountain or peak you plan to visit. The slopes exposed to the winds will tend to be wet and blustery, those on the lee side will tend to be dry (though chinook or gap winds could still make conditions unpleasant).

The actual weather forecast should yield information on expected precipitation and sky cover, snow or freezing levels, high and low temperatures (at least in the major passes), and expected pass winds. Typically, this forecast will only cover 24 hours. Consider the following:

> *Mountains: Partly cloudy today with increasing clouds and an increasing chance of showers late in the day, mainly on west-facing slopes. Snow level dropping to 3000 feet. Pass highs in the low to mid 30s. Lows tonight in the mid to upper 20s. Pass winds easterly 15 to 25 miles per hour.*

To get a sense of longer-range trends, look at the long-range forecast for a nearby city. It will tell you if forecasters expect a wet or dry weather pattern and if temperatures will be warming or cooling. That can be applied, at least in a general sense, to pass temperatures and freezing or snow levels.

Using Radio Weather Broadcasts

Most radio weather broadcasts tend to focus on the immediate metro area over the next 24 hours. Occasionally, some will offer specific mountain forecasts. If not, consider contacting your favorite station—

particularly if it offers ski reports—and suggest that including mountain forecasts is just as important as current ski reports (and perhaps less optimistic). The information you want to hear will include the following:

- Any current severe weather watches, warnings, or advisories
- Forecast precipitation
- Pass temperatures
- Pass winds
- Snow or freezing levels

Perhaps your best radio option for weather information is NOAA Weather Radio (NWR). It usually requires a separate radio (though frequencies are occasionally built into other radios or devices). NWR forecasts will include all the points mentioned, and typically they include longer-range trends for the mountains, as well as current weather conditions in the passes. Recognizing the importance of good information in the wilderness, NWR is working to improve transmission to such areas. Locations within mountain ranges may still cause reception problems, but check anyway. If weight is a major consideration, such as for backpackers or climbers, you may choose to leave the radio in your car, but it can give you a last-minute weather update before heading out on a trail.

Using Television Weather Broadcasts

Television allows you the opportunity to immediately see as well as listen to weather information. You will have the opportunity to look at current radar displays of precipitation and see time-lapse loops of satellite motion that will give you the best sense of where clouds and specific storms or fronts are headed. While timing such features can be challenging, good forecasters will give estimates of both when and where such disturbances are expected and, possibly, their degree of uncertainty. Animated graphics may show the position and location of the jet stream. Current as well as forecast mountain conditions should also be shown. Given the highly localized nature of mountain or wilderness weather, the jet stream may or may not be a major influence.

If a broadcast meteorologist you otherwise trust does not provide sufficient detail, consider contacting him or her with a friendly, tactful suggestion regarding how they could make their broadcasts even more useful. Recognize that some television stations give their meteorologists or weathercasters more time and latitude than others to determine what to insert in their broadcasts. Look for the following elements:

- Current weather watches, warnings, or advisories
- Current mountain or backcountry weather conditions
- Satellite loops for cloud motion relative to your destination
- Jet stream or winds aloft relative to your destination, including the same factors listed for Using Newspaper Weather Information (see page 139)
- Mountain forecasts with snow/freezing levels, pass temperatures, and winds
- What the forecasters say, as well as what they show

Experienced meteorologists will often sandwich important nuances in forecasts as they move from graphic to graphic. Many users "surprised" by "unexpected" weather simply did not listen to or watch the broadcast very closely.

Using the Internet for Weather Information

The skills needed to properly utilize weather information found on the Internet can necessitate a degree in meteorology. That can be one of this source's downfalls: a lot of information with little guidance. The following sections present methods for interpreting some key types of weather information. Keep in mind that the websites used in examples and offered for reference may change their addresses. A good search engine can usually direct you to a current address or to an equivalent site. Since some people want the quickest possible weather briefing while others enjoy delving deeply into the mysteries of the atmosphere, the following information offers approaches for both types of weather researchers.

A Quick Approach to Gathering Weather Information

Remember the Four A's of Thunderstorm Safety? *Anticipate, Assess, Act,* and *Aid.* Pre-trip weather briefings utilize three of those steps. *Anticipation* involves searching for pertinent weather information, *assessing* that data allows you to use that information to determine whether conditions favor your planned outing, and *acting* on that information involves making the proper decision. The correct decision should prevent the need for any *aid.*

The best source for the broad range of weather information and forecasts needed for most trips is the website for the local U.S. National Weather Service Forecast Office or for Environment Canada. The following screen capture shows the homepage for the website of the National Weather Service Forecast Office in Salt Lake City, Utah (*newweb.wrh.noaa.gov/slc*). While the exact format may change, the information available will remain mostly the same. Notice the map displaying active watches, warnings, and advisories with current radar and satellite images. The menu on the left side shows the range of information available

In certain instances, you will want to check some additional sources, but your briefing should begin with a search for any special watches, warnings, advisories, or statements. These deal with hazardous weather: severe thunderstorms, high winds, flash floods, or blizzards—the kind of weather that would make an outing inadvisable. In the absence of immediate hazardous weather, proceed to the information in the following list:

1. Severe weather watches, warnings, advisories, or statements
2. Current weather observations
3. Zone, state, or provincial forecasts
4. Extended outlooks
5. Avalanche forecasts (as appropriate, in season)

The U.S. National Weather Service has developed several levels of alerts relating to different types of severe weather. Environment Canada and weather services in other countries have developed similar types of watches, warnings, and advisories. Check for any such alerts before heading into the backcountry. If any of these watches, warnings, or advisories are posted for your area of interest, delay your trip or choose a different destination.

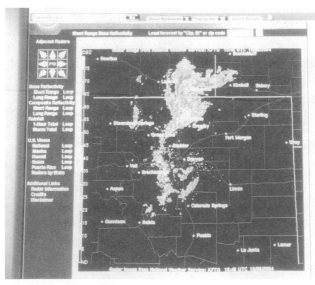

Typical National Weather Service Forecast Office website homepage

NATIONAL WEATHER SERVICE WATCHES, WARNINGS, AND ADVISORIES

- *Severe Thunderstorm Watch:* Conditions are favorable in the watch area described for thunderstorms strong enough to produce wind gusts to 58 miles per hour (97 kilometers per hour) or greater, hail 0.75 inch (1.9 centimeters) or larger, or tornadoes. None have actually been spotted in the watch area. [Such watches typically are issued for 4 to 6 hours at a time, and for a number of counties.]
- *Severe Thunderstorm Warnings:* A severe thunderstorm has been detected [by radar, or by a trained spotter], or is imminent. Take cover immediately!
- *Tornado Watch:* Tornadoes are possible in the watch area described. Remain alert for approaching storms.
- *Tornado Warning:* A tornado has been seen or indicated by weather radar and is imminent. Move to a place of safety immediately.
- *Flash Flood Watch:* Flash flooding is possible in the watch area described. Remain alert and be prepared to move promptly to a safer location.
- *Flash Flood Warning:* Take action immediately to save yourself. Flooding is imminent or already occurring. You have only minutes or seconds to act.
- *High Wind Watch:* Sustained winds of 40 miles per hour or gusts of 58 miles per hour (67 or 97 kilometers per hour) or more are possible for an hour or more.
- *High Wind Warning:* Sustained winds of 40 miles per hour or gusts of 58 miles per hour (67 or 97 kilometers per hour) or more lasting an hour or more are imminent or occurring.
- *Winter Storm Watch:* More than 4 inches of snow (and/or sleet) (10 centimeters), freezing rain accumulation of 0.25 inch (.6 centimeter) or more within 12 hours, enough ice accumulation to damage trees or powerlines, or a life-threatening combination of snow and/or ice accumulation with wind is possible within 48 hours.
- *Winter Storm Warning:* Winter storm conditions as defined above are imminent or occurring.

- *Blizzard Warning:* Snow and/or blowing snow reducing visibility to 0.75 mile (.6 kilometer) or less for 3 or more hours and sustained winds or frequent gusts of 35 miles per hour (58 kilometers per hour) or greater are occurring or expected within the next 18 hours.
- *Wind Chill Warning:* Wind chills of −30°F (−35°C) or lower are expected.

Using Watches and Warnings

If a watch or warning is posted for your destination, either delay the trip or select a different destination. Keep in mind that, by definition, the backcountry is a remote area and radio reception will tend to be either poor or nonexistent, as will cell phone reception. Do not count on these tools being able to receive a severe weather watch or warning for you. The time to act on such a watch or warning is before you leave home and commit yourself and possibly others to an exposed location in hazardous weather. Because of the short-term nature of these alerts, you will need to get them from an up-to-date broadcast source such as radio, television, or the Internet. In a local forecast given by NOAA Weather Radio, an Internet weather site, or a television or radio meteorologist, a typical watch would read as follows:

THE STORM PREDICTION CENTER HAS ISSUED A SEVERE THUNDER-STORM WATCH FOR PORTIONS OF EASTERN AND CENTRAL ARIZONA . . . NORTHERN AND WESTERN NEW MEXICO

EFFECTIVE THIS THURSDAY AFTERNOON FROM 1:00 P.M. UNTIL 6:00 P.M. MST.

HAIL TO 2 INCHES IN DIAMETER . . . THUNDERSTORM WIND GUSTS TO 60 MPH AND DANGEROUS LIGHTNING ARE POSSIBLE IN THESE AREAS.

THE SEVERE THUNDERSTORM WATCH AREA IS ALONG AND 40 STATUTE MILES NORTH AND SOUTH OF A LINE FROM 25 MILES WEST OF FLAGSTAFF ARIZONA TO 10 MILES EAST OF GALLUP, NEW MEXICO.

REMEMBER . . . A SEVERE THUNDERSTORM WATCH MEANS CONDI-TIONS ARE FAVORABLE FOR SEVERE THUNDERSTORMS IN AND CLOSE TO THE WATCH AREA. PERSONS IN THESE AREAS SHOULD BE

ON THE LOOKOUT FOR THREATENING WEATHER CONDITIONS AND LISTEN FOR LATER STATEMENTS AND POSSIBLE WARNINGS.

The specific information given in such a watch or warning helps users assess the likely impact of the expected thunderstorms, flash floods, tornadoes, high winds, or heavy snow on their planned outing. The next step after checking for short-term watches and warnings should be to examine current weather conditions, and then the longer-term potential for severe weather, which typically would be available in either a state or zone forecast.

Current Weather Conditions

Interpreting current conditions given in a radio or television broadcast is straightforward. Those given on an Internet website will look something like the following.

VERMONT STATE WEATHER ROUNDUP

National Weather Service Burlington VT
100 AM EST Thu Dec 18 2003
Note: "fair" indicates few or no clouds below 12,000 feet with no significant weather and/or obstructions to visibility

City	Sky/Wx	tmp	dp	rh	wind	pres	remarks
Burlington	lgt snow	31	30	96	NW9	29.29F	vsb ¾ 6 hr min temp: 30; 6 hr max temp: 33; 6 hr pcp: 0.53
Montpelier	lgt snow	29	28	96	NW14 G24	29.16F	vsb ¾ 6 hr min temp: 29; 6 hr max temp: 33; 6 hr pcp: 0.62
Morrisville	lgt snow	30	29	96	Calm	29.17F	vsb ¾ 6 hr min temp: 30; 6 hr max temp: 33; 6 hr pcp 0.57
St. Johnsbury	N/A	30	30	100	vrb 5	29.12F	6 hr min temp: 30; 6 hr max temp: 33; 6 hr pcp: 0.81
Rutland	Cloudy	28	27	93	W13 G21	29.22S	wci 18 6 hr min temp: 30; 6 hr max temp: 34; 6 hr pcp: 0.04

Springfield	Cloudy	33	26	75	W12 G18	29.18S	6 hr min temp: 33; 6 hr max temp: 37; 6 hr prp: 0.80
Bennington	lgt snow	29	25	85	W10	29.28S	fog wci 20 6 hr min temp: 29; 6 hr max temp: 33; 6 hr pcp: 0.24

Key
vsb — visibility in miloc
wci — wind chill index

Burlington, for example, is reporting light snow with a temperature of 31°F and a dew point of 30. The closeness of those two numbers suggests the atmosphere is close to saturation: The relative humidity of 96 percent is not surprising, nor is the fact that visibility is only three-quarters of a mile, as shown in the "remarks" column. Winds are from the northwest at 9 miles per hour, and barometric pressure is 29.29 inches and falling. The minimum temperature over the last 6 hours was 30°F, while the maximum over that same period was 33°F and precipitation totaled 0.53 inch. Since temperatures have been close to or below freezing, much if not all of that precipitation was probably in the form of snow. As noted in Chapter 6, on average 1 inch of rain yields 10 inches of snow. Because precipitation gauges are typically heated, the snow will be melted to yield a measurement in inches of liquid water. Multiplying that number by 10 will yield a reasonable estimate of snowfall. In this case, 0.53 x 10 yields 5.3 inches.

It is also worthwhile to scan the observations for significant variations in air pressure. In the preceding example, Bennington (with a stable pressure) and Burlington are reporting similar pressures, while the reported pressure for St. Johnsbury to the east is considerably lower. That moderately strong difference in pressures from west to east could generate some gusty gap or channeled winds and is probably responsible for the gusty winds in Rutland and Springfield. If the pressure difference increases, winds are likely to become even stronger in both those locations and near any other notches, gaps, or passes.

Interpreting Local Forecasts

The zone forecasts issued by the National Weather Service typically extend over a five-day period and cover a specific geographic area, collection of counties, or metropolitan area that will have similar weather. The forecast language for the first two days will be much more specific than for the next three. Again, TV and radio broadcasts, together with Internet websites, will be the best sources for such forecasts. Zone or state forecasts offer you the opportunity to see how well the forecasters are doing. Check the forecast a few days before your trip, and then check to see what happens the next day. Was the forecast correct? If so, you can have more confidence in the forecast for your trip. If it was wrong, you will want to regard the forecast with more caution. A typical zone forecast looks like this:

INTERIOR NORTHERN CALIFORNIA ZONE FORECASTS

NATIONAL WEATHER SERVICE SACRAMENTO CALIFORNIA
505 PM THU NOV 4 2004
CAZO13-021430
SHASTA LAKE AREA/NORTHERN SHASTA COUNTY-
INCLUDING . . . SHASTA DAM
505 PM THU NOV 4 2004
. . . SNOW ADVISORY FOR FRIDAY . . .
TONIGHT . . . BREEZY. RAIN AND SNOW SHOWERS. SNOW LEVEL
3500 FEET. SNOW ACCUMULATION UP TO 2 INCHES. LOWS 28 TO
36. SOUTHWEST WINDS 20 TO 25 MPH.
FRIDAY . . . RAIN OR SNOW SHOWER. SNOW LEVEL 2000 TO 2500
FEET. SNOW ACCUMULATION UP TO 4 INCHES. HIGHS 30 TO 43.
GUSTY WEST WINDS 20 TO 30 MPH OVER RIDGES.
FRIDAY NIGHT . . . MOSTLY CLOUDY. COOLER. CHANCE OF SNOW
SHOWERS. LOWS 18 TO 32.
SATURDAY . . . MOSTLY CLOUDY. A LITTLE WARMER. RAIN OR
SNOW SHOWERS. SNOW LEVEL 4000 FEET. HIGHS 35 TO 45.

	TEMPERATURE			/	PRECIPITATION			
SHASTA DAM	32	41	28	44	/	70	70	40	30

The text portion of the forecast is self-explanatory. The temperatures listed for Shasta Dam are specific for each forecast period. In this example, it is 32 for Thursday evening and 41 for Friday. The numbers given for precipitation are the forecaster's estimates of the probability that measurable precipitation will fall at the specified location for each forecast period—for example, a 70 percent chance of precipitation for both Thursday evening and Friday, decreasing Friday evening and Saturday. If winds begin diminishing Thursday evening, showers end, and skies clear, Friday may actually offer better weather than forecast. If not, bundle up and be prepared for challenging weather.

Avalanche Forecasts

Most people set off the avalanches that trap or kill them. That simple, stark fact, together with the availability of avalanche forecasts such as the following one, suggest that backcountry travelers have more control over their fate than most would suspect. The establishment of avalanche forecast centers confirmed that as more backcountry skiers and climbers followed the guidance available, the number of avalanche fatalities decreased. After a few years, however, deaths and injuries from snowslides began to increase again. That mystified everyone from avalanche experts to park rangers. After some thought and investigation, an explanation emerged: New groups were pushing into the winter backcountry, and skiers and climbers now shared mountains with snowshoers, snowboarders, and snowmobilers. Their enthusiasm often was not tempered with education and awareness of avalanche hazards. Their first mistake was often their last.

Avalanche centers cover much of the western United States and Canada, with one in the northeastern United States (see Appendix V). It takes just a few minutes to check the latest avalanche forecast and statement. Obviously this step will not be necessary if you are planning a snowshoe trek in the Boundary Waters region of northern Minnesota, but it is critical in the mountainous West and even parts of the Northeast. The following is a sample of one such forecast:

FOREST SERVICE NORTHWEST WEATHER AND AVALANCHE CENTER ISSUED THROUGH NATIONAL WEATHER SERVICE SEATTLE, WA SUMMARY BACKCOUNTRY AVALANCHE FORECAST FOR THE OLYMPICS AND WASHINGTON CASCADES
These forecasts apply to backcountry avalanche terrain below 7000 feet. They do not apply to highways or operating ski areas.
0830 AM PST Friday, January 02, 2004
ZONE AVALANCHE FORECASTS. . . .

OLYMPICS . . . WASHINGTON CASCADES . . .
Moderate avalanche danger below 7000 feet Friday, slightly decreasing through early Friday night. Danger gradually increasing Saturday, remaining moderate below 7000 feet but locally considerable above 5000 feet on easterly facing slopes. Danger

slowly decreasing late Saturday and Saturday night.
OUTLOOK SUNDAY . . .
Moderate avalanche danger below 7000 feet expected Sunday,
with a locally greater danger developing on mainly westerly facing
slopes near the Cascade passes.

The sample forecast from the Northwest Avalanche Center suggests that you might be wise to avoid easterly facing slopes, particularly trails or sections above 5000 feet on Saturday because of the increased avalanche hazard. The snowpack is expected to become more stable in those areas on Sunday, so you could switch to the higher easterly facing slopes then. If you enjoy venturing into the backcountry during winter, consider taking an avalanche course from trained experts. Some resources, together with books specifically dealing with avalanche hazards, are listed in Appendixes V and VI.

WEATHER BRIEFINGS FOR THE OVERACHIEVING OUTDOORS ENTHUSIAST

The previous section covered the basic elements of weather information needed to form a reasonably thorough picture of current and expected weather for your planned trip. Surprises can and will happen. The atmosphere, after all, will not fit into a test tube, and that precludes the precision of laboratory sciences (which sometimes yield surprises of their own). Other sources of information can be useful, particularly for those with either a strong interest in weather or just a little added intellectual curiosity. If, like Sergeant Joe Friday in the old *Dragnet* TV series you want "Just the facts," skip to the sample briefings. Come back to this section when curiosity prompts you. Otherwise, read on.

Forecast Discussions: Getting Inside the Forecaster's Head

Forecast discussions are primarily intended for other meteorologists. They explain the forecaster's interpretation of the weather patterns and computer guidance behind the zone forecast and express the forecaster's level of confidence in the forecast issued. The added information can be invaluable for anyone heading into the mountains or backcountry.

AREA FORECAST DISCUSSION
NATIONAL WEATHER SERVICE MISSOULA MT
UPDATE . . . CURRENT WINTER STORM WARNINGS AND ADVISORIES WILL REMAIN IN EFFECT THROUGH FRIDAY MORNING WITH

VIGOROUS WINTER STORM MOVING THROUGH THE NORTHERN ROCKIES THIS EVENING.
UPPER LEVEL TROUGH AND SURFACE LOW PRESSURE SYSTEM STACKED VERTICALLY OVER THE IDAHO PANHANDLE THIS EVENING . . . WITH COLD FRONT MOVING THROUGH CENTRAL IDAHO AND INTO WESTERN MONTANA . . . WITH CONVECTIVE HEAVIER SNOW SHOWERS OCCURRING WITH COLD FRONT. THE COLD FRONT WILL PASS THROUGH WESTERN MONTANA BEFORE MIDNIGHT . . . WITH DEFORMATION SNOWS CONTINUING OVERNIGHT OVER NORTH-WEST MONTANA. SOME LOCAL GUSTY SOUTHWEST WINDS SHOULD OCCUR AS THE FRONT PASSES FROM MISSOULA SOUTH-WARD. WIND AND SNOW SHOULD BEGIN TO TAPER OFF SHORTLY AFTER MIDNIGHT FROM MISSOULA SOUTHWARD. GUSTY NORTH-EAST WINDS WILL CONTINUE OVERNIGHT IN NORTHWEST MON-TANA. THE UPPER LEVEL AND SURFACE LOW WILL MOVE INTO NORTHWEST MONTANA BY DAYBREAK FRIDAY AND WEAKEN. LIGHT SNOW SHOULD COME TO END OVER EXTREME NORTHWEST MONTANA BY FRIDAY AFTERNOON WITH AREAS OF CONVECTIVE SNOW SHOWERS CONTINUING ELSEWHERE AS THE AIR MASS REMAINS UNSTABLE.

Certainly these forecast discussions contain some jargon that may be confusing to non-meteorologists (and perhaps seem to be bordering on gibberish), but nonetheless they offer a degree of detail not always included in an actual forecast. The preceding forecast discussion explains when the heaviest snow showers are expected (western Montana just before midnight) and specifically where snow is most likely to continue after the cold front zips through. It also mentions where the strongest winds are likely and for how long—all useful tips for helping you select a destination for your outing.

Forecast Winds/Temperatures Aloft
Zone forecasts include estimated winds, but those projections rarely apply to passes or ridgelines, unless specifically stated. Anyone who has spent much time in the high country knows there can be a world of difference between wind speeds in the flatlands and in the mountains, and that difference can lead to a world of hurt. The aviation section of the National Weather Service website includes winds aloft: typically for 6, 12, 18, and occasionally 24 hours in the future. You can find these by selecting the aviation heading on the homepage, then searching for the winds aloft forecast section. Such forecasts will look like this:

6Hr Upper Winds
FDUW01 KWBC 130213
DATA BASED ON 130000Z
VALID 130600Z FOR USE 0500-0900Z. TEMPS NEG ABOVE 24000

FT	3000	6000	9000	12000	18000
PHX	0406	1006+11	0906+04	9900-03	2816-17
PRC			9900+03	9900-04	2914-17
TUS		1007+12	1208+04	9900-02	2912-17
DEN			9900+03	3310-04	3013-19

The preceding forecast is for winds aloft 6 hours in the future, in this case at 6 Greenwich Mean Time. The phrase "130600Z" refers to the date and time of the wind forecast: "13" is the date and "0600Z" is the time (1:00 A.M. Eastern Standard Time, midnight Central Standard Time, 11:00 P.M. Mountain Time, and 10:00 P.M. Pacific Standard Time). The altitudes along the top are given in feet above mean sea level (i.e., 3000 feet, 6000 feet, etc.), until 18,000 feet, when the number changes to what is called *pressure altitude*. That simply means the elevation is determined by setting the altimeter to 29.92 inches or 1013.2 millibars, instead of actual local pressure. That will not be a consideration for most users rooted in terra firma. The column to the far left lists specific terminals. You will need to know the abbreviation for local airports, which are usually listed elsewhere within a website. In the case of Denver (DEN), notice that nothing is given for an altitude until 9000 feet. That is because no winds are forecast within 1500 feet of the terminal or station elevation. Phoenix (PHX) shows a wind forecast at 3000 feet of 0406. The first two digits are direction: 04 means 040° (the last zero is omitted), while 06 means 6 knots. Remember: 1 knot is equivalent to 1.15 statute miles per hour. The next elevation for Phoenix, 6000 feet, shows 1006—that is, winds are from 100° at 6 knots. The +11 is the temperature: 11°C (52°F). Temperatures are not given for the 3000-foot level or for any elevation within 2500 feet of the ground. Notice that at 12,000 feet, the winds forecast above Phoenix are 9900, which signifies light and variable. This wind forecast does not show significant winds at any of the elevations, but checking this forecast can help you spot a potentially dangerous weather condition that normal zone forecasts will not include.

Satellite Images

It is overstated and trite but still essentially true: A picture *can* be worth a thousand words. That especially applies to satellite images. A quick glance shows whether your destination is about to be wrapped in the

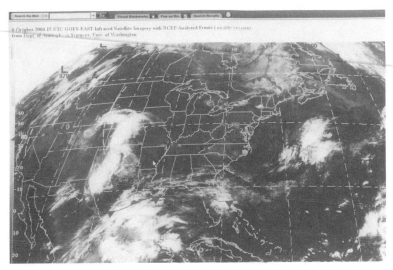

Sample satellite photo

tentacles of an approaching low, assaulted by a squall line, or peppered by air mass thunderstorms. All the National Weather Service websites offer current satellite images and sometimes even time-lapse loops. So do some television station, university, and commercial weather web pages For further discussion of fronts, etc., see Chapter 2.

Radar Images
Current radar images offer valuable short-term guidance. They can prevent you from getting thoroughly drenched and hypothermic as you set off down the trail but will be of little use on a multiday backpack trip (unless you are hauling along a laptop computer with satellite access to the Internet!). Images showing the reflectivity of storms are normally offered on National Weather Service or other websites. Simply put, those images show the intensity of precipitation. The more intense the precipitation, the greater the reflectivity of the radar beam. A scale, such as the following, is shown at the base of the radar image (see page 143). When you begin seeing colors verging toward or beyond yellow in the middle of the scale to the side, the potential for hail and thunderstorms becomes much greater.

FOLLOWING A PLAN WITH A PURPOSE
Given the many sources and types of weather information, it is easy to lose sight of the core message contained in that information. Information by

itself is of little use. Information gathered with a purpose is of great use.

To best assess the suitability of weather for your planned trip in the backcountry, follow a plan. The following checklist helps formulate one such plan. Use it, modify it, develop one best suited to your needs. The key is to organize your information so it is easy to review data and to determine whether conditions favor your planned trip. Several examples follow to help you use such a plan effectively.

MOUNTAIN AND WILDERNESS WEATHER CHECKLIST

Planned Route/Destination:
Today's Date:
Date(s) of Travel:
Preferred Weather Websites/Sources:
Watches/Warnings/Advisories:
Synopsis:

Observations:

CITY	SKY/WX	TMP	DP	RH	WIND	PRES	REMARKS

Winds Aloft Forecast Location/Time:

Altitude	Wind Direction	Wind Speed	Temperatures
3000'			
6000'			
9000'			
12,000'			
15,000'			
18,000'			

Freezing/Snow Level(s):

Zone Forecast(s)
Date/Time:
Sky:
Weather:
Temps:

Extended Outlook:
Avalanche Outlook:
Additional Notes:
Analysis:

Using a Plan Effectively

Do not wait to formulate your plan until just a few hours before you leave. Obviously, some information is better than no information, but consider getting weather data at least one day—and preferably two days—before your planned departure. That will give you a chance to verify the forecasts with observed conditions. If the forecasts are pretty close to what you observe, you can proceed with more confidence than if the forecast and observed weather conditions are completely contradictory. A suggested sequence for gathering information follows.

Two Days Before the Trip
1. Large-scale pattern and synopsis
2. Projected weather for the next two days

One Day Before the Trip
1. Current weather to evaluate the previous day's forecasts
2. Large-scale weather pattern
3. Projected weather for the next two days

Day of the Trip
1. Current weather to evaluate the previous day's forecasts
2. Projected weather to fill out the Mountain and Wilderness Weather Checklist

Let's take an example to see how such a plan can be used effectively.

MOUNTAIN AND WILDERNESS WEATHER CHECKLIST: EXAMPLE 1

Planned Route/Destination: Longs Peak, Rocky Mountain National Park, Colorado

Today's Date: 7/1

Date(s) of Travel: 7/2 in to Battle Mountain, overnighting 7/2 and 3, out 7/4

Preferred Weather Websites/Sources: National Weather Service Forecast Office—Denver–Boulder, CO

Watches/Warnings/Advisories: None posted

Synopsis: A large surface high that has brought several days of dry weather with mostly sunny skies is moving from the Rockies toward the Plains states. That will result in a shift from dry northwesterly winds to south or southeasterly winds, directing warmer, more moist air toward the Front Range by 7/3.

---

continued on next page

Observations:

NORTHERN COLORADO FRONT RANGE

CITY	SKY/WX	TMP	DP	RH	WIND	PRES	REMARKS
Denver	FAIR	74	42	31	NW7	30.02F	
Aurora	PTCLDY	76	40	27	NW5	30.04F	
Centennial	PTCLDY	73	43	34	N6	30.05F	
Broomfield	FAIR	72	42	33	NW3	30.02F	
Loveland	PTCLDY	68	40	34	NW8	30.04F	

NORTHEAST COLORADO

Greeley Arpt	FAIR	74	41	29	N4	30.05F	
Akron	PTCLDY	75	42	30	NW5	30.03F	
Burlington	PTCLDY	74	42	31	NW3	30.07F	

Winds Aloft Forecast Location/Time:

Altitude	Wind Direction	Wind Speed	Temperature
9000'	300	15	+12
12,000'	300	21	+03
15,000'	280	23	-01

Freezing/Snow Level(s): 14,000' FL

Zone Forecast(s):

Date/Time: 7/1 PM	**Date/Time:** 7/2 AM	**Date/Time:** 7/2 PM
Sky: M. Clear	Sky: P. Cldy	Sky: P. Cldy
Weather: None	Weather: None	Weather: None
Temps: 75–80	Temps: 50–55	Temps: 77–83

Extended Outlook: Partly cloudy with a slight chance of afternoon thundershowers developing 7/3, greater chance 7/4. Thundershowers likely 7/5 with cooler temps following a cold front.

Avalanche Outlook: Not available

Additional Notes: Barometer at home showing a slow drop: about .04 inch over 6 hours. Some high clouds drifting through; cloud streaks oriented from WSW to ENE. Forecast for today had been for clear skies with highs in the upper 60s to low 70s.

Analysis: Weather today is not threatening with minimal high clouds and no precipitation. The pressure drop on the home barometer is not significant at this point, as it is well within what is normally seen with daytime warming. But the appearance of clouds ahead of schedule, along with warmer-than-forecast temperatures, suggest the surface high is shifting eastward faster than expected. The orientation of cirrus streaks from WSW to ENE indicates the upper ridge is already to the east, with a trough of low pressure to the west.

This likely means southerly winds will draw warmer, moist air up the backside of the high into the area sooner than forecast, meaning the threat of thunderstorms will increase earlier than expected, and the cold front expected on the 7/5 could also arrive earlier. There are a couple of sensible alternatives: The first is to continue with the trip but be prepared to reduce the length of the outing to a single night at Battle Mountain should cumulus clouds near the peak begin to show significant upward growth on the 2nd; the second, given the high and exposed nature of the route, is to select a different, less exposed destination that involves a shorter hike (offering a faster retreat to the trailhead). A check of weather observations to the west in Utah would show some showers already developing over the mountains, which would also be confirmed by a look at a regional satellite image. It always pays to look at the larger weather picture, beyond and especially upwind of your area (based on the winds aloft that will steer such storms).

MOUNTAIN AND WILDERNESS WEATHER CHECKLIST: EXAMPLE 2

Planned Route/Destination: Big Meadows Campground/AT Trail, Shenandoah National Park
Today's Date: 10/2
Date(s) of Travel: 10/3 drive to the park and day hike connected nature trails, 10/4 out on the stretch of the AT trail toward Fisher's Gap, 10/5 back and drive home.
Preferred Weather Websites/Sources: National Weather Service Forecast Office—Baltimore/Washington, DC; also Blacksburg, VA, Charleston, WV, and Raleigh, NC.
Watches/Warnings/Advisories: None posted
Synopsis: The eastern end of a weak warm front is approaching today with areas of light rain expected as it pushes north from

continued on next page

North Carolina into Virginia. It is expected to push into central Pennsylvania by early morning on the 10/3. The cold front is forecast to remain well to the west, with hazy skies and above normal temperatures expected for the next several days.

Observations:

IN WESTERN VIRGINIA

CITY	SKY/WX	TMP	DP	RH	WIND	PRES	REMARKS
Charlottesville	MOCLDY	56	46	42	SSE10	N/A	
Staunton	MOCLDY	55	44	68	S7	29.99F	
Hot Springs	NOT AVBL						
Roanoke	MOCLDY	58	51	76	S12	29.98F	
Lynchburg	MOCLDY	59	51	72	SSE11	29.98F	
Danville	CLDY	60	53	78	S14	29.97F	

IN WESTERN NORTH CAROLINA

Asheville	RAIN	62	61	97	S12	29.95S	
Jefferson	RAIN	61	59	97	S10	29.96F	
Mount Airy	CLDY	59	55	86	SSE12	29.97F	

IN CENTRAL NORTH CAROLINA

Greensboro	RAIN	62	60	97	S9	29.96F	
Winston-Salem	RAIN	62	60	97	S7	29.96F	
Raleigh-Durham	RAIN	61	60	99	S6	29.96F	

Forecast Winds Aloft:

Altitude	Wind Direction	Wind Speed	Temperature
3000'	170	14	
6000'	180	18	+12
9000'	190	20	+09

Freezing/Snow Level(s): None given in zone forecasts

Zone Forecast(s):

Date/Time: 10/2PM	**Date/Time: 10/3 AM**	**Date/Time: 10/3 PM**
Sky: Cldy	Sky: M. Cldy	Sky: P. Cldy
Weather: Rain	Weather: None	Weather: None
Temps: 58–62	Temps: 60–65	Temps: 52–57

Extended Outlook: P. Cldy 10/4 with a slight chance of a T-shower. Highs mid 60s. P. Cldy 10/5 with a slight chance of a T-shower. Highs mid 60s.

Avalanche Outlook: Not available/applicable
Additional Notes: Long fingers of cirrus clouds moved almost directly from south to north early this morning, expanding into broader cirrostratus, then lowering into altostratus. Home barometer showing slow but steady drop last 12 hours.
Analysis: Current observations show thickening clouds to the south: one of the benefits of (and reasons for) checking weather conditions beyond your immediate area and in the direction of any approaching weather. Pressures lower to the south in the vicinity of the warm front, with rain just south of the Virginia/North Carolina state line. A quick check of the satellite or radar images on the websites mentioned would confirm this trend. Winds at the surface and aloft are not strong enough to pose much of a problem (but still remember the tent stakes!), supported by the relatively slight drop in pressure to the south. This seems to support the forecast arrival of precipitation in the Charlottesville area near the park later today.

A check of conditions farther south (in South Carolina and northern Georgia) would show if rain does stop behind the warm front and whether any thundershowers have popped up. An occasional glance at satellite images could also confirm that the cold front to the west is staying there, with little motion to the east. Overall, a promising forecast for your planned trip—just watch for signs of developing thunderstorms!

MOUNTAIN AND WILDERNESS WEATHER CHECKLIST: EXAMPLE 3

Planned Route/Destination: Climb to Camp Muir on Mount Rainier from Paradise, 5000 feet to 10,000 feet, ski descent upon return
Today's Date: 2/10
Date(s) of Travel: 2/11
Preferred Weather Websites/Sources: National Weather Service Seattle website, Northwest Avalanche Center, FAA Flight Service
Watches/Warnings/Advisories: None
Weather Synopsis: A modified Arctic air mass has kept temperatures well below normal. Occasional weak disturbances have brought

continued on next page

periods of snow at low elevations—1000 to 2000 feet above sea level. An approaching low from the subtropical Pacific has brought warming today with a rapidly rising snow level: It is already up to 5000 feet and likely to top out around 7000 feet. The strong contrast between high pressure in eastern Washington and the low offshore has generated some strong winds. The warm front producing today's precipitation is expected to shift north by this evening, leading to a dry, mild day tomorrow.

Current Observations:

CITY	SKY/WX	TMP	DP	RH	WIND	PRES	REMARKS
Bellingham	cldy/snow	29	20	67	E27G40	29.98F	
Everett	cldy/rain	42	40	94	S12	29.94F	
Seattle	cldy/rain	43	41	95	SE19G27	29.94F	
Tacoma	cldy/rain	43	41	95	SE 14	29.92F	
Olympia	cldy	45	40	84	S9	29.90F	
Stampede Pass	fzg rain/snow	30	28	94	E21G29	30.11S	
Yakima	cldy/fog	27	27	100	Calm	30.14S	

Forecast Winds Aloft:

Altitude	Wind Direction	Wind Speed	Temperature
3000'	200	29 knots	
6000'	210	37 knots	+02
9000'	210	48 knots	-02
12,000'	220	54 knots	-06
15,000'	230	62 knots	-11

Freezing/Snow Level(s): 5000 feet, forecast to rise to 7000 feet 2/11

Zone Forecast(s):

Date/Time:	2/10 PM	2/11 AM	2/11 PM
Sky:	Cldy	Mstly Cldy	Ptly Cldy
Weather:	Rain/Snow	— — — —	— — — —
Snow/Freezing Level:	6000' SL	8000' FL	8000' FL
Temps:	35–39	33–37	40–43
Winds:	S 25–40	S 20–30	S 15–25

Extended Outlook: Increasing clouds 2/12 with a chance of rain late; rain at times 2/13, changing to showers with snow level falling to 3000 feet. Occasional snow showers 2/14 and 2/15.
Avalanche Outlook: Avalanche hazard moderate at/above 4000 feet, high on north-facing slopes—gradually becoming high later

tonight and tomorrow at/above 3000 feet. Avalanche watch posted for tomorrow.

Additional Notes: Mountain pass reports indicate freezing rain Snoqualmie Pass/I-90.

Analysis: The avalanche outlook alone should be enough to make you think twice about this trip. An avalanche watch is posted for the day of your trip, with the hazard expected to be high. That is especially troubling in the big-mountain environment of Mount Rainier, particularly given the exposed nature of the route up to Camp Muir, with plenty of snow (and much of it apparently ready to slide) above you.

That said, some nuggets are worth further discussion here. The fact that temperatures are cold in eastern Washington (Yakima) and in the northwest corner (Bellingham) suggest that previous snowfall was of very light density. The warmer temperatures now moving into the area guarantee the new precipitation is either wet, heavy snow, or rain. That is a very unstable pattern. Remember the peanut-butter-over-jelly analogy in Chapter 6? This is a perfect example of that: a situation ripe for avalanches. It might seem confusing that the snow level is at 5000 feet and rising, but Stampede Pass at 4000 feet is below freezing and reporting a mix of snow and freezing rain, as is Snoqualmie Pass at 3000 feet. The cold air is trapped in the basin east of the Cascades, and higher pressure there is forcing that cold air through the passes toward lower pressure in the west. That is resulting in a thin layer of cold air, with warmer air above. That is why snow and freezing rain are reported in the lower passes, while rain is falling a short distance above. That is also why Bellingham is still experiencing snow in western Washington; cold Arctic air is shooting through the Fraser River Canyon from the interior of British Columbia, undercutting the warm, moist air there.

The wise choice in this situation would be to postpone your trip. Given a forecast snow level of 7000 feet, even the developed ski areas are likely to experience rain—not most people's idea of a fun day on the snow! Notice the forecast calls for falling snow levels as the cold front pushes through late on the 2/12 and 2/13. Continue to check the avalanche hazards; conditions are likely to stabilize afterward with the promise of some lighter, fresh snow. The Northwest Weather and Avalanche Center says it best on its website: "Make every trip a round trip!" Given the conditions cited above, that is doubtful on the 2/12.

The preceding examples show how personal observations, paired with official weather observations and forecasts and a measure of weather know-how, can produce good decisions: sometimes to go with confidence, at other times to change your destination, and occasionally stay at home. Each of the examples show how local patterns can have a major impact on your plans that may not always be obvious in the forecasts. This leads to the next chapter, which discusses localized weather patterns, divided by regions. I call it "Trail Notes." Reading it is a little like having an experienced local meteorologist sitting at your kitchen table as you plan your trip.

Trail Notes: Regional Weather Guidance

"Toto, I don't think we're in Kansas anymore!"
Dorothy, in *The Wizard of Oz*

We've all shared Dorothy's sense of disorientation, and it does not require transport by tornado. Even familiar territory, with moderately bad weather, can leave the most experienced hiker or skier humbled and confused. Place that same backcountry traveler in new territory with unfamiliar weather, and he or she may echo another of little Dorothy's feelings: "There's no place like home!"

LOCAL WEATHER WISDOM: NOT JUST FOR LOCALS

Gathering the pre-trip weather information and forecasts detailed in Chapter 7 will go a long way toward keeping you safe in the backcountry. Most forecasts give you the big picture, and while often that is enough, at other times knowing local weather patterns will help you plan a trip with more confidence, especially when traveling farther afield. That is the purpose of this chapter: to give you more confidence in visiting new areas, and perhaps to add to your outdoors wisdom at home. The knowledge in each regional section comes not only from my own research and experience but also from knowledgeable local meteorologists and wilderness guides. This information can help you to avoid the wet side of the mountains, to find the time of day when thunderstorms are most likely, and to pick the ski area most likely to offer fresh powder. When everyone else at your office, school, or coffee shop complains about their weekend outdoor ordeal, you can smile sweetly and respond, "That does sound terrible, but I had a wonderful trip!"

This chapter is divided into a series of regional subsections, each organized in the same way:

1. Regional climate
2. The big picture (basic storm tracks and associated weather)
3. Local weather phenomena and maps
4. Trail notes and a map (with weather problems plotted by location and season)

Begin by reading the regional overview. You will find information here that will help you avoid planning a dry Southwest getaway to Arizona's Mogollon Rim during monsoon season or a springtime hike up New Hampshire's Mount Washington only to find the trails buried under snow. When you begin looking over weather data for your pre-trip forecast, compare the position and track of weather disturbances on satellite pictures with the storm track maps provided. That will give you important clues to the likely duration and intensity of storms, average snow or freezing levels, areas that will tend to be the wettest, and those that will be in rain shadows, as well as those that might expose you to the added trauma of wind chill or heat stress (see Appendixes I and II). Keep in mind that the average snow or freezing levels given are for areas beneath the jet stream or storm track. Areas farther north will have lower levels, while areas to the south will experience higher snow or freezing levels.

Next is a discussion of key local weather phenomena. This section examines local weather patterns of particular interest, such as glacier winds in Alaska. That is followed by the planning map and the actual trail notes.

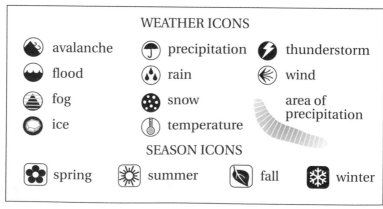

WEATHER ICONS

avalanche   precipitation   thunderstorm

flood   rain   wind

fog   snow   area of precipitation

ice   temperature

SEASON ICONS

spring   summer   fall   winter

Icons specify key weather challenges, and the seasons such challenges most frequently occur are placed after the appropriate weather icon in the trail notes paragraphs. Match those with the trail notes to see if a particular weather pattern is likely to pose a problem for your planned trip. The atmosphere is always full of surprises, particularly in the mountains, but these trail notes should help you minimize such surprises.

THE FAR NORTH: ALASKA AND THE YUKON

> *As the clouds lifted, leaving the vast snow-mantled mountain clear, I seated myself and gazed for more than an hour on the sublime panorama. There was not a breath of wind, and no sound except the faint murmur of the creek far below, and the cannonading and crashing roar of avalanches thundering down the mountain walls.*
> Charles Sheldon,
> *The Wilderness of Denali*

> *He was quick and alert in the things of life, but only in the things, and not in the significances. Fifty degrees below zero meant eighty-odd degrees of frost. Such fact impressed him as being cold and uncomfortable, and that was all. It did not lead him to meditate upon his frailty as a creature of temperature, and upon man's frailty in general.*
> Jack London, *To Build a Fire*

The name "Alaska" is derived from a native Aleut word which means "The Great Land." It is just that: Alaska's size beggars the imagination. Consider that one national park in Alaska, Wrangell–St. Elias, is more than five times the size of Yellowstone and larger than the combined states of Massachusetts, Rhode Island, and Connecticut. Alaska's coastline spans 33,000 miles, greater than that of the entire Lower 48. The presence of oceans and seas on three sides, together with the highest mountains in North America, produce weather that defines the term "extreme." While some of the variation in weather can be explained by the proximity of ocean and ice or latitudinal location, much is due to the complicated geology of both Alaska and the Yukon, reflected by the complex skeins of mountains that weave through the region. The Coast Range is the backbone of the Panhandle in the southeast, terminating in the towering St. Elias Mountains to the north: the greatest concentration of 16,000-foot-plus

peaks in North America. Maritime climate dominates this area that runs from Prince of Wales Island in the south to Icy Bay and encompasses thousands of islands and islets, some of which barely emerge above water at high tide. Annual precipitation averages 221 inches on Baranof Island. When the number of consecutive dry days fills the fingers on one hand, it is considered a drought. This climate zone continues 1500 miles along the Gulf of Alaska coast, which arcs from the ancient totem poles and rain forests of the southeast, past the St. Elias and Wrangell Mountains, and beyond the Chugach and Kenai Ranges farther west, eventually terminating along the partially submerged volcanoes of the Aleutians. Although precipitation amounts decrease over the western part of this zone, wind speeds can exceed 100 miles per hour any month of the year.

These coastal or near-coastal ranges act as a barrier both to Arctic air masses coming from the north and to moisture moving north off the Pacific and the Gulf of Alaska. That is why average yearly precipitation also decreases to the immediate north, which represents a transition to the continental climate of the interior: Yearly precipitation may average just 12 inches. The Alaska Range arcs northward from the Aleutian Range and reaches an apex at 20,320 feet on the summit of Denali (Mount McKinley). To keep track of all the convoluted mountain ranges in Alaska, it is helpful to possess the mental agility of a soap opera analyst. The largest ranges beyond the Alaska Range are the Kuskokwims to the northwest and the Brooks Range in the far north. True Arctic climate is found to the north of the Brooks. Barrow averages just 4 inches of precipitation. (Remember: 1 inch of liquid precipitation is roughly equivalent to 10 inches of snow.) Temperatures near or above the Arctic Circle may remain below freezing for seven months. If you spend much time in the interior or the far north or on one of the impossibly immense peaks—such as Denali, where temperatures can plummet to 40°F, 50°F, or even 60°F below (sometimes for weeks at a time)—you will understand why some may believe it can become too cold to snow. You will also learn that is not true. Winds can exceed 100 miles per hour, typically in the mountains and in narrow passes. Climbers, some in well-anchored tents, have literally been blown off mountains. Alaska, like the Yukon, demands that visitors know how to read the signs of weather: the changes in cloud cover, wind speed, wind direction, and air pressure already covered throughout this book. To paraphrase Jack London, this is an area that requires an understanding of the significance of weather changes, not just mere observation of their presence.

To the east of the St. Elias Mountains in the Yukon lie the Pelly, Selwyn, and Mackenzie Mountains, all of which are roughly parallel. Progressing to the northeast, the British and Richardson Mountains adjoin Mackenzie Bay on the Beaufort Sea. Because coastal mountains effectively drain clouds of moisture, the air that sinks over the St. Elias Range generally produces arid or semi-arid conditions over the southwestern Yukon. The continental climate east of the Wrangell and St. Elias Mountains tends to produce more thunderstorms in the Yukon during the summer than in points farther west. Although disturbances weaken and become less frequent during the summer, brisk fronts still can move through both Alaska and the Yukon. Once such fronts cross the various coastal ranges, they may become indistinct before evolving into a band of thundershowers later in the day. As they move farther inland, the cloud band may redevelop with increased precipitation over the Mackenzie Mountains. The Ogilvies, roughly in the middle of the territory, tend to block Arctic air from flooding farther south during winter, though on occasion such Arctic air can and does surge throughout the Yukon and on into British Columbia.

As harsh as the weather can be in Alaska and the Yukon, this is also a region of unsurpassed beauty: the metallic gold of the setting sun reflected from massive glaciers, the rose and purple alpenglow that follows, the shimmering curtains of the aurora borealis. Towering Sitka spruce, hemlock, and cedar leave only filtered sunlight in the southeast rain forests even when clouds vanish. Farther inland, less moisture, bigger variations in temperature, and the presence of permafrost create a harsher environment: Less luxuriant stands of black spruce, larch, birch, and willow are found in the lower elevations of Denali National Park. In the farther northern reaches of the state, such as in Gates of the Arctic, stunted, more scattered black spruce and poplar are found. It may require a hundred years for a black spruce to reach a diameter of 2 inches. Farther north or farther upslope, the trees give way to small shrubs, mosses, and lichens.

Moose. Caribou. Wolf. Musk ox. Black bear. Grizzly bear. Kodiak bear. Polar bear. Bald eagle. Goshawk. Goose. Snowy owl. Salmon. Mosquito. Blackfly. With the exception perhaps of the last two creatures, it is the wildlife, along with the vistas, that draws visitors to this remarkable region, keeps them returning, or prevents them from leaving. Magic permeates this great land. As you might suspect, it has cast a spell over me on numerous occasions that include whale watching in the mist-covered fjords of southeast Alaska; observing hulking Alaska brown bear along the treeless, windswept McNeil River Bear Sanctuary; and cross-country skiing on a –30°F night in the Yukon. Trips here change visitors. After you have seen the smokelike herds of caribou materialize over a ridge, it is no longer difficult to accept that these creatures far outnumber the people of Alaska. (We already know the mosquitos do!) Meteorologists have unraveled much of the story of mountain weather in Alaska and the Yukon. Pilots and climbers have contributed pieces of the puzzle as well. But the lack of people, as well as the complexity of the land and its impact on incoming weather systems, leaves more localized weather patterns unexplained or unknown than in other states and provinces. Still, much is known, and that is the subject of this section.

Alaska and the Yukon: The Big Picture

The *Aleutian low* is the preeminent source of storms along the Pacific coast. It should come as no surprise that it plays a major role in the

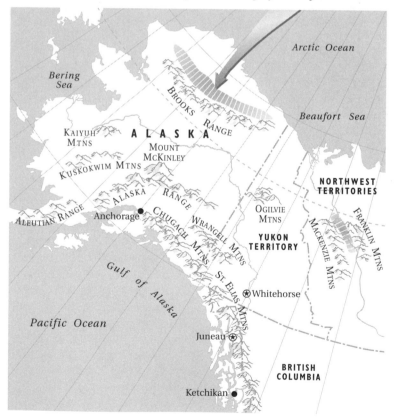

Storm track from the north to northwest

weather of the great country of Alaska and of its Canadian neighbor, the Yukon. This regional low-pressure system is a cradle of bad weather. It forms near the Aleutian Islands, an archipelago of partially submerged volcanoes stretching westward more than a thousand miles from the Alaska Peninsula toward the Kamchatka Peninsula. It is the result of air chilled by the Bering Sea moving over the warmer surface waters of the North Pacific. Relatively subtle shifts in the position of the Aleutian Low can result in major changes in weather affecting this region. During winter, an average of ten to fifteen different disturbances will swing through this region each month. Experienced forecasters pay close attention to these shifts, as well as the path smaller disturbances travel—so does anyone who spends much time outdoors. That is why the examination of this region's weather begins with a look at the big picture: the major storm tracks and their influence on the weather. Those are shown in the

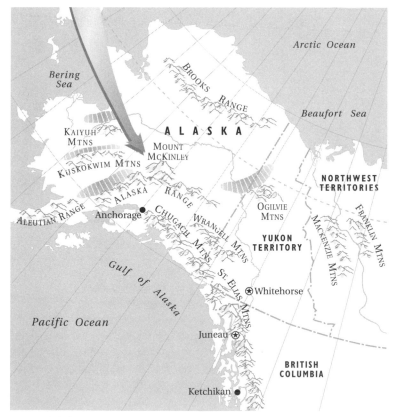

Storm track from the west to northwest

illustrations that follow, together with the areas that tend to get the most precipitation and the least. The illustrations mirror what you would be likely to see in a satellite image. A brief description follows, including the duration and intensity of each pattern.

A storm track from the north or northwest is most typical when a large ridge of high pressure, the *Arctic high,* is centered over eastern Siberia or western Alaska. The resulting northerly flow is dry and very cold. Winter temperatures over the interior may drop to −40°F or colder. This pattern can persist for weeks. During warmer months, moisture from the Beaufort Sea can produce significant precipitation over the northern slopes of the Brooks Range.

A storm track from the west–northwest that moves over the Bering Sea side of the Aleutians carries more precipitation over the interior into the Alaska Range as far north as Denali, and to a lesser extent into the Yukon.

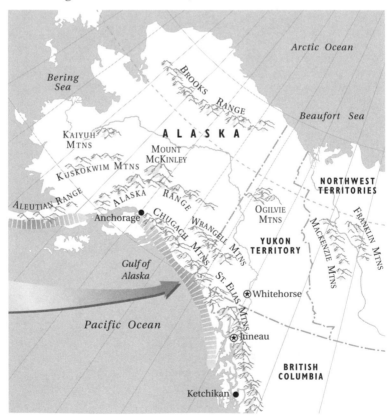

Storm track from the west to southwest

This area will receive more precipitation (rain or snow) from late spring through early autumn, and more snow later in autumn through much of spring, than the coastal regions of south-central and southeastern Alaska. During winter, this pattern usually brings very cold air over the southern interior of the Yukon.

A storm track from the west–southwest that moves south of the Alaska peninsula into the Gulf of Alaska and toward southeast Alaska directs most precipitation to the southern and southeastern coastal regions of Alaska, less to the south central region just inland. Again, this area will receive more precipitation from late spring through early autumn and more snow later in autumn, in winter, and in much of spring than interior regions. The Chugach Mountains will typically receive heavy snow or rain but act as a barrier, effectively removing much of the moisture before it can reach points farther east, such as the Wrangell Mountains.

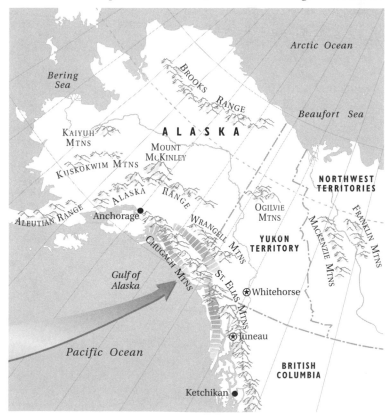

Storm track from the southwest

A *storm track from the southwest* carries low-pressure systems into the Gulf of Alaska and inland from the Chugach Mountains, most frequently in late August or September. The result is abnormally warm, wet weather. Flooding can occur, though typically these lows do not clear the Wrangell Mountains, resulting in drier weather farther inland. Some of the heaviest precipitation occurs when a dying Pacific typhoon wanders into the Gulf of Alaska. Fortunately, this does not happen every year.

A *storm track from the south–southwest* is often called the "Pineapple Express" because it draws moist tropical or subtropical air northward, sometimes from as far south as the Hawaiian Islands. The earliest this pattern will typically affect this region is during the late summer or early autumn months. The early-season target of this storm track is

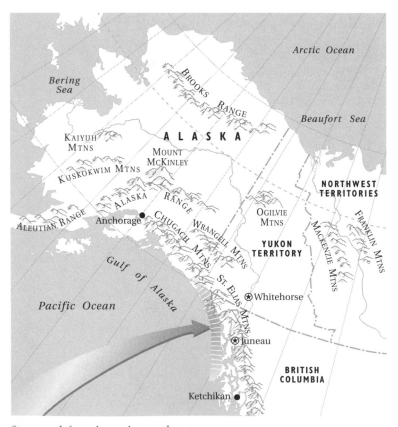

Storm track from the south to southwest

Storm track, or surface winds, from the east

usually the north Panhandle. Later into the autumn the focus is usually farther south, into the Stikine River Valley. Such a tropical visitation may persist for days, resulting in very high snow levels, strong winds, heavy rain, and flooding. Winds may reach 70 miles per hour with gusts over 100. After October, this pattern is usually directed farther south into Washington and Oregon.

A storm track from the east typically occurs when a low moves into the east end of the Gulf of Alaska. The return flow around the low that occurs inland brings much of the moisture along the east slopes of the Wrangell and St. Elias Mountains and into the Yukon's Kluane National Park. Such moisture typically will not extend farther north than Tok in Alaska or Pelly Crossing in the Yukon. The western slopes will offer drier conditions.

Alaska and the Yukon: Local Weather Phenomena You Need to Understand

Glacier winds are one form of *katabatic* wind. (The term "katabatic" simply refers to any wind flowing down an incline.) Glacier winds occur when there is a difference in temperature between the air that is physically in contact with the glacier or snowfield and air at the same altitude that is not touching the snow. The bigger the difference in temperature, the stronger the glacier wind. Such winds are not steady but often come in pulses. The exact strength and depth of such winds depends upon the shape of the terrain and the length of the glacier. Such winds reach peak velocity during the early to mid-afternoon hours but can blow at all hours during summer months. Peak speeds can range from a few miles (or kilometers) per hour to more than a hundred in extreme cases. However, glacier winds tend to be shallow. Climbers moving upslope finding themselves buffeted and chilled by such winds can at times feel warmer air simply by extending an arm overhead.

A related phenomenon is called a *cold air avalanche*. Cold air may build up on a peak or plateau, reach some critical mass, and then pulse downslope in intervals ranging from a few minutes to an hour or so. These cold air avalanches are most common when skies are clear and prevailing winds are light. Both phenomena are good reasons to make certain your tent is well anchored.

An *ice blowout* is a dangerous phenomenon that occurs when a deep freeze is followed by sudden warming, often in November. High pressure over the interior may produce temperatures of −40°F (also

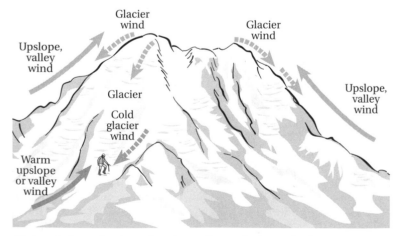

Glacier winds can flow beneath upslope valley winds during the day.

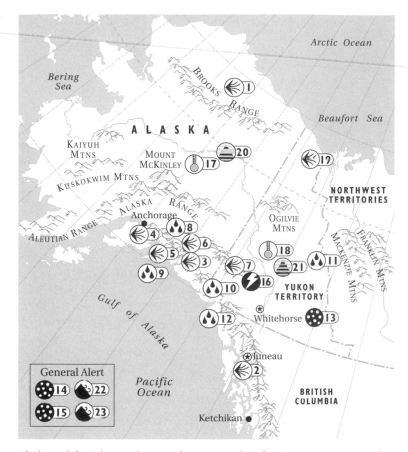

Alaska and the Yukon trail notes reference map (icon locations are approximate)

–40°C) or colder, quickly freezing creeks. If an approaching low directs warmer air into an area, any snow falling may change to rain, resulting in an abrupt rise in the water level, which may carry an ice jam downstream, leading to widespread flooding in a valley. McCarthy Creek is a common location for such blowouts.

The following point is aimed specifically at climbers. The highest peaks in Alaska and the Yukon reach the top of the troposphere, which is found at lower elevations at more northerly latitudes. While severe weather can certainly be found on peaks 14,000 to 15,000 feet or higher over the continental United States and Europe, Arctic conditions should be expected as a matter of course on such peaks in Alaska and the Yukon. Denali, for example, extends well into the stratosphere.

The combination of subzero temperatures and strong winds can drive conditions off the end of the wind-chill chart! It is imperative for climbers to carry clothing appropriate for such Arctic conditions.

Alaska and the Yukon: Trail Notes
Brooks Range: Barrier Jet (1)

Northerly winds produce what is called a *barrier jet* along the northern slopes of the Brooks Range. Because barrier jets turn to the left, the strong winds will be found along the north slopes of the Endicott and Philip Smith Mountains.

Taku Straits: Gap Winds (2)

Higher pressure over the interior of British Columbia will generate strong gap winds through the Taku Straits just south of Juneau. Watch for strong pressure differences between Whitehorse and Juneau. Such winds will be strongest during winter. However, when low pressure develops over the Yukon during hot weather in the Yukon, gap winds will be strongest inland. Similar gap winds occur throughout the Coast Mountains.

Copper River Valley: Gap Winds (3)

Higher pressure over the interior of Alaska compared to the coast will generate strong gap winds through the Copper River Valley east of Cordova and through Wood Canyon. Watch for strong pressure differences between Cordova and Fairbanks or for the approach of a strong low along the coast. Such winds will be strongest during winter, with the highest winds on the Copper River Delta. Huge snowdrifts may develop overnight.

Turnagain Arm: Gap Winds (4)

Higher pressure over the interior of Alaska compared to the coast will generate strong gap winds through Turnagain Arm south of Anchorage. Such winds will be strongest during winter. Watch for the approach of a strong low along the coast or for strong pressure differences between Anchorage and Fairbanks.

Thompson Pass: Gap Winds (5)

Higher pressure over the interior of Alaska compared to the coast will generate strong gap winds through Thompson Pass in the Chugach Mountains north of Valdez. Such winds will be strongest during winter, possibly reaching hurricane force. Watch for the approach of a strong low along the coast or for strong pressure differences between Valdez and Fairbanks.

Kennicott River Valley: Chinook Winds (6)

High pressure near the Alaska Range and lower pressure near the coast can generate chinook winds over the Wrangell Mountains into the Kennicott Valley toward McCarthy that result in rapid warming and, in turn, melting snow. Watch for the development of northerly winds aloft. This typically occurs only a few times each year.

Slims River Valley: Gap Winds (7)

The Slims River Valley generates very strong winds into the south end of Kluane Lake. When prevailing winds are from the south to southwest or pressures are higher along the coast than inland at Whitehorse, expect strong and gusty winds in this area.

Copper River Valley: Rainfall (8)

At the north end of a valley opening to the south, 10,000-foot-plus peaks tend to concentrate incoming moisture, resulting in very persistent and heavy rain compared to nearby areas. Local flooding can also occur. Expect when prevailing winds are from the south.

Valdez Arm: Rainfall (9)

Beyond the northeast end of this channel, 10,000-foot-plus peaks tend to concentrate incoming moisture, resulting in very persistent and heavy rain compared to nearby areas. Local flooding also can occur. This pattern also can produce significant snow in winter. Expect this to occur when winds are from the south to southwest.

Yakutat Bay: Rainfall (10)

At the northeast end of a valley, 10,000-foot-plus peaks flowing to the south tend to concentrate incoming moisture, resulting in very persistent and heavy rain compared to nearby areas. Local flooding can also occur. Expect when winds are from the south to southwest.

Mackenzie Mountains: Upslope Rain (11)

Weak cloud bands from dissipating fronts may redevelop with increasing precipitation as they move upslope along the west slopes of the Mackenzie Mountains in the Yukon.

Glacier Bay: Rainfall (12)

At the northeast end of a valley flowing to the south, 10,000-foot-plus peaks tend to concentrate incoming moisture, resulting in very persistent and heavy rain compared to nearby areas. Local flooding can also occur. Expect when winds are from the south to southwest.

Teslin/Watson Lake: Snowfall (13)

Snow and frequently heavy snow can occur from late summer through early spring in the area from Teslin to Watson Lake in the southeast section of the Yukon. Watch for snowstorms developing near Anchorage, which will likely track into this region of the Yukon.

Glacier Snow Bridge: Crevasse Risk (14)

The spring thaw begins late in spring and early summer as the hours of daylight increase. Meltwater seeps into the snowpack, resulting in highly unstable snow bridges. This tendency begins at lower elevations, then moves higher with passing weeks. Wind-stiffened snow bridges may look stable but can collapse suddenly, particularly during the afternoon. Snow bridges in coastal ranges are often fairly stable and usually will last well into the summer, when weakened conditions are fairly easy to see. Snow bridges in the interior ranges tend to be thinner and therefore can be dangerous throughout the year, especially when the spring melt begins. A good general rule is to expect the worst of snow bridges until proven otherwise. Crevasses open by midsummer in most years.

Glacier Snow Bridge: Crevasse Risk (15)

Most snow falls during late summer and early autumn as winters here tend to be cold and relatively dry. The reduced hours of daylight and cooler temperatures gradually rebuild snow bridges and make them stronger. However, the first few snowfalls only tend to insulate unstable snow bridges from the cold and hide their instability. This is especially true in the coastal ranges. As mentioned in the previous section, snow bridges in the interior ranges can be dangerous throughout the year. Expect the worst, and probe carefully.

The Yukon: Thunderstorms (16)

Showers and thundershowers develop most frequently during the afternoon or at night over the Yukon east of the Wrangell and St. Elias Mountains. Such thunderstorms typically move along the valleys. The main period for such thunderstorms is from mid-June to mid-August. Such thundershowers will tend to be heaviest and most frequent over Joe Mountain to the northeast of Whitehorse and east of Lake Laberge. Watch for upward-growing cumulus in the morning as a clue to likely thunderstorms in the afternoon.

Alaska Interior near Fairbanks: Temperature Risks (17)

The combination of long winter nights, highly reflective snow, and the arrival of an Arctic front can lead to frigid, subzero temperatures with stagnant air trapped beneath a strong dome of high pressure that can last for weeks. The layer of the coldest air is often fairly shallow; temperatures can be significantly warmer a few hundred feet up the surrounding ridges. *A special warning for travelers in November:* −40°F weather can come right on the heels of relatively comfortable conditions, so always go prepared for the deep freeze.

Yukon Interior: Temperature Risks (18)

The combination of long winter nights, highly reflective snow, and the arrival of an Arctic front can lead to frigid, subzero temperatures with stagnant air trapped beneath a strong dome of high pressure that can last for weeks. Temperatures can be slightly warmer a few hundred feet up.

British/Richardson Mountains: Winds (19)

A storm track that moves from the Bering Sea across the Beaufort Sea will bring warm temperatures and strong southwest winds through the British and Richardson Mountains. Watch satellite images or listen to weather forecasts for evidence of a slow-moving front along the Beaufort Sea coast.

Alaska Interior: Ice Fog (20)

A persistent Arctic air mass within a strong high-pressure system can produce dense ice fog with very little moisture. Even the breath of a caribou herd can produce sufficient moisture at the subzero temperatures that typically occur, sometimes down to –60°F (also –60°C). Such fogs can also develop near open water sources.

Yukon Interior: Ice Fog (21)

A persistent Arctic air mass within a strong high-pressure system can produce dense ice fog with very little moisture. Even the breath of a caribou herd can produce sufficient moisture at the subzero temperatures that typically occur, sometimes down to –60°F (also –60°C). Such fogs can also develop near open water sources.

The Coast: Winter Avalanche Hazard (22)

This region tends to experience wet, heavy snowfalls accumulating at fairly mild temperatures. For that reason, direct-action and wet, soft-slab avalanches pose the biggest risk. Be particularly careful when snow has fallen at a rate of an inch or more per hour, the snow level has been rising, or fresh snow has fallen on a layer of crust. Be certain to obtain updated avalanche and mountain weather forecasts.

General Note: Spring Avalanche Hazard (23)

During spring, melting snow will percolate into the snowpack, lubricating buried layers and priming the trigger for avalanches, particularly on sun-warmed, south-facing slopes. Ski or ride on these slopes early in the day, moving to shaded northern or eastern slopes as the sun gets higher. As always, carefully check avalanche forecasts.

THE CANADIAN COAST RANGE AND ROCKIES: BRITISH COLUMBIA AND ALBERTA

*Near thirty miles we had struggled up the pass, and still far ahead,
nameless, tented peaks of snow shone in the late light like windowed
castles at sunset . . . darkness rushed up the tottering gorges, stars
came out overhead in the narrow fillet from east to west, and tendrils of the aurora rose and sank over the northern heights.*

Ernest Ingersoll,
To the Pacific through Canada

*These mountains are our temples, our sanctuaries and our resting
places. They are a place of hope, a place of vision, a very special
and holy place where the Great Spirit speaks with us.*

First Nations Stoney Chief John Snow,
These Mountains Are Our Sacred Places

The mountains of western Canada can make visitors feel insignificantly small and evanescent, yet at the same time part of something immeasurably grand and everlasting. Whether entering from the Okanagan to the west or the plains of Alberta to the east, time seems almost suspended here. The impression is more of entering the toothy gates of a land still actively being created, burdened by the presence of an almost eternal winter.

Seasons come to pass here, but each is tinged with the presence of winter. It can snow anytime. Evidence of ice ages past can be seen in the U-shaped valleys carved by glaciers. But in British Columbia and Alberta, the Ice Age continues to flourish. Even in summer, walkers strolling along the gentle path bordering Lake Louise are startled by the crash of ice falls plunging off hanging glaciers on nearby peaks. The line between civilization and wilderness here is a fine one; with the exception perhaps of Alaska and the Yukon, no other area exists so much on the edge of meteorological consent as this one. This demands cautious attention to detail. Another short hike from the elegant Chateau Lake Louise to what is called the Lake Agnes "Tea House" may bring unexpectedly close encounters with a grizzly bear. Yet wildlife and the stunning scenery are part of the enchantment of this special region. While bears hibernate in winter, bighorn sheep migrate to lower terrain where it is easier to uncover vegetation. Winter travel is more difficult for elk and moose; during the summer they graze at will, often causing lengthy traffic jams. If you do not see wildlife here, you probably are not looking very hard.

Winter, at least as it is defined by the calendar, is without question a time of snow and cold. Days are short, with the sun skimming above the horizon in the northern part of these provinces. Frequent systems rip through, most from across the Pacific. This is why the heaviest snow falls over the coastal ranges on Vancouver Island and on the British Columbia mainland. The heaviest snow on mountains located along the many West Coast/ocean inlets tends to occur as a low or trough is approaching. Those places closer to the U.S. border will receive more snowfall following such disturbances because the moist and unstable air is not blocked by the Vancouver Island Range. By the time the system moves inland, those ranges have wrung much of the moisture born by those clouds. Farther inland, it is the depth of cold air trapped in valleys that determines whether precipitation will fall as snow or quickly transition to rain or even to freezing rain if temperatures are moderating. If that cold air mass is even a few hundred feet, extending up to 5000 feet (1500 meters), the result is likely to be snow. The Okanagan is one prime example of this situation. Because of the narrow valleys, the existence of cold air typically means winds are relatively light near the valley bottoms during significant snowfalls.

Avalanches can be notoriously difficult to predict particularly in the interior of this region. It suffices here to say that the conditions leading to elevated avalanche potential in the Vancouver Island and Coast Ranges are entirely different from those in the Columbia Mountains, such as the Selkirks, Cariboos, and Monashees, which in turn are considerably different from the Rockies farther east near Banff and Lake Louise. (See also Local Weather Phenomena You Need to Understand.)

As winter transitions into spring, upper troughs of low pressure can bring the towering cumulus clouds that produce heavy snowfall and excellent skiing, particularly in March and early April in the Rockies. In the Coast and Columbia Mountains, the best skiing is earlier—usually from January through mid-March. However, good powder can be found in April in the Coast Mountains north of Terrace. The development of these showers also presents the potential for lightning and wild up-and-down plunges in the snow level, though lightning is most common after May.

Summer is thunderstorm season in the mountains. While some thunderstorms are produced by the closed lows that can produce damp weather for days, air mass thunderstorms are most frequent in the mountain ranges of British Columbia and Alberta. The really severe activity is found just east of the Rockies in a belt running between Red Deer and Calgary. When thunderstorms are forecast in the mountains, or when cumulus clouds are seen swelling rapidly upward, hikers and climbers should be off the major peaks and ridges by midafternoon. Farther north, thunderstorms typically die along the west slopes of the Cariboos, with only weak remnants farther to the east in Jasper National Park. Narrow valleys typically prevent thunderstorms from becoming better organized and severe. However, the taller peaks—such as Mount Robson, Mount Athabasca, and Mount Forbes—can easily generate their own thunderstorms. The arrival of a trough, with southeasterly winds near the surface and southwesterly winds aloft can generate not only thunder and lightning but also lots of hail.

Colors change here from late summer to early autumn, and while snow can fall anytime of the year, it begins to fall in earnest on occasion in September and certainly October. Backpackers should be versed in winter camping skills and entirely equipped for very cold weather. Even in summer, warm afternoons can easily give way to temperatures well below freezing at night.

British Columbia and Alberta: The Big Picture

The *Aleutian low* is the preeminent source of storms along the Pacific coast. It should come as no surprise that it plays a major role in the weather both of British Columbia and its neighbor to the east, Alberta. Relatively subtle shifts in the position of the Aleutian low can result in large changes in the weather affecting this region. As many as a dozen disturbances move through these two provinces each month during winter especially over the Coast and Columbia Mountains. The Aleutian systems often weaken substantially by the time they cross the Purcell Mountains, prior to arriving over the Rockies. Experienced forecasters pay close attention to these shifts, as well as to the paths smaller disturbances travel. So should anyone who spends much time outdoors. Thus this examination of this region's weather begins with a look at the major storm tracks and their influence on the weather. The illustrations that follow are indicative of what you would be likely to see in satellite images. A brief description follows, including the duration and intensity of each pattern.

A storm track from the north to northwest is most typical when the Arctic high is centered over Alaska, directing air over the Beaufort Sea and down into northern British Columbia and Alberta. The resulting flow is dry and very cold: Winter temperatures over the interior may drop well below 0°F (–20°C). The coldest air initially slides east of the Rockies, accompanied by gusty winds. This air mass can generate strong outflow winds through east–west passes and may persist for a week or more.

A *storm track from the west to northwest* moves over the Bering Sea side of the Aleutians to the southeast into northern British Columbia and Alberta. These areas will receive more precipitation (rain or snow)

Storm track or surface winds from the north to northwest

from late spring through early autumn and more snow later in autumn through much of spring than the coastal regions of British Columbia. During winter, this pattern usually brings very cold air over both northern British Columbia and Alberta, as well as the southern interior of the Yukon.

A *storm track from the west to southwest* that moves south of the Alaska peninsula into the Gulf of Alaska generates more precipitation farther south from the U.S. border north to Fort St. John. The

Storm track from the west to northwest

western slopes of the Coast Range will receive more precipitation than the interior ranges from this pattern, though it will bring significant snowfall to the western slopes of the Monashees and Selkirks. Such a pattern can literally dampen hopes for summerlike weather from May into mid-July because it often directs a series of cold lows that bring persistent clouds and rain.

   A *storm track from the south to southwest* is often called the "Pineapple Express" because it draws moist tropical or subtropical air north-

Storm track from the west to southwest

ward, sometimes from as far south as the Hawaiian Island**s**. The earliest this pattern will typically affect this region is during the late summer or early autumn months. The early-season target of this storm track is usually north of the Stikine River Valley. Later, a more common focus will be the Queen Charlotte Islands and Vancouver Island. Such a tropical visitation may persist for days, resulting in very high snow levels, strong winds, heavy rain, and flooding. Winds may easily reach 60 miles per hour (100 kilometers per hour), with gusts in excess of 75 miles per hour (120 kilometers per hour). Typically, the

Storm track from the south to southwest

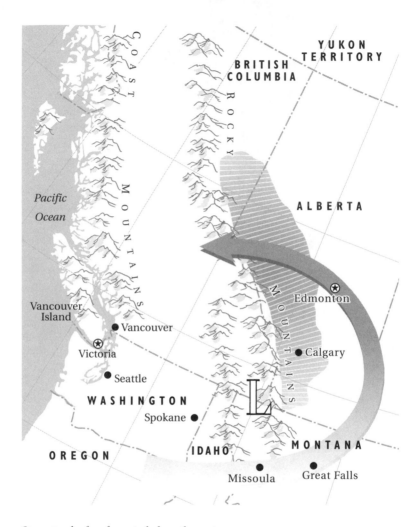

Storm track of surface winds from the east

strongest winds will occur ahead of the actual low, especially in areas subject to easterly outflow winds. A second band of strong winds typically occurs just after the cold front. If this pattern develops after November, it will primarily affect the Vancouver Island Range or from Mount Waddington south in the Coast Range. While skiers and snowboarders may curse the rising snow levels along the Coast Range, this same pattern can produce significant snowfall at Red Mountain and Fernie if Arctic air is already in place. Backcountry skiers and snowboarders must understand this pattern can set off a very strong cycle of avalanches.

A *storm track from the east* typically occurs when a large low moves through the North Pacific and tracks inland near the U.S. border. Eastern slopes just north of the actual track will receive the heaviest precipitation. Western slopes will offer drier conditions, especially after the low crosses the Coast Range or Rocky Mountains. Skiers and snowboarders in Banff and Lake Louise hope for this because it brings the heaviest snow there. This is especially common there in April.

British Columbia and Alberta: Local Weather Phenomena You Need to Understand

Backcountry travelers in British Columbia and Alberta are likely to encounter *avalanche terrain*. As discussed in Chapter 6, appearances can be deceiving and deadly. The sparkling white slope that exudes tranquility may conceal internal stresses waiting for a trigger. This is true not only during winter but also in autumn and spring. (The Canadian Avalanche Association is an excellent source of mountain weather and avalanche guidance. It also offers contacts for training courses *imperative* for anyone venturing into the snow-covered backcountry. See Appendix V for contact information.) A simple look at a map shows the variation encompassed by this region—from the coastal alpine zone of the Vancouver Island Range and Coast Mountains to the eastern alpine zone of the Canadian Rockies. This results in a wide variety of avalanche hazards: direct-action or wet, soft-slab avalanches near the coast, to the direct-action or soft-slab avalanches in the British Columbia interior such as in the Selkirks, to the notorious delayed-action slides of the Rockies spanning the border of the two provinces. It is important to understand that what may indicate safe slope conditions in one area may fail to point out hazardous conditions elsewhere, as well as that changes in season or even elevation can demand entirely different considerations. High pressure settling in from late winter into early spring can result in strong temperature inversions. Cold and seemingly safe conditions for ice climbing on frozen waterfalls at the base may mask much warmer air aloft. That, together with the higher elevation reached by the sun, can lead to melting and sudden ice avalanches above. Stratus trapped in valleys may produce heavy hoarfrost in a bathtublike ring that will produce buried weak layers after additional snowfalls. The lack of single, big snowfalls typical of the interior allows weaknesses to persist within the snowpack for a long time, although some areas, such as Rogers Pass, can mimic coastal snow patterns. The answer is to obtain solid training, check

British Columbia and Alberta, with rough outlines of alpine zones for avalanche assessment

public avalanche bulletins, and exercise caution and good judgment in the field.

Snow is not the only substance that can avalanche here. Mountain travelers may encounter what is called a *cold air avalanche*. Cold air may build up on a peak or plateau, reach some critical mass, and then pulse downslope in intervals ranging from a few minutes to an hour or so. These cold air avalanches are most common when skies are clear and prevailing winds are light.

Downslope winds and cold air avalanches are good reasons to make certain your tent is well staked. I spent a very chilly and breezy night camped near the terminus of a glacier near Rogers Pass. Choosing a different campsite would have resulted in a more comfortable evening. Of course, that was the same evening my stove chose to stop working!

British Columbia and Alberta: Trail Notes
Crows Nest Pass: Gap Winds, Backdoor Cold Front (1)

When Arctic air slides east of the divide, strong gap winds push through Crows Nest Pass in the Lizard Range near Fernie. As this cold air encounters somewhat warmer, moist air approaching from the west, locally heavy snow can occur within the pass in what is called a

British Columbia and Alberta trail notes reference map (icon locations are approximate)

backdoor cold front. That name comes from the fact that cold air is moving from east to west, instead of the usual west to east direction of cold fronts. Expect this pattern when colder air is moving east of the divide and winds within the pass become easterly.

Yoho National Park: Gap Winds (2)

Arctic air sliding east of the divide can generate strong, gusty winds between Golden and Banff. This condition is commonly referred to as a "Yoho blow." The winds, together with snowfall, can result in blizzard conditions. Expect this pattern when colder air slides east of the divide in Alberta and winds within this region shift to easterly.

British Columbia: Chinook Winds (3)

When winds aloft are from the west to southwest, conditions favor chinook winds and rapid warming along and beyond the eastern slopes of the Coast Mountains. Carefully check forecast and reported winds aloft near 10,000 feet (3300 meters): If they are from the west to southwest and in excess of 40 miles per hour (60 kilometers per hour), expect chinook conditions on leeward slopes east of the crest with rapid warming, snowmelt, and destabilizing conditions on snow-covered slopes, snow bridges, and ice fields.

Alberta: Chinook Winds (4)

Anytime winds aloft are from the west to southwest, conditions favor chinook winds and rapid warming on the eastern slopes of the Canadian Rockies. Carefully check forecast and reported winds aloft near 10,000 feet: If they are from the west to southwest and in excess of 40 miles per hour (60 kilometers per hour), expect chinook conditions on leeward slopes east of the divide with rapid warming, snowmelt, and destabilizing conditions on snow bridges and ice fields.

Fraser River Canyon: Winds (5)

An Arctic push with high pressure building over the interior of British Columbia can produce extremely strong winds through the Fraser River Canyon. If pressures are significantly higher at Hope than at Abbotsford, be prepared for a real blow. An approaching disturbance that brings moisture can produce heavy snow in the mountains. If the moisture is accompanied by significantly warmer air, persistent freezing rain can develop near Chilliwack.

Howe Sound: Winds (6)

An Arctic push with high pressure building over the interior of British Columbia can produce strong winds affecting the mountains on either side of Highway 99. Expect such winds if pressures are significantly higher in Squamish or Pemberton than at Bowen Island. An approaching disturbance that brings moisture can produce heavy snow in the mountains.

Coquihalla Highway: Heavy Snow (7)

The heaviest snow can fall following a cold front along the Coquihalla Highway as moist and unstable air pushes inland with a westerly wind.

Cypress, Grouse Mountain, and Seymour Mountain Ski Areas: Heaviest Snow (8)

An easterly flow of cold air down the Fraser Valley colliding with moisture from a low-pressure system approaching from the west tends to produce the most significant snow at the Cypress and Grouse Mountain Ski Areas near Vancouver. Watch for reported or forecast easterly winds at Abbotsford and a band of clouds moving inland from the Pacific on satellite images.

Whistler/Blackcomb Ski Areas: Heaviest Snow (9)

A northeasterly flow of cold air into Howe Sound colliding with moisture from a low-pressure system approaching from the west tends to produce the most significant snow at Whistler and Blackcomb. Watch for reported or forecast northeasterly winds at Squamish and a band of clouds moving inland from the Pacific on satellite images.

Vancouver Island Range: Heaviest Snow (10)

The heaviest snow along the Vancouver Island Range from Strathcona Provincial Park south tends to occur as a trough or closed low moves inland, with south to southeasterly winds circulating moist and unstable air up against the eastern slopes. West to southwesterly winds following such a disturbance will produce heavy snow along the western slopes.

Interior British Columbia: Flash Flooding (11)

Strong nocturnal or cold-front thunderstorms can generate amazingly rapid flash flooding in the central and northeastern interiors of British Columbia. Watch for such flash floods from late spring to early summer, particularly when cold lows slowly inch across British Columbia into Alberta. Thunderstorms generated by such lows can fire up as early as 9:00 A.M. When such conditions threaten, select campsites well above streams or rivers confined to narrow channels.

Coastal British Columbia: Flash Flooding (12)

Flash flooding is most common along the Vancouver Island Range or Coast Mountains with the arrival of the autumn rainy season. When freezing/snow levels are rising and moderate to heavy rain is forecast, be especially cautious. Storm tracks from the southwest to south–southwest, such as the Pineapple Express, are major culprits.

Vancouver Island, Coast Mountains: Air Mass Thunderstorms (13)

Air mass thunderstorms generated by cooler air lying on top of significantly warmer air near the surface are most common along the Vancouver Island Range and Coast Mountains. These reach a peak from June through August. Watch carefully for strongly building cumulus clouds. It is best to be off peaks and ridges by midafternoon in such conditions.

Interior of British Columbia: Thunderstorms (14)

A southwesterly flow, together with a cold front, can generate more organized, longer-lasting thunderstorms from Williams Lake and Prince George northward.

British Columbia and Alberta Rockies: Air Mass Thunderstorms (15)

Air mass thunderstorms are most common in the Monashees and Cariboos during summer, as well as in Glacier, Kootenay, Banff, and Lake Louise National Parks. Watch carefully for cumulus clouds building strongly. It is best to be off peaks and ridges by midafternoon in such conditions, as thunderstorms typically reach maturity by 3:00 to 4:00 P.M.

Okanagan Valley: Fog and Stratus (16)

Descending into the Okanagan Valley on Highway 97C can result in an abrupt and eerie reduction in visibility as drivers descend into fog or stratus clouds in the colder air below. Start slowing down before you drop into this zone.

Rocky Mountain Trench: Arctic Outbreak (17)

An Arctic outbreak from the north will typically produce the coldest temperatures from Golden to Cranbrook in the Rocky Mountain Trench. Temperatures may drop to –20°F to –30°F (also –20°C to –30°C), with this bitter cold persisting for 2 to 5 days. Such outbreaks require extreme caution when dressing, moving slowly to prevent perspiration, and keeping a watchful eye for signs of frostbite or hypothermia.

THE PACIFIC NORTHWEST COAST: WASHINGTON AND OREGON

Of all the fire mountains which, like beacons, once blazed along the Pacific Coast, Mount Rainier is the noblest in form, has the most interesting forest cover, and . . . is the highest and most flowery.
John Muir

The best winter I ever had was the summer I spent in Puget Sound.
Samuel Clemens (aka Mark Twain)

No question: The Pacific Northwest can be soggy. Rare to nonexistent is the hiker, camper, or climber who has not been transformed into a walking sponge, including this author. However, I have also spent October evenings in shirtsleeves and shorts camped on the shoulders of Mount Rainier at elevations of 6000 to 7000 feet. No, I was not in the end stages of hypothermia and I'm not a charter member of the Polar Bear Club. It can be that warm—occasionally. There is, however, a reason the Northwest's major volcanic peaks serve as test pieces for climbers preparing for Himalayan expeditions, just as there is a reason local residents selfishly (but understandably) play up

Rainier's reputation for foul weather: They want to keep its oft cloud-veiled beauty for themselves.

The Pacific Northwest is a region born of the fire of volcanism and sculpted by water and ice. Mount Rainier (originally called "Tahoma") towers over all other peaks at 14,410 feet (4392 meters) and serves as the dominant icon for the region. Mount Rainier, together with other Northwest mountains, supports the most extensive system of glaciers in the contiguous United States. The Mount St. Helens eruption in 1980, followed by its reawakening in 2004, serves as a pointed reminder that fire does indeed still dwell beneath the ice.

Visitors flying into the Northwest on clear days (which admittedly can be scarce) enjoy spectacular vistas. The blue waters of the North Pacific give way to rugged headlands: The Coast Range of Oregon drops precipitously into the sea, breached by the expansive Columbia River to the north. The young Olympic Mountains rise just inland in Washington, separated from British Columbia's Vancouver Island Range by the Strait of Juan de Fuca. The geologically older Cascade Range runs parallel to the east, separated by a broad trough sculpted in Washington State by Ice Age glaciers. This trough begins with Oregon's Willamette Valley in the south, continues into the Puget Sound basin in Washington, and submerges into British Columbia's Hecate and Georgia Straits. The Cascades extend from northern California through Oregon and into Washington, merging with British Columbia's Coast Mountains and punctuated with massive volcanoes. The Cascades typically confine the moist, marine air to the west and dry, continental air to the east. The result is an astonishing difference in climates, more typical of different regions than different parts of the same state. Two great river valleys cleave these mountains: the Fraser in British Columbia and the Columbia between Washington and Oregon. Those chasms, together with a series of east–west passes and frequent visits by the jet stream, help produce some of the most complicated weather in North America.

The mountains of the Pacific Northwest Coast are highly efficient at wringing moisture from inbound clouds making landfall along their west slopes. Water is much more scarce to the east. The dense, towering stands of Douglas fir and western red cedar give way to drought-tolerant lodgepole pine and, eventually, sagebrush. The cool waters offshore tend to moderate weather systems, resulting in fewer and less powerful thunderstorms but giving birth to intense lows that batter this region almost yearly with hurricane-force winds. That is not to say thunderstorms do not occur here: They are most frequent along the west slopes *after* a cold front passes, particularly with a pronounced drop in the freezing/snow level and a brief period of partial clearing. Head east of the crest to avoid these heavy showers and thunderstorms. However, during summer, a trough of low pressure may extend northward from the interior of California. If thunderstorms are occurring just to the east of that trough, they will typically move northward into Washington and Oregon along with the hot air, particularly along the east slopes of the Cascades.

Snow is more plentiful here than any other place in North America. Mount Baker set the world record of 1140 inches during the winter of 1998–99: It replaced the record of a bigger Washington State volcano: Mount Rainier. But thanks (or perhaps no thanks) to the proximity of the Pacific Ocean, the snow can be very dense. The nickname "Cascade concrete" is not an exaggeration. Northwest skiers give their legs a thorough workout. The region's famous wet weather is most pronounced during the months of November, December, January, and February. The odds of dry, sunny weather are greatest during the second half of July and the first half of August, but autumn is the great secret in the Pacific Northwest Coast: The crowds are gone, and the weather is often beautiful (notice I say often, not always—this is the Northwest!).

Washington and Oregon: The Big Picture

It is not surprising that the Pacific Ocean is the birthplace of most of the storms that hit the Northwest. What might be startling is that seemingly small variations in the path of those storms can result in huge differences in the weather and on its impact on outdoor recreation. Experienced forecasters pay close attention both to where the weather systems develop and the path those storms travel. So does anyone who spends much time outdoors, which is why our examination of the Pacific Northwest's weather begins with a look at the big picture: the major storm tracks and their influence on the weather. Nitpicking over the number of such patterns would lead to a meaningless polyglot of patterns, but essentially four are worth understanding. Those are shown in the illustrations that follow, together with the areas that tend to get the most precipitation and the least. The illustrations mirror what you would likely see in a satellite image. A brief description follows, including the duration and intensity of each pattern, and each pattern's effect on the freezing level.

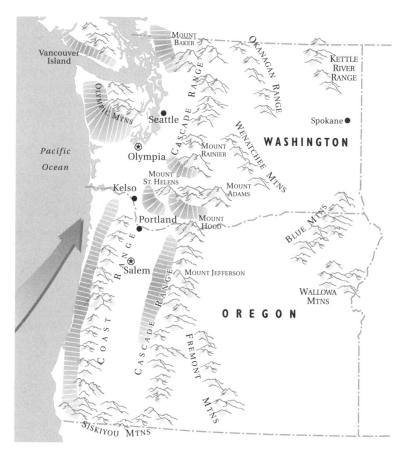

Storm track from the south to southwest

A storm track from the south to southwest is often called a "Pineapple Express." That nickname comes as no surprise once you look at a satellite image: Clouds often stretch all the way from the Hawaiian Islands to the Pacific Northwest. The arrival of that warm, moist, subtropical air results in a great deal of rain: 1 to 2 inches (2.5 to 5 centimeters) in the Puget Sound in Washington and the Willamette Valley in Oregon. That is far exceeded by the rain that falls on the west slopes of the Olympics in Washington, the Coast Range in Oregon, and the Cascades in both states: 3 to 4 inches (about 1.5 centimeters) per day and often much more. This storm track tends to persist for several days as new disturbances develop and ripple along this band of clouds. The mild air also results in unseasonably high freezing levels: 6000 to 9000 feet (1500 to

Storm track from the southwest to west

2400 meters) or more. Snow melts rapidly in the mountains, serious flooding often develops, snow bridges weaken, and the avalanche hazard may become high or extreme. A shorter south to southwesterly flow that doesn't reach the tropics can produce intense storms with hurricane-force winds.

A *storm track from the southwest to west* is more common than the Pineapple Express. The rain is not as persistent or as intense. A break usually occurs between disturbances, sometimes lasting only a few hours, occasionally a full day. If cold air has an icy grip on the Northwest, the precipitation carried by this storm track may begin as snow but then change to rain. Freezing levels associated with this pattern vary from season to season: 3000 to 6000 feet (900 to 1500 meters) is typical

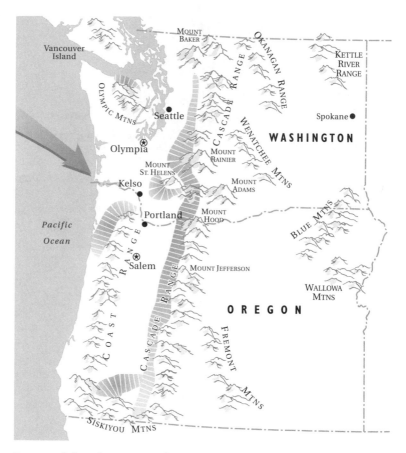

Storm track from the west to northwest

in winter, 5000 to 8000 feet (1500 to 2100 meters) in autumn or spring. The result is slushy, wet snow at or near pass elevations, elevated avalanche hazards and weakening snow bridges. However, rain shadows are likely just to the east of the region's mountain ranges, offering sunshine to the selective backcountry traveler.

A *storm track from the northwest* results in fast-moving weather disturbances, often with little warning to backcountry travelers. Although storms move through quickly with fairly rapid clearing, the colder air from Siberia and Alaska behind a front can lead to thundershowers, especially along the western slopes of the Cascades. Unlike other regions of North America, thunderstorms are most frequent *after* a cold front moves through. Expect freezing levels from just above sea level to

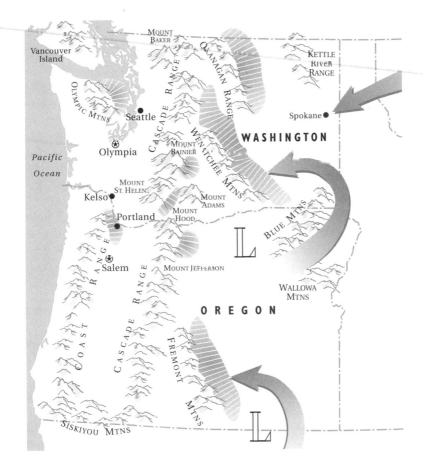

Storm track or surface winds from the northeast to east

2000 feet (900 meters) in winter and 3000 to 5000 feet (900 to 1500 meters) in autumn and spring. This pattern produces excellent-quality snow in the mountains and usually lots of it. Again, rain shadows are likely to the east of the Cascades, with drier and often sunnier weather.

A surface flow from the northeast to east has a split personality: In summer it produces dry, sunny, and warm weather on both sides of the Cascades because the air originates over land, not over water. The air moving from this large high-pressure system slides down the west slopes of the Cascades, which compresses and warms the air. It is a very different story during winter. The dominant feature of this pattern is a large high over the eastern Pacific that directs very cold air southward from the interior of British Columbia or the Yukon. A zone of low pressure, a *trough,* drops southward along the coast, helping the cold air from the interior to squirt through gaps in the terrain, the Fraser River in particular, and then to circulate over the Pacific just long enough to pick up moisture but not long enough to warm the air very much. Snow falls at or just above sea level, often making its way from Vancouver to Bellingham to Seattle and sometimes Portland. Because the northerly winds aloft are sliding past, not against, the Cascades, more snow may actually fall in the cities than in the mountains. However, heavy snow may fall over the north and east slopes of the Olympics. What does fall is dry powder, the stuff normally found farther east in the Rockies. Another winter pattern involves a surface low that tracks inland just to the south, and the counterclockwise flow around that low directs air up the east slopes of the Cascades. That will generate the heaviest precipitation along the east slopes of the Cascades and much drier conditions along the west slopes. A surface low moving inland near the California–Oregon border will produce the heaviest precipitation along the east slopes of the Cascades, especially from Klamath Falls north. One moving inland along the Columbia River will produce the heaviest precipitation from Mount Adams north to the Mission Ridge ski area.

Washington and Oregon: Local Weather Phenomena You Need to Understand

Name a type of weather phenomena found in or near mountains, and odds are you will find it in the Pacific Northwest. However, this region—like most others—possesses unique patterns that merit specific explanation in addition to the more general descriptions provided in other chapters.

The Puget Sound Convergence Zone may be the focus of heavy precipitation while other areas just a few miles to the north or south are enjoying sunshine. This zone often develops after the passage of a cold front, as high pressure building along the coast produces coastal winds from the west–southwest to northwest.

When the onshore flow of air runs into the Olympic Mountains, it splits, some flowing through the Strait of Juan de Fuca to the north, some through the Chehalis Gap to the south. The Cascades present an almost insurmountable barrier to the east, so some of the air moving through the strait is forced south into Puget Sound, while some of the air moving through the Chehalis Gap is forced north. These two opposing currents collide, forcing some of the air to rise, and then it is pushed into the Cascades by the winds passing over the Olympics.

This convergence zone tends to range from Everett south to Tacoma. Coastal winds from the northwest tend to push it between Seattle and Tacoma, while those from the west to southwest will result

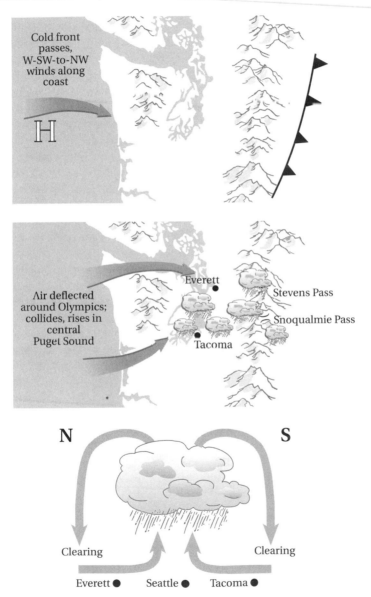

Elements of the Puget Sound Convergence Zone

in a zone north of Seattle to Everett. A weak convergence zone may produce only thicker clouds more resistant to clearing, but a stronger zone can produce locally heavy rain or snowfall and possibly even thundershowers. Convergence zones have produced as much as 10 to 20 inches (25 to 51 centimeters) of snow at Stevens Pass, while only 2 to 3 inches (5 to 8 centimeters) of snow fell at Snoqualmie Pass, less than 50 miles (80 kilometers) away. The reverse can also occur, depending upon where the convergence zone forms and how it moves.

Generally, the Puget Sound Convergence Zone ranges between Stevens and Snoqualmie Passes, although it may reach from Mount Pilchuck to Huckleberry Mountain. Because the air that rises within this zone sinks to the north and south, occasional clearing and distinctly reduced precipitation occur. The best plan if a convergence zone is active or likely to be active, is to head to the eastern slopes of the Cascades. If that is not possible, plan your outing from Glacier Peak north or from Mount Rainier south. Usually the precipitation will be less intense.

Similar convergence zones occur elsewhere in the Northwest. Onshore winds also split when they encounter the segment of the Coast Range in southwestern Washington State, converging near the Toutle Range to the east. Northwesterly winds flowing around the Vancouver Island Range produce increased precipitation in a convergence zone that extends roughly from Everett to Mount Vernon, or from Glacier Peak north to Eldorado Peak in the southern end of North Cascades National Park. This pattern can contribute to Mount Baker's record-setting snowfall. Wily skiers also know southwesterly winds flowing around Mount Rainier converge upon the Chinook Pass area but provide the Crystal Mountain Ski Area with wonderful light powder snow.

Oregon and Washington: Trail Notes
Fraser River: Outflow (1)

Arctic air pouring from the interior of British Columbia can generate hurricane-force winds here. Watch for subzero temperatures over the British Columbia interior, as well as a forecast for north–northeasterly winds, especially when pressures between Hope, British Columbia, and Bellingham, Washington, near or exceed 10 millibars.

Stevens Pass: Gap Winds (2)

A strong difference in pressures between eastern and western Washington

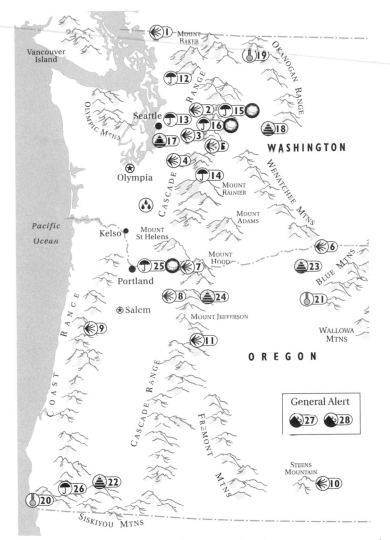

Washington and Oregon trail notes reference map (icon locations are approximate)

can generate strong winds through the pass, especially near the entrances, with lower pressure. Watch for pressure differences between Wenatchee and Everett of 6 to 8 millibars or more. Westerlies will occur when lower pressure is to the east, with the strongest winds just east of Stevens Pass, while easterlies will occur when lower pressure is to the west, with the strongest winds west of Stevens Pass.

Snoqualmie Pass: Gap Winds (3)

A strong difference in pressures between eastern and western Washington can generate strong winds through the pass, especially near the entrances, with lower pressure. Watch for pressure differences between Yakima and Seattle of 6 to 8 millibars or more. Westerlies will occur when lower pressure is to the east, with the strongest winds near Cle Elum and Ellensburg. Easterlies will occur when lower pressure is to the west, with the strongest winds near North Bend.

Naches Pass: Gap Winds (4)

A strong difference in pressures between eastern and western Washington can generate strong winds through the pass, especially on the side, with lower pressure. Easterly winds will be strong near Greenwater toward Enumclaw. This pattern can also produce strong ridgetop winds at Crystal Mountain. Watch for pressure differences between Yakima and Seattle of 6 to 8 millibars or more.

East Slope: Chinook Winds (5)

Moderate to strong westerly winds aloft will produce strong winds along the east slopes of the Cascades with marked warming. This phenomenon is most notable from Stevens Pass southward.

Blue Mountains: Chinook Winds (6)

South to southeasterly winds aloft can produce moderate to strong chinook conditions along the north and northwesterly slopes of the Blue Mountains leading toward Walla Walla and Pendleton. Expect abrupt warming and locally stronger winds in southeast–northwest-oriented valleys and canyons.

Columbia Gorge: Winds (7)

The Columbia Gorge became the popular windsurfing destination it is because of the frequency of strong winds. A strong difference in pressure between western and eastern Oregon can generate stiff winds in the Gorge. Watch for differences of 8 millibars or more between Astoria and The Dalles. Strong westerlies are most common from late spring to early fall when eastern Oregon is sizzling hot and lower pressure lies to the east. Easterlies are most common from late fall to early spring when cold, dense air settles east of the Cascades and lower pressure lies to the west. The strongest winds will occur near the end with lower pressure.

Mount Hood Highway: Backdoor Cold Front (8)

Higher pressure east of the Cascades can also generate strong easterly winds to the south of Mount Hood. Typically the Timberline Ski Area and Government Camp are much more exposed to cold winds in this pattern than is Mount Hood Meadows. Again, use pressure differences between Astoria and The Dalles of 8 millibars or more as a warning sign.

Coast Range/Corvallis: Gap Winds (9)

A gap in the Coast Range leading from Newport along the coast to Corvallis along US 20 can generate locally strong winds down the east slopes along the Tumtum and Marys Rivers toward Corvallis. Watch for pressure differences of 4 to 6 millibars or more between Newport and Salem, with the higher pressure along the coast.

Steens Mountain: Downslope Winds (10)

Downcanyon winds of 20 miles per hour or more can occur off Steens Mountain. Watch for these when westerly winds are blowing. Make sure your tent is well staked. Such winds typically drain into the Alvord Desert.

Oregon Cascades (East Slopes): Chinook Winds (11)

Westerly winds aloft can produce moderate to strong chinook conditions along the east slopes of the Cascades, especially from Bend north to The Dalles. Again, abrupt warming is likely.

Vancouver Island: Convergence Zone (12)

Northwest winds off the coast converge beyond the south end of Vancouver Island, resulting in increased rain/snow from Glacier Peak to Eldorado Peak. Head north or south of this zone, or into it if you are looking for snow in winter. The Mount Baker Ski Area can benefit from this pattern.

Puget Sound: Convergence Zone (13)

West–southwesterly winds off the coast converge beyond the Olympic Mountains, resulting in increased rain, snow, and thundershowers in the vicinity of Stevens Pass. Northwest coastal winds will steer this toward Snoqualmie Pass. This is most common after cold front passage. Watch for west to northwest surface winds at Everett, southwest winds farther south.

Mount Rainier: Convergence Zone (14)

Southwest winds split around Mount Rainier, then converge near Chinook Pass, most commonly after a cold front passes. Expect increased rain and snow in this area. Fine, light powder commonly falls on the Crystal Mountain Ski Area in this pattern.

Stevens Pass: Backdoor Cold Front (15)

Colder, high-pressure air moves through the pass and encounters warmer, moist air. The result is localized snow even though the snow level is above pass elevation. Look for daytime temperatures well below freezing in eastern Washington, pass temperatures at or below freezing, a pressure difference between Wenatchee and Everett of 6 millibars or more, humidities in western Washington of 60 percent or more, and snow levels 1000 feet or more above pass elevation. Freezing rain is possible as easterly winds diminish and the cold air layer thins.

Snoqualmie Pass: Backdoor Cold Front (16)

Colder, high-pressure air moves through the pass and encounters warmer, moist air. The result is localized snow even though the snow level is above pass elevation. Look for daytime temperatures well below freezing in eastern Washington, pass temperatures at or below freezing, lower pressure to the west with humidities 60 percent or more, and snow levels 1000 feet or more above pass elevation. Freezing rain is possible as easterly winds diminish, and the cold air layer thins.

Washington/Oregon Cascades (West Slopes): Upslope Fog/ Stratus (17)

Low Stratus or fog is most likely from late spring to early autumn following unseasonably warm weather moving into the Puget Sound basin in Washington and the Willamette Valley in Oregon. Watch for reports of fog moving northward along the coast and a wind shift from east or calm winds to west winds through the Strait of Juan de Fuca and the Columbia River. These conditions are typically found at or below 4000 feet.

Washington/Oregon Cascades (East Slopes): Upslope Fog/Stratus (18)

Low Stratus or fog is most likely during winter. Cold air from building high pressure surges westward against the Cascades, and moisture condenses as it moves upslope. A mix of flurries, drizzle, freezing drizzle, or fog is possible. This pattern may expand throughout eastern Washington as high pressure builds.

North Central Washington: Arctic Cold (19)

Cold air draining off the North Cascades can produce extreme cold in the Methow River Valley. Watch for high pressure settling directly over this area. Temperatures can easily drop below zero Fahrenheit.

Southern Oregon, Brookings Area: Banana Belt (20)

Expect unusually warm temperatures when brisk northeasterly winds move over Sexton Mountain and the Coast Range toward Brookings on the coast—hence the nickname "Banana Belt." Brookings may reach 90°F while North Bend a short distance up the coast is still in the 50s.

Northeast Oregon: Arctic Outbreak and Arctic Cold (21)

Cold air draining off the Blue Mountains in western Grant and southwestern Umatilla Counties during an Arctic outbreak produces the coldest temperatures in the state (−54°F in Ukiah, Seneca, and Bates).

Rogue River Valley: Radiation Fog (22)

Clearing after precipitation and light winds will produce dense and persistent fog extending from the Rogue River Valley southeast to Medford and Ashland.

Pendleton Area: Radiation Fog (23)

Clearing after precipitation and light winds will produce dense and persistent fog northwest of the Blue Mountains near Pendleton.

Cascades (East Slopes): Upslope Fog (24)

Cold air from building high pressure surges eastward against the Cascades, and moisture condenses as it moves upslope. A mix of flurries, drizzle, freezing drizzle, or fog is possible. This phenomena is most pronounced along US 26 but can be found from The Dalles south to Madras.

Columbia River Gorge: Silver Thaw (25)

Snow in the Gorge can give way to freezing rain as easterly winds drive colder air through the Gorge, undercutting warmer, moist air approaching from the west. Expect this with an Arctic air mass over eastern Oregon/Washington with pressures 8 to 10 millibars higher in Pendleton than Astoria, and a low-pressure system approaching the coast. May last a few hours or more than a day. Sleet is likely at Troutdale, with freezing rain near Portland International Airport and rain in Beaverton.

Rogue and Illinois Rivers: Flash Flooding (26)

Heavy rains, typically from thundershowers, can cause abrupt and rapid rises in the Illinois and Rogue Rivers. Be especially cautious if thundershowers are forecast.

All Areas: Winter Direct-Action Avalanches (27)

Because of the maritime climate of the Pacific Northwest, most—though certainly not all—avalanches here tend to be of the direct-action or wet, soft-slab variety. Snow falling at a rate of an inch or more an hour, particularly if the snow level is rising, produces the greatest hazard. Check avalanche forecasts carefully, and allow at least a day for the snow to consolidate.

All Areas: Spring Avalanches (28)

During spring, melting snow will percolate into the snowpack, lubricating buried layers and priming the trigger for avalanches, particularly on sun-warmed, south-facing slopes. Ski or ride on these slopes early in the day, moving to shaded northern or eastern slopes as the sun gets higher. As always, check avalanche forecasts carefully.

THE NORTHERN U.S. ROCKIES: MONTANA, IDAHO, AND WYOMING

Soon after a torrent of rain and hail fell more violent than ever I saw before, the rain fell like one volley of water falling from the heavens and gave us time only to get out of the way of a torrent of water which was poreing down the hill in the river with emence force tareing everything before it taking with it large rocks & mud.

William Clark, *The Journals of*
Lewis and Clark, June 29, 1805

Like many fly fishermen in western Montana where the summer days are almost Arctic in length, I often do not start fishing until the cool of the evening. Then in the Arctic half-light of the canyon, all existence fades to a being with my soul.

Norman Maclean,
A River Runs Through It

It has been said that in the northern U.S. Rockies, particularly in Montana, winter lasts nine months of the year: The other three months bring tourists. That is an exaggeration, of course, but seven feet of snow have fallen as late as June in the mountains. Missoula has picked up 8 inches during what is supposed to be the first month of summer,  Bozeman 1 foot. And it can begin snowing again in late August or September, though prolonged snow typically waits until early November in Montana and Wyoming, and a little later in central Idaho.

The ranges here have storied names: the Tetons, Wind Rivers, Bighorns, Bitterroots, Absarokas, and Lewises. Ski, climb, or backpack here and you are apt to literally be walking in the footsteps of Lewis and Clark. As those explorers came to learn, it is the westerlies carrying moisture inland from the Pacific that generate most of the precipitation here. During winter, Aleutian lows moving from the northwest generate much of the fabled powder snow, particularly when the jet stream is just to the south of your destination. The repeated movement over mountain ranges wrings out the soggier stuff over the Olympics and the Cascades to the west. What falls as "Cascade concrete" there often falls as feathery fluff here.

Glacier National Park in northwestern Montana is living proof of how snow, consolidating through the endless winters of the Ice Age, shaped this region—and snow can sculpt a landscape even in the course of a single day. What are called *direct-action avalanches* can occur in the midst of or shortly after a big snow. *Delayed-action avalanches* can release suddenly following days of clear, cold weather. What happens in late autumn and early winter can set the tone for the stability and safety of the backcountry for weeks to come, if not much of the season. Plentiful snow in November can build up a thick snowpack that retards the formation of weak layers that lead to avalanches. Sparse snowfall, together with clear, cold weather early in the season results in an unstable snowpack that can persist much of the season. Some basic guidelines can be found in this section's trail notes, but it is important to recognize that nothing can substitute for obtaining current, thorough avalanche forecasts *and following them*. This region combines aspects of the different alpine zones: good reason to be conservative and seek expert guidance. Fortunately, world-class avalanche forecast centers are located here, as is the preeminent snow science research facility at Montana State University in Bozeman.

During spring and early summer, lows move more slowly through the Northern Rockies, generating sustained heavy precipitation, including late-season snows and, of course, thunderstorms. That is the major forecast problem during the relatively short warm season. Although the thunderstorms are not as strong as those to the south in Colorado, it only takes one lightning bolt to ruin an outing. The accident cited in Chapter 1 is just one example. Summer air mass or "popcorn" thunderstorms typically develop by 1:00 or 2:00 in the afternoon. Storms produce extensive lightning from June through August, but the larger hailstorms tend to occur more in July and August. Even spells of sunny, warm weather can be hazardous. Hikers may set out ill-prepared for the sudden onset of an overnight deep freeze. Days that hit 90°F may include overnight temperatures below freezing.

Of course there is the storied chinook. The origin and characteristics of this powerful wind is described in detail in Chapter 5. Suffice it to say that chinooks can produce radically different weather over short distances. It may be cold and snowing in West Glacier while it is 55°F, sunny, and blowing madly in and beyond East Glacier. This complex braid of mountains can produce wide variations in weather over short distances, particularly near the two large "kinks" in the range: the first in southwestern Montana, the second in southwestern Wyoming. Jackson Hole, surrounded by peaks, receives much less precipitation than nearby areas. Forecasts tend to both overestimate and rush precipitation for this area. Without question, weather in the northern Rockies can be good or bad, but it is rarely indifferent.

Montana, Idaho, and Wyoming: The Big Picture

Although the northern Rockies in a sense gets "hand me down" storms that move inland from the Pacific coast, nothing is second rate in the strength of storms that sweep these high peaks with such ferocity. Credit that to the wildly differing conditions that often exist on either side of the Continental Divide. Experienced forecasters pay close attention both to where the weather systems develop and the path those storms travel. So does anyone who spends much time outdoors. It can make a big difference in the success or misery of your outing. That is why our examination of this region's weather begins with a look at the big picture: the major storm tracks and their influence on the weather. Essentially, five patterns are worth understanding. They are shown in

Storm track, or surface winds, from the north

Storm track from the northwest

the illustrations that follow, together with the areas that tend to get the most precipitation and the least. The illustrations mirror what you would be likely to see in a satellite image. A brief description follows, including the duration and intensity of each pattern and its effect on the freezing level.

A *storm track from the north* essentially means an Arctic outbreak during winter. This extremely cold and dry air mass moves east of the divide first. If it is deep enough, the Arctic air will then move west of the divide. A gradual shift to a more moist northwesterly flow can produce extensive snow that persists as long as the cold air remains trapped in place and moist air continues to flow. A shift to southwesterly winds aloft will typically moderate temperatures more rapidly. During the summer months, a northerly flow aloft brings dry, sunny weather west of the divide. Cool and cloudy weather can prevail east of the divide, sometimes slopping over the crest (usually this is true just west of the divide. Cool, cloudy, upslope conditions can prevail east of the divide, and at times along and just to the west side of the divide.

A *storm track from the northwest* brings somewhat lighter, more

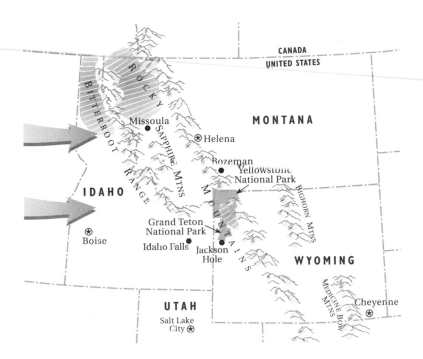

Storm track from the west

powdery snow than a westerly track and tends to produce the most significant snow in central and southern Montana: from Missoula to Butte and Bozeman with the promise of good skiing at Big Sky and Bridger Bowl. If cold air is in place from a prior Arctic outbreak, this pattern can bring prolonged snowfall, with the heaviest snow along north- and east-facing slopes. This pattern tends to bring very cold temperatures, particularly to upper elevations. This pattern is also a frequent source of storms in summer, resulting in both rain and thunderstorms.

A *storm track from the west* tends to produce the heaviest snow over the Idaho Panhandle and northwest Montana when the jet stream is cruising near the Canadian border, often with a succession of fronts. It can also bring significant snow to the Snake River Range in Idaho, the Bitterroots in Montana, and the Jackson Hole area in Wyoming if the jet stream is cruising farther south, through southern Washington and Oregon. The best powder snow will come when the jet stream is located just to the south of your intended destination. However, westerly flows also bring chinooks to the eastern slopes if wind speeds reach or exceed

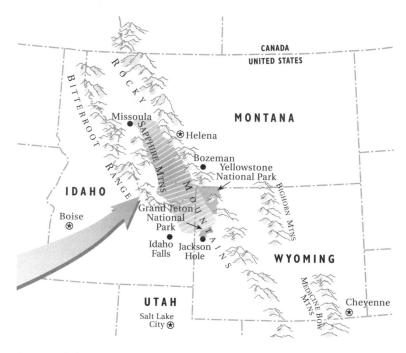

Storm track from the southwest

40 to 50 miles per hour. For further discussion of problem areas, see the Unique Weather Phenomena and the Trail Notes sections for this region.

A storm track from the southwest that carries disturbances across northern California and through Utah will often have its greatest impact once the actual surface low moves east of the Rockies, as easterly winds generate upslope snow over the eastern slopes of the Medicine Bow, Laramie, and Bighorn Mountains in Wyoming, and to a lesser extent over the Wind River Range. Lander, Wyoming, may receive several inches of snow while it is sunny in Jackson Hole. However, this pattern can produce some of the heaviest snows, albeit with higher snow levels from Missoula south in Montana and over the Snake River Range in Idaho and into northwest Wyoming. Occasionally such a storm may bring some precipitation to the east slopes of the divide in northern Montana. Although these storms can occur anytime, they are most common from March through May. While snow levels can be high south and east of the track, they will drop very low to the north and west of it.

A storm track from the south–southwest is called a "Pineapple Express" here just as it is along the West Coast: The results are similar—

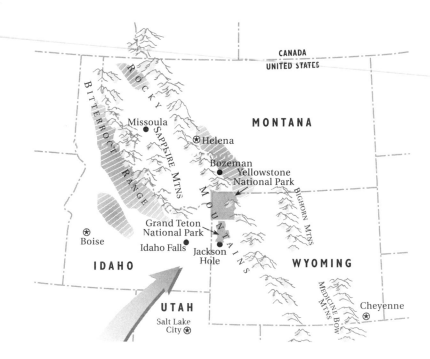

Storm track from the south to southwest

namely rain or wet, heavy snow. Rain is most likely in the valleys with a transition to snow at about 6000 to 7000 feet. However, in extreme conditions the snow level may be as high as 10,000 feet. Large amounts of precipitation may fall for several days, and avalanche conditions may become high or extreme. Such conditions are not frequent in this area, occurring perhaps once every few years. During summer, a southerly to southwesterly flow can bring enough monsoon moisture from the southwest to generate almost daily thunderstorms.

Montana, Idaho, and Wyoming: Unique Weather Phenomena You Need to Understand

Waiting for a Chinook is not only one of cowboy artist Charley Russell's best known works: It also perfectly captures the timing and promise of downslope winds. A skeletal steer, weakened by hunger to the point of collapse, is shown staggering through the snow while wolves patiently await the animal's almost certain demise. Only a chinook, and the rapid warming and snowmelt it generates, can expose enough vegetation for the beleaguered creature to survive. The timely arrival of such downslope winds has in fact saved more than one cattleman's brisket. "Chinook" is just one name for downslope winds, which do in fact bring rapid warming and snowmelt. Native Americans living in or near the Rockies used to call such winds "Snow Eaters." Sudden warming of 30°F to 60°F can easily melt inches of snowpack in a single day, resulting in abrupt flooding. Whatever they are called, such warm winds can weaken both snow bridges and the overall snowpack. The avalanche hazard may jump from moderate to high or even extreme. Backcountry travelers not anticipating such an event can find themselves inconvenienced at the least and very possibly endangered. This is particularly true for ice climbers. The winds are capable of considerable damage, easily reaching sustained speeds of 40 to 70 miles per hour. Peak gusts of 100 miles per hour have been reported. These winds are most frequent from November through March, when the strongest chinooks (see the illustration on page 94) may blast 60 to 80 miles beyond the east slopes and out onto the plains.

Such downslope winds are the result of several different factors: a large difference in surface air pressure across a mountain range, strong winds aloft crossing that range, and precipitation falling over the upwind slopes. Although winds flowing from the northwest to southwest may produce chinooks, most occur when winds aloft are from the west to northwest and speeds range from 40 to 50 miles per hour or more. Before setting out, check reported and forecast winds aloft at 10,000 feet (see Chapter 7). Strong westerly winds aloft, together with higher surface pressures west of the divide than to the east in Cut Bank or Helena point to likely downslope winds, particularly if precipitation is falling along the west slopes of the Continental Divide. When such conditions exist, anticipate damaging winds, abrupt warming (a rapid increase of 30°F to 60°F is possible), an elevated avalanche hazard, and unsafe ice climbing conditions. Avoid lee slopes. If Arctic air is already in place east of the divide, a chinook may engage in a sort of tug-of-war with the frigid air mass, which may pulse back and forth from the east slopes of the divide, resulting in alternate extreme warming and cooling. In the field, watch for the appearance of lenticular clouds (check the cloud charts in Appendix III) and also for the appearance of chinook wall clouds.

Montana, Idaho, and Wyoming: Trail Notes
Marias Pass: Gap Winds (1)

An outbreak of Arctic air into eastern Montana with higher pressures

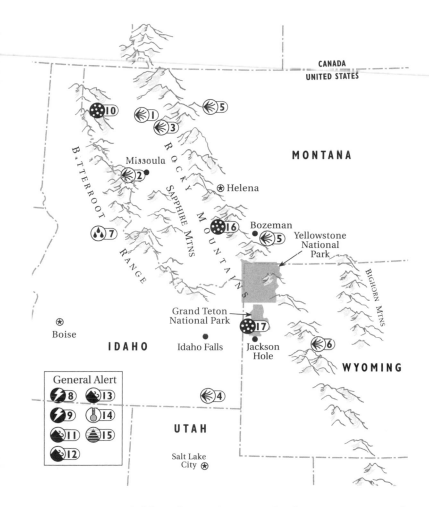

Montana, Wyoming and Idaho trail notes reference map (icon locations are approximate)

east of the Continental Divide can produce strong winds exceeding 50 miles per hour through and to the west of Marias Pass toward West Glacier, and even as far as Kalispell. Winds will be particularly strong if a low is approaching from the west.

Missoula Area: Gap Winds (2)

An outbreak of Arctic air into eastern Montana with higher pressures east of the Continental Divide can produce strong winds reaching or exceeding 50 miles per hour from the Blackfoot through Hell Gate Canyon. Watch for higher pressures in Helena compared to Missoula in such a situation.

Logan Pass: Gap Winds (3)

Westerly winds produced by higher pressures to the west of the Continental Divide can generate strong gap winds through Logan Pass in Glacier National Park. Wind speeds of 100 miles per hour have been recorded. Look for strong gap winds here when air pressure is higher in Kalispell than in Browning or Cut Bank.

Snake River: Outflow (4)

Higher pressure over Idaho's Snake River Plain can produce strong canyon winds between the Bannock and Aspen Ranges in southeast Idaho down into northern Utah. Check for higher pressure at Pocatello compared to Logan: a difference of 6 to 8 millibars or more makes such strong winds likely.

Livingston Area and Great Falls to Cut Bank: Chinook Winds (5)

Strong west to northwesterly winds aloft will produce the strongest chinooks in this area. Sustained wind speeds of 40 to 70 miles per hour are common with peak gusts as high as 100 miles per hour. Temperature fluctuations of 30°F to 60°F are not uncommon and can result in rapid snowmelt and flooding. Watch for reported and forecast westerly to northwesterly winds aloft at 10,000 feet as a clue for the development of chinooks. In the field, watch for evidence of a chinook wall cloud hanging over the mountains as signs of an imminent chinook. Livingston is one common area for chinooks in southwest Montana. Bridger Bowl near Bozeman can also host strong downslope winds. Farther north, the strongest chinooks occur in a zone from west of Great Falls north to Browning and Cut Bank.

Absaroka and Wind River Mountains, Wyoming: Chinook Winds (6)

Strong westerly to even southwesterly winds will produce the strongest chinooks along the east slopes of these two ranges. Look for a high-pressure system to the west of the Continental Divide and winds aloft of 45 to 50 miles per hour or more. Reported and forecast winds at 10,000 feet will give a good indication of the potential for such downslope winds. Temperature fluctuations of 30°F to 60°F are not uncommon and can result in rapid snowmelt and flooding.

Montana and Northern Idaho: Closed Low Rainfall (7)

May and June can produce what are called closed lows: The cloud patterns resemble a whirlpool on satellite photos. They often begin over the eastern Pacific and slowly drift eastward over the northern Rockies. The wettest conditions tend to occur from the Salmon River Mountains in Idaho northward and over most of Montana. If you see this kind of whirlpool-like cloud pattern on a satellite photo, expect prolonged wet, cool weather with lowered snow levels and probable thunderstorms. Such patterns have produced significant snow in Missoula and Bozeman as late as June.

All Areas: Spring Thunderstorms (8)

Although spring thunderstorms will not be as strong as those farther south in Colorado, the same dangers of lightning, gusty winds, heavy downpours, and flash flooding exist in the northern Rockies. Spring air mass thunderstorms tend to develop earlier, by about midday, so plan to get off ridges by lunchtime if cumulus clouds are swelling rapidly. The approach of either a cold front or a trough of low pressure in the upper atmosphere is a common trigger for spring thunderstorms. Such thunderstorms are most common from the middle of May through June.

Summer Thunderstorms (9)

Summer thunderstorms that occur in July and August tend to develop a bit later than those that form in spring but also tend to produce more lightning and hail. When the air is warm and humid and winds tend toward the south, expect thunderstorms to begin developing by about 1:00 or 2:00 in the afternoon, with the heaviest activity from about 3:00 P.M. Wise climbers and hikers are off mountain ridges and peaks by 2:00 P.M. Occasional cold fronts crossing the Rockies can also trigger thunderstorms as they approach, but this source typically disappears by late July.

Northern Idaho and Northwestern Montana: Heavy Snow (10)

Some of the heaviest snow tends to occur from the Cabinet Mountains to the west side of Glacier National Park and also over the Clearwaters in Idaho when winds aloft are westerly and the jet stream is along or near the Canadian border. The same wind direction but with the jet stream farther south will tend to shift the heaviest snow south to the Bitterroots.

Early Season Avalanche Hazard (11)

Substantial, sustained snow in November and December—3 feet or more—tends to prevent weak layers from forming. However, a shallow snowpack with clear, cold weather promotes formation of surface hoar. This weak layer, buried by later snowfall, can persist for weeks. Depth hoar can also develop, making this a very dangerous time to travel in the mountains. Delayed-action slab avalanches can occur, involving layers extending to bare ground.

Midwinter Avalanche Hazard (12)

By midwinter, avalanche activity becomes less random, involving new snow that slides above the old snow. Hoar formation is most common on north-facing slopes. Areas that receive heavy snow that deposits into drifts from moderate to strong wind are most prone to large, direct-action soft-slab avalanches, with most action on north- and east-facing slopes.

Late Season Avalanche Hazard (13)

Increased sunshine and warmer temperatures shift the prime hazard to south-facing slopes. It is best to avoid south- and west-facing slopes, particularly during the afternoon. Rain can destabilize the snowpack very quickly.

Summer Frosts in Valleys (14)

Even the warmest days in the northern Rockies can be followed by nighttime lows dropping below freezing in valleys and along lakeshores. It is not necessary to travel far to enjoy warmer nighttime temperatures at your campsite. Moving 300 to 400 feet upslope can result in temperatures 15°F to 20°F warmer.

Valley Radiation Fog (15)

Valleys tend to experience dense fog when high pressure settles overhead following substantial rain or snow followed by rising temperatures aloft. The saturated air mass may initially be shallow but can reach depths of 3000 to 4000 feet if the pattern continues for several days. Such fog may persist four to five days and is most common from late November through mid February. Choose a destination with an elevation of 3000 feet or more above the valley floor.

Southwest Montana: Heavy Snow (16)

Some of the heaviest snow and the best skiing at Big Sky and Bridger Bowl come with a storm track directing a low from the southwest. This pattern brings more powder snow than a westerly track. Overall, it tends to produce the heaviest snowfall from Missoula down to Bozeman. Feet of fresh powder can fall. A northwesterly storm track is most favorable for snow from Missoula to Butte but may occasionally extend to Bozeman.

Jackson Hole: Moderate to Heavy Snow (17)

Some of the best snow in the Jackson Hole area occurs when a westerly storm track is cruising through northern Oregon or southern Washington. Often this pattern brings a series of fronts with plenty of snow. Keep in mind that the combination of colder temperatures and brisk winds provides a firsthand definition of "wind chill."

THE PACIFIC SOUTHWEST: CALIFORNIA AND NEVADA

The mighty Sierra, miles in height, reposing like a smooth cumulus cloud in the sunny sky . . . so luminous it seems to be not clothed with light, but wholly composed of it, like the wall of some celestial city.

John Muir, *The Mountains of California*

On nights like that, every booze party ends in a fight, meek little wives feel the edge of a carving knife and study their husbands' necks . . . anything can happen.

Raymond Chandler, mystery writer,
on Santa Ana winds in southern
California

The mountainscapes of California and Nevada range from the sublime to the severe, yet even in their sunbaked severity, a subtle yet palpable beauty can be experienced. A sunset following a session of bouldering in Joshua Tree National Monument can be just as pleasing as the incandescent, soul-filling splendor of Yosemite Valley. It has a way of bringing out the best in wilderness travelers. After deciphering maps for a visiting group of Italian climbers, I was both amazed and pleased to see them exuberantly produce a checkered tablecloth and a bottle of Chianti and wine glasses, together with an insistent invitation to join them for a toast to the desert sunset (which was accepted!).

To be certain, the weather here can be almost as grim as the Pacific Northwest (consider the Donner Party), but California also boasts the most moderate temperatures and reliable sunshine in the Lower 48, though certainly not in the same areas. To understand these variations, some orientation is in order. The ranges of northern and central California resemble a stretched, backward letter C. The spine of the C is formed by the aptly named Sierra Nevada, Spanish for "Snow White Mountains," though the word "sierra" can also refer to a saw. At a length of 500 miles and an average of 70 miles in width, the peaks of the Sierra range from 7000 to over 14,000 feet in height. The Sierras merge with the Cascades to the north, which in turn intersect with the Coast Range to the west. The gap in the C represents San Francisco Bay, the Central Valley comprises the interior. On a map, the short hop eastward from the coast to the Great Basin represents a soaring leap in terms of variations in plant and animal life. The fog-shrouded redwoods are found on the seaward slopes of the Coast Range, just inland of the more salt- and wind-tolerant spruce, fir, and hemlock. These ancient giants give way to the Jeffrey pines and red and white firs of the Sierra, which in turn yield to the ultimate of survivors, the gnarled bristlecone pines in the Great Basin ranges to the east. These distinctions in plant life reflect differences in local climate, and in turn support varying animal life.

At the base of the C, the mountains of southern California can be represented by an upside down, backward-dogleg L. The Transverse Range runs east to west, intersecting the Peninsular Range trending northward from the Mexican border. The highest peaks of both ranges are just 20 miles apart, near the junction of the two ranges. This angular combination of ranges confines ocean air and pollutants close to the coast, resulting in an effective moisture barrier that gives rise to the inland deserts to the east. Like the mountains farther north, the decrease in rainfall and increased variation in temperature are reflected by an obvious transition in plant and animal life to the east. Coastal oak woodlands, chaparral, and sage scrub give way to pinyons, Joshua trees, palms, and cholla cactus, as well as pines and firs at the higher elevations of the San Gabriels and neighboring ranges. Coyotes, mule deer, and king snakes are found to the west, desert sidewinders and tortoises to the east.

When the storm track drops southward into California, the western slopes of first the Coast Range and then the Sierra wring out most of the moisture. Annual precipitation can easily exceed 50 inches in these areas, even approaching 100 inches along the north Coast Range. To the lee of the Coast Range in the Sacramento Valley, that figure drops to about 15 inches, and to just single digits east of the Sierra. The vast Pacific high deflects most disturbances well north during the summer, resulting in mostly dry weather. However smog reaches a maximum during the summer months in coastal southern California, including, of course, the L.A. basin. The exception to the summer dry pattern occurs when moist air drifts northward from the Gulf of California or the Gulf of Mexico, a pattern that frequently generates thundershowers over the mountains. As the Pacific high weakens and retreats southward during winter, rainfall increases: mainly over northern and central California. Although winter tends to be nice in southern California, the reverse can be true during El Niño years. That is when a change in sea surface temperatures deflects both ocean currents and the jet stream, often directing the storm track into southern California. The result can be persistent heavy rain, flooding, and even landslides. Autumn may still be marked by persistent smog in coastal southern California, particularly in the L.A. basin, while the best weather in the Sierra tends to occur from late September into early October, but by mid-October snow can fall, particularly in the northern Sierra. That makes an extra fleece or down garment particularly welcome. Perhaps the most reliable good weather in the high Sierras comes in the late spring and early summer months, after the last of the winter storms have departed and before the summer monsoon has started.

Both the Sierra and the Peninsular Ranges cast a long rain shadow, reaching into and across Nevada. Although largely a plateau classified as part of the Great Basin, several mountain ranges, most of which run north to south, are found here. Still, most streams disappear into lakes (if they make it that far), with the exception of those in the northeast, which drain into the Columbia River Basin, and the far southeast, which flow into the Colorado River. The generally dry climate leads to wide swings between daytime heat and nighttime lows. Recorded extremes range from 120°F to –50°F. Precipitation peaks during winter in the western and south-central parts of Nevada, during spring in the central and north-eastern sections, and during summer near the eastern border shared with Utah and Arizona. Amounts range from less than 5 inches in the lee of the Sierra to the east to more than 70 inches within the Sierra.

California and Nevada: The Big Picture

It is not surprising that the Pacific Ocean is the birthplace of most of the storms that hit California and Nevada. What might be startling is

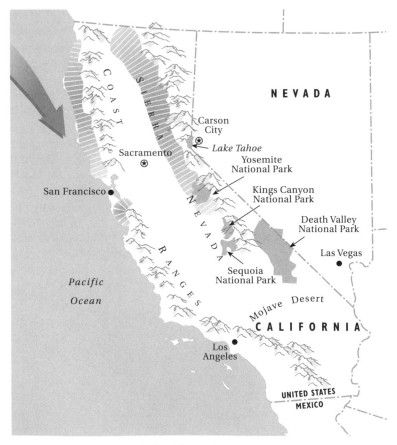

Storm track, or surface winds, from the north to northwest

that seemingly small variations in the path of those storms can result in huge differences in the weather and its impact on outdoor recreation. Experienced forecasters pay close attention both to where the weather systems develop and to the paths those storms travel—as does anyone who spends much time outdoors. Thus our examination of this region's weather begins with a look at the big picture: the major storm tracks and their influence on the weather. Essentially, four patterns are important to understand and are shown in the illustrations that follow, together with the areas that tend to get the most precipitation and the least. The illustrations mirror what you likely would see in a satellite image. A brief description follows, including the duration and intensity and the effect on the freezing level of each pattern.

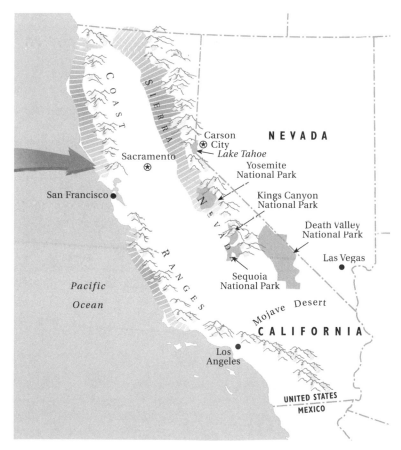

Storm track from the west

A storm track from the north to northwest can bring a mix of weather. From the north, it can bring cold, dry air in winter, although the barrier formed by the Siskiyou and Klamath Mountains in southern Oregon typically prevents much of an incursion into California, with the colder air being diverted east of the Sierra into the Great Basin of Nevada. However, once a decade or so, Arctic air plunges into southern California, kicking up dust in the interior valley and occasionally driving temperatures into the teens as far south as the Imperial Valley. If the track is from the northwest, it not only brings cold air in winter but also low snow levels. Moisture moving off the Pacific can produce snow levels as low as 2000 feet in both the Coast Mountains and the Sierra. Fine, light powder at the ski areas can be nothing short of heavenly.

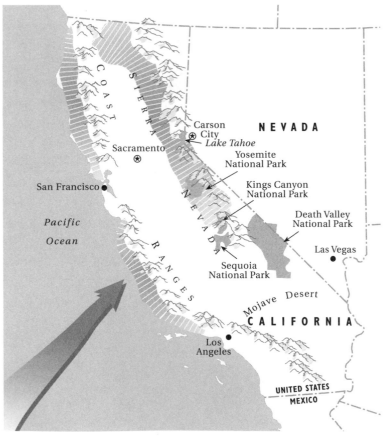

Storm track from the southwest

Even a few inches may accumulate on summits in the greater San Francisco Bay area, such as Mount Diablo and Mount Tamalpais. Less rain will be found to the east of the Coast Mountains and, naturally, to the east of the Sierra. Rarely, a disturbance may back into the region from the north to northeast, which can bring snow almost down to sea level.

A storm track from the west can bring rain, most typically when the jet stream drops southward into northern California and Nevada. Although forays into central and southern California are much less frequent, the jet stream can bring rain in torrents during the stronger El Niño years. Such years will rarely come as a surprise, since they typically receive considerable publicity in the news media. Even when the jet stream remains to the north of Santa Barbara on the coast and the

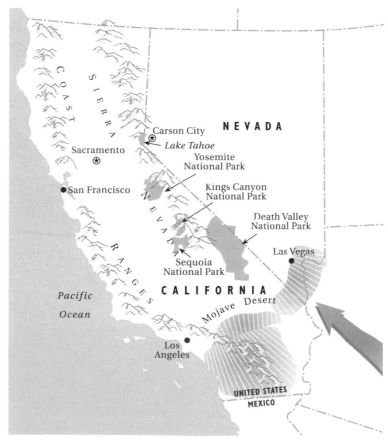

Storm track, or flow, from the south to southeast

Tehachapi Mountains inland, it can induce strong pushes of ocean air into southern California, resulting in damp, chilly weather. Typical snow levels range from 4000 to 6000 feet.

A storm track from the southwest often generates rain in winter and sea fog that can sometimes persist a week (though that is rare). It can tap into subtropical moisture capable of generating heavy downpours, which can make it seem as though it is time to begin building an ark. Snow levels may soar as high as 8000 feet or more.

A storm track from the south to southeast is not so much a storm track as it is a flow of moisture aloft. It is most typical when a large ridge of high pressure is over the Rockies or to the east—generally during the summer months. If it originates more from the south, this pattern frequently generates thundershowers during summer and can also draw remnants of tropical storms or hurricanes into southern California later in summer or autumn. A more southeasterly flow typically occurs when a ridge of high pressure drifts farther east over the United States, directing some of the Southwest's monsoon moisture into southern California from San Diego to Los Angeles. Thunderstorms are also typical of this pattern.

California and Nevada: Unique Weather Phenomena You Need to Understand

Outside of dry weather and sunshine, or the persistent summer stratus along the coast, perhaps the weather pattern most associated with California is the Santa Ana.

The Santa Ana has enjoyed much literary fame, from a Raymond Chandler detective yarn to Richard Henry Dana. It has been blamed for aggravating homicidal tendencies—and for fanning fires out of control—but the Santa Ana is also credited for scouring smog from the L.A. basin. Similar to the sirocco wind that blows out of the Sahara toward the Mediterranean, the Santa Ana blows from the Mojave Desert toward Los Angeles and the rest of coastal southern California to the southwest. The lack of low passes in the Sierra Nevada tends to prevent Santa Ana conditions in that region.

The critical ingredient is strong high pressure forming east in the Great Basin, typically after a vigorous storm moves through central California in autumn or winter. This reverses the typical onshore flow in southern California. The easterly flow drives air through Cajon Pass between the San Gabriel and San Bernardino Mountains, Banning Pass between the San Bernardinos and the San Jacintos, the Santa Clara River Valley to the north, and through Santa Ana Canyon. As this air moves downslope, it warms further: about 5.5°F (about 3°C) per 1000 feet. That can give southern California the hottest temperatures in the United States, as well as extremely dry air: Relative humidities have been measured in single digits. Exceptionally strong Santa Anas can produce gale-force winds along the coast and hurricane-force winds in the mountains. One such outburst in 1919 produced winds of 90

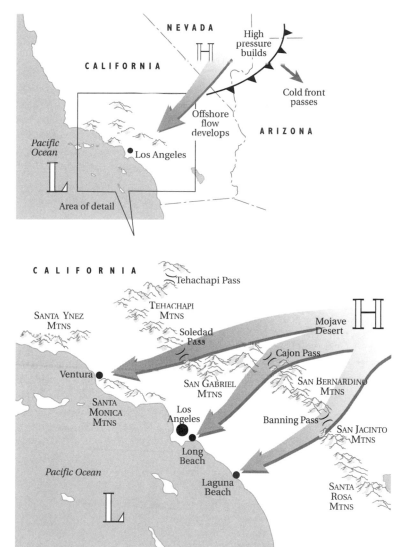

The development of the Santa Ana wind pattern

miles per hour at Mount Wilson. Other, more recent Santa Anas have torn off roofs and littered streets with large branches. The hot, dry air can whip small brushfires into raging infernos. In 1961, Santa Ana–driven flames destroyed 496 homes in the exclusive Bel Air neighborhood of Los Angeles.

California and Nevada: Trail Notes
Santa Ana Winds and Gap Winds (1)

If high pressure builds over the Great Basin to the east after a moderate to strong low tracks inland, Santa Ana winds typically follow. Expect strong easterly winds through Banning and Cajon Passes, along the exposed slopes of the adjacent mountain ranges, and through the Santa Clara River Valley. Watch for significantly higher pressures at Barstow or Palm Springs than at locations in the L.A. basin.

Trinity Alps: Barrier Jet (2)

Moderate to strong southerly winds flowing up the north end of the Sacramento Valley can produce locally heavy precipitation along the east side of the Trinity Alps, as well as blustery winds. Watch for reports of strong southerly winds in Redding and evidence of cloud cover in satellite images.

Bishop: Chinook Winds (3)

Westerly winds flowing over the Sierras can produce strong chinook winds over the east slopes that lead to rapid warming and snowmelt. A westerly storm track or jet stream transiting the area is one good sign, with strong winds aloft. In the field, watch for a chinook wall cloud drooping over the range or rotor clouds downwind of the range that appear to rotate about a horizontal axis. Both serve as an alert to strong, turbulent winds, particularly near Bishop.

Santa Barbara: Sundowner Winds (4)

The Santa Barbara area can experience strong winds and abruptly warmer temperatures when north to northeasterly winds cross the Santa Ynez Mountains. It is relatively rare for such winds to reach destructive strength within the city, though such cases have occurred,

California and Nevada trail notes reference map (icon locations are approximate)

including New Year's Eve Day in 1995. Such winds can measure 20 to 35 miles per hour along the southern slopes with higher gusts. Winds of 15 to 25 miles per hour along the coastal plain are not uncommon. Although Sundowner winds can occur throughout the year, when they develop during the summer months, temperatures can exceed 100°F in Santa Barbara, and they have reached 115°F west of the city. This pattern can produce a rapid boost in the fire danger. Watch for higher pressures at Santa Maria or Bakersfield compared to Santa Barbara.

Mojave Desert: Sandstorms (5)

Strong lows driven by westerly winds aloft in winter and spring may not generate much, if any, precipitation beyond the Sierras, but they can kick up nasty sand and dust storms in the Owens Valley and the Mojave Desert beyond, ranging from Mount Whitney to the north and the San Bernardino Mountains to the south. Consider delaying your trip until high pressure has settled in, and by all means stake your tent well.

Tehachapi Pass: Gap Winds (6)

Winds accelerate through the pass toward the troughs of low pressure called heat lows that develop during summer. When the air pressure between Bakersfield becomes significantly higher than Edwards to the south (perhaps 6 millibars), expect gusty winds through the pass and toward the direction of lower pressure.

Southern Nevada: Sand or Dust Storms (7)

Storms move through southern Nevada more frequently during spring, which in turn leads to more frequent sand or dust storms. Forecasts of an approaching cold front should lead to caution in planning outings in this area.

Northern California: and Nevada Low (8)

A storm track that carries a low through the Bay Area will produce locally heavy rains along the east slopes of the Sierra, typically north of Yosemite.

Southern California and Nevada Low (9)

A storm track that carries a low toward Los Angeles will produce locally heavy rains along the east slopes of the Sierra from Kings Canyon and Sequoia National Parks to Yosemite.

Southern California: Monsoon Rains (10)

Moist air flowing from the Gulf of California to the south and occasionally the Gulf of Mexico to the east, especially in midsummer, can produce afternoon thundershowers over the eastern slopes of the Laguna, Santa Ana, San Jacinto, Santa Rosa, and San Bernardino Mountains. Thunderstorm activity can even develop over the southern slopes of the San Gabriels. Evaluate satellite photos for evidence that such thunderstorms are moving from Arizona toward southern California and Nevada.

Yosemite Valley: Heat (11)

During the peak of summer hot spells, the highest temperatures will be found along valley floors. Temperatures will cool 4°F to 5°F for every 1000 feet of altitude gained. Higher elevations will bring relief from both the heat and crowds.

Kings Canyon: Heat (12)

During the peak of summer hot spells, the highest temperatures will be found along valley floors. Temperatures will cool 4°F to 5°F for every 1000 feet of altitude gain. Higher elevations will bring relief from both the heat and crowds.

Nevada: Flash Floods (13)

Thunderstorms can release torrential rains, triggering flash flooding. Watch out for streams and rivers in confined channels or canyons when thunderstorms are forecast. Camping in dry desert washes exposes you to a considerable risk of flash floods, even if thunderstorms are only evident in the distance. Stay out of them.

California and Nevada: Winter Avalanche Hazard (14)

This region tends to experience wet, heavy snowfalls accumulating at fairly mild temperatures. For that reason, direct-action and wet, soft-slab avalanches pose the biggest risk. Be particularly careful when snow has fallen at a rate of an inch or more per hour, the snow level has been rising, and the fresh snow has fallen on a layer of crust. Be certain to obtain updated avalanche and mountain weather forecasts.

California and Nevada: Spring Avalanche Hazard (15)

During spring, melting snow will percolate into the snowpack, lubricating buried layers and priming the trigger for avalanches, particularly on sun-warmed, south-facing slopes. Ski or ride on these slopes early in the day, moving to shaded northern or eastern slopes as the sun gets higher. As always, carefully check avalanche forecasts.

THE DESERT SOUTHWEST: ARIZONA, NEW MEXICO, AND WEST TEXAS

> *The wind will not stop. Gusts of sand swirl before me, stinging my face. But there is still too much to see and marvel at. . . . it seems to me that the strangeness and wonder of existence are emphasized here, in the desert, by the comparative sparsity of the flora and fauna.*
>
> Edward Abbey, *Desert Solitaire*

> *The mountain of the west they fastened to the earth with a sunbeam. They adorned it with abalone shell, with black clouds, he-rain, yellow corn and all sorts of wild animals.*
>
> Navajo creation story about the San Francisco Peaks

The Southwest's geology and geography combine to produce copious sunshine and warmth, which make this region highly attractive to visitors (and certainly residents), yet it is an environment not without risk and challenge. Explore the long-abandoned cliff dwellings of the ancient Anasazi at Canyon

de Chelly in northeastern Arizona or Pueblo Bonito in northwestern New Mexico, and the difficulties of subsistence living in a mostly arid region are clear. It is impossible not to experience profound admiration for the resourcefulness, wisdom, and skill of these mysteriously vanished people. That challenge to survival continues undiminished for anyone who ventures very far from air-conditioned urban oases. Heat and lack of water are the most obvious challenges, yet the Southwest can exhibit wide swings in temperature in the space of a single day, as well as sudden downpours that can unleash life-threatening floods. Ignore swelling cumulus clouds, miss an abrupt change in water clarity in a slot canyon, or fail to carry enough water on a hot day, and you will pay for it dearly. This region's weather defies simple characterization, evidenced by rich variation in vegetation and wildlife. It also demands care by those traveling into the backcountry.

Travel east from the wooded rim of the Grand Canyon, and the stands of ponderosa and pinyon pine and oak give way to sparse sage, grasses, tumbleweed, cactus, prickly pear, and yucca. As Edward Abbey notes, the clear, dry desert air makes each stand out vividly. Mesas rise in the red haze, like dinosaurs from another time. Climb higher onto the Colorado Plateau and trees reappear. Deer, bear, and avian life varied enough to delight any birder dwell here. So do those champions of desert survival, the rattlesnake, javelina, and armadillo. The fascinating differences in this region are due in part to changes in elevation. Variations in altitude here mimic changes in latitude as surely as elsewhere across the globe. Simply stated, an elevation gain of 1000 feet is roughly equivalent to traveling 5° northward in latitude, a distance of approximately 300 miles. Snow that might seem unthinkable in lowland deserts becomes a common sight above 5000 feet in winter, both on the Colorado Plateau and within the Sangre de Cristo and San Juan Mountains that extend southward into New Mexico. Such snow may persist into April. Daytime heat vanishes with the sun, particularly in the high country, giving way to astonishing cold. Understand that an arid region is one that averages less than 10 inches of rain each year, such as the Sonoran Desert, which extends northward into Arizona, and the Chihuahan Desert, which encompasses both southern New Mexico and west Texas. Semi-arid conditions exist at the higher elevations of the Colorado Plateau, which averages 10 to 20 inches of rain each year. Dry air leads to large swings in temperature, often 40° or more from day to night. Be certain to carry sufficient water and enough clothing for the chilly desert night. One more item is important: sunscreen. Ultraviolet radiation is particularly strong in the dry air, and visitors will burn even faster at higher elevations. A common rule of thumb is that UV radiation will increase by 2 percent for every 1000 feet of elevation gain. *Do not just carry sunscreen: Apply it frequently.*

Due to a lack of dense vegetation, an exploration of almost any area here not only reveals the geologic history of the Southwest: It confronts you. It would be a rare and unimaginative traveler who could look at the multihued layers within the Grand Canyon and not wonder about the story behind these ancient layers of sediments. The span of time represented by these strata can be expressed mathematically, in the precise language of science, but not easily absorbed viscerally. The Canyon walls, like the other wonders of this region, are very much like a brilliantly illustrated storybook that invites the visitor to explore ever more deeply. Explore for long and you will recognize these pages have been opened largely by water. They were first turned by the waters of ancient oceans, then the mostly patient but irresistible force of rivers, fed by the torrential downpours of booming thunderstorms. Multifingered lightning strikes cleave the sky here in a way rarely seen elsewhere. Although annual rainfall is slight, when it rains in the Southwest, it rains hard. Flash flooding poses a major threat throughout the region, both in the washes to the south and the slot canyons to the north. Maintaining a close watch on the sky is important here, but so too is understanding the lay of the land. Unlike most areas, it is not just the storm overhead that will hammer you: The one that unleashes a torrent of rain a dozen or more miles away may send floodwaters twisting and turning through myriad channels, washes, and slot canyons, growing as they approach. Such flooding is most common during the monsoon of summer but also can occur when a dying tropical storm or hurricane nears in early autumn. About half of the annual precipitation in southern Arizona, southern New Mexico, and west Texas—and perhaps one-third of the annual precipitation in northern Arizona and northern New Mexico—comes from summer thunderstorms. Pay close attention to forecasts and apply the sky-reading skills presented previously in this book (see Chapter 7), and you will avoid most trouble.

Arizona, New Mexico, and West Texas: The Big Picture

Although much of the Southwest's precipitation comes from thunderstorms, some also comes from transient lows and the associated fronts that are directed by specific storm tracks. Even the thunderstorm activity tends to wax and wane with shifts in seasonal patterns. Experienced forecasters pay close attention to these shifts and the paths smaller disturbances travel. So does anyone who spends much time outdoors. Thus our examination of this region's weather begins with a look at the big picture: the major storm tracks and their influence on the weather, which are shown in the illustrations that follow, together with the areas that tend to get the most precipitation and the least. The illustrations mirror what you would be likely to see in a satellite image. Brief descriptions follow, including the duration and intensity of each pattern.

A storm track from the south to southeast is not a storm track in the sense of winds aloft carrying a disturbance into west Texas, New

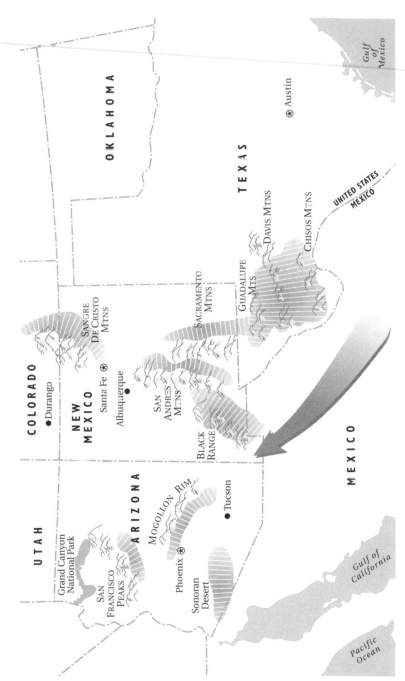

Storm track, or surface winds, from the south to southeast

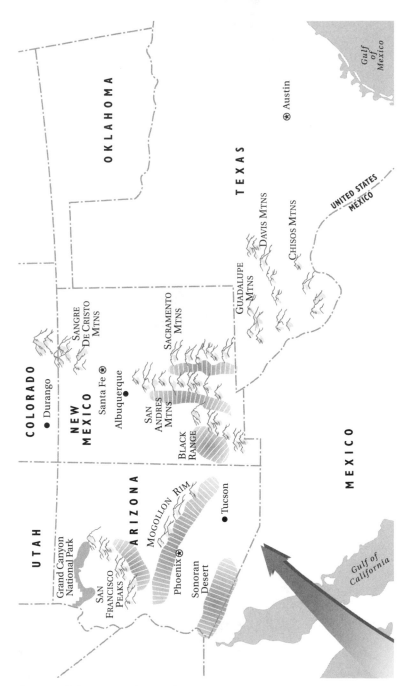

Storm track from the south to southwest

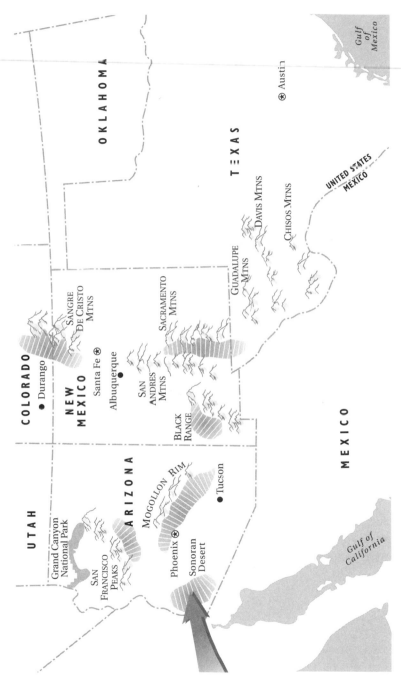

Storm track from the southwest to west

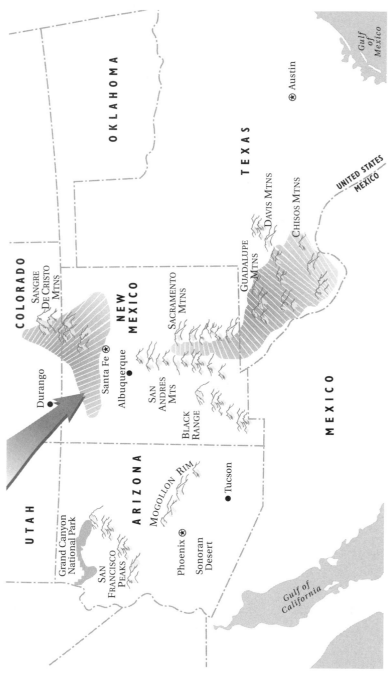

Storm track from the northwest to north

Mexico, or Arizona: Rather, it occurs when a surface high directs moist air from the Gulf of Mexico and possibly the Gulf of California into the Southwest. As discussed in the following section, this summer pattern typically produces afternoon thunderstorms.

A storm track from the south to southwest can occur when a large trough of low pressure in the upper atmosphere sits off the Pacific coast of the United States and Mexico and directs a moist flow of tropical air into the region. This can generate thundershowers, widespread rain, or both. Such a pattern can also direct the dying (but not totally defunct) remnants of a tropical storm or hurricane from over Baja California into the Southwest. This situation can produce widespread flooding, usually during autumn. The tracks of such dying hurricanes or tropical storms can be tricky to forecast, requiring particular vigilance, attention to updated forecasts, and caution. Satellite images are especially useful for monitoring this pattern.

A storm track from the southwest to west is most common during spring and will bring a surface low with rain over the region. This track may also occur at the end of the summer monsoon season and—combined with the remaining moist air near the ground—will set off thundershowers. This is best tracked by watching local weather forecasts, satellite imagery, and certainly the movement of long-fingered cirrus clouds across the sky.

A storm track from the northwest to north is most common from autumn through winter in New Mexico and western Texas. A ridge of high pressure along the coast can send a cold front sprinting within the space of a day or less from Montana through Wyoming and Colorado into New Mexico and Texas. These fast-moving systems can produce snow, gusty winds, and a sudden, large drop in temperature.

Arizona, New Mexico, and West Texas: Local Weather Phenomena You Need to Understand

Think of the Southwest, and you think of heat: dry heat. That makes it seem all the more ironic that what is called the *monsoon* is the defining weather pattern of the Southwest: It brings concentrated thunderstorms to Arizona, New Mexico, and west Texas (and the deserts of southeastern California, too) during summer. This not only brings needed rainfall to a region in which water is a scarce and treasured resource, it can also generate surprisingly sizeable and abrupt rises in river levels, resulting in dangerous flash flooding. The slot canyons so irresistible to hikers receive the worst flooding: Walls of water 20 feet high can sweep everything in their path. The thunderstorm

How the Mexican monsoon develops in the Southwest

responsible for such flash floods may not even be directly over the canyon.

The genesis of the *Mexican monsoon* originates far to the east over the subtropical Atlantic. The Bermuda high builds northward during late spring and summer as the sun's warming rays become more direct over the Northern Hemisphere. The clockwise circulation around this high draws moisture from the Gulf of Mexico and directs it northward into the northern Mexican states of Sonora, Chihuahua, Coahuila, Nuevo Leone, and Tamaulpas. As that moist air rises over the spare, sunbaked slopes of the Sierra Madre and on into Arizona, New Mexico, and west Texas, a major shift in seasonal weather patterns ensues. Research shows that this pattern also pulls moisture from over the eastern Pacific and Gulf of California. Whatever the source of its moisture, the monsoon's entrance is dramatic: a sudden transition from hot, dry weather to towering thunderstorms, mesmerizing lightning displays, and occasionally drenching downpours. The air becomes more humid: The arrival of the monsoon in Phoenix is defined by the dew point reaching 55. That's a big deal because dew points are typically in the 20s to 30s. (Remember: Dew points measure the moisture content in the air.) In Tucson, 1200 feet higher than Phoenix, three consecutive days of 54°F dew points signal its arrival. The monsoon season typically begins earliest in New Mexico and west Texas, usually in May and occasionally June, tapering off in July. It develops a little later in Arizona, usually around the beginning of July, dwindling by early September. Those, of course, are the most popular months to explore the natural beauty of the Southwest, thanks to summer vacation schedules. (Hikers and canyoneers in particular should re-read Chapters 3 and 4.)

Experienced Southwest hikers and climbers know you can almost set your watch by the development of thunderstorms over the major peaks during the monsoon season, typically during early afternoon. If buildups develop by 1:00 P.M. one day, odds are that the same will happen for the next day or two.

Arizona, New Mexico, and West Texas: Trail Notes
San Francisco Peaks: Gap Winds (1)

Northerly winds moving through the San Francisco Peaks can accelerate, generating increased wind speeds to the south near Flagstaff. Anticipate such gap winds both by watching for forecasts of moderate to strong northerly winds near the surface, as well as northerly winds aloft.

Arizona, New Mexico and western Texas trail notes reference map (icon locations are approximate)

Sonoran Desert: Sandstorms (2)

Strong gusty winds anytime of the year can kick up an amazing volume of sand, dust, and grit. Such sandstorms seem to be most frequent during spring. If forecasts call for strong, gusty winds, either delay your outing or be prepared to seek shelter rapidly.

Northern New Mexico and Arizona: Backdoor Cold Front (3)

A low-pressure system that moves from the eastern slopes of the Colorado Rockies into Kansas and Nebraska can force a cold front back into northern New Mexico and at times into northern Arizona. At times they may even move into the southern parts of both states. The greatest potential for precipitation will be along the eastern slopes of the Sangre de Cristo Mountains in northern New Mexico and, if the cold front holds together, north of the Mogollon Rim in Arizona. During the winter, such fronts are typically dry, but bring gusty easterly winds and blowing dust.

Arizona: Monsoon Gulf Surge (4)

The Gulf surge is a monsoon event in summer and is named for its origin in the Gulf of California. If satellite images show a large band of clouds or thunderstorms along the gulf, expect this surge to progress eastward to both the Phoenix and Tucson areas, bringing clouds and occasionally heavy rainfall. Flash flooding can result in washes and canyons. A tropical storm or hurricane in the southern Gulf of California can also direct heavy rainfall into the deserts of Arizona.

San Francisco Peaks: Thunderstorms (5)

The arrival of the summer monsoon, usually in July, brings frequent afternoon thunderstorms to this area. Hikers should watch carefully for the upward development of initially innocent-looking cumulus clouds, typically in early afternoon. Such thunderstorms tend to redevelop at the same time for days. Outings earlier in the day are a wise choice.

Mogollon Rim: Thunderstorms (6)

The arrival of the summer monsoon, usually in July, brings frequent afternoon thunderstorms to this area. Watch carefully for the upward development of initially innocent-looking cumulus clouds. Thunderstorms here tend to develop in early to midafternoon and shift southward over time. Such thunderstorms tend to redevelop at the same time for days. Outings earlier in the day are a wise choice.

Sky Island: Thunderstorms (7)

The presence of the monsoon, together with the large peaks in southeastern Arizona and southwestern New Mexico called the "Sky Islands," can set off some awe-inspiring thunderstorms with intense lightning activity. Watch for thunderstorms here to develop during the afternoon, with maximum activity typically from early to midafternoon, with storms drifting away from higher terrain and into lower elevations during the late afternoon to early evening. The earlier you begin your hike, the better.

Texas: Dry Line Thunderstorms (8)

Strong thunderstorms can form as drier air off the high plateau of New Mexico collides with moist air circulating inland from the Gulf of Mexico. The line of thunderstorms that develops can persist for days, drifting east during the day, and then drifting back west at night. Keep this movement in mind if you note a line of thunderstorms near your location or if you check radar on the Internet before setting out.

Sabino and Madera Canyons: Flash Flooding (9)

Thunderstorms produced by the summer monsoon or remnants of tropical storms and hurricanes can trigger rapid rises in the water level in Sabino Canyon northeast of Tucson and Madera Canyon to the south, moving boulders with little warning. Similar flooding can occur in any of the many washes in this area. Paying close attention to the sky for evidence of swelling cumulus that may develop into thunderstorms, as well as to forecasts before setting out, are important safety precautions. Avoid committing yourself to a location from which quick escape will be difficult if such conditions threaten.

Skeleton Canyon: Flash Flooding (10)

Thunderstorms produced by the summer monsoon or remnants of tropical storms and hurricanes can trigger rapid rises in the water level in

Skeleton Canyon in southwestern New Mexico, moving boulders with little warning. Similar flooding can occur in any of the many washes in this area. Close attention to the sky for evidence of swelling cumulus that may develop into thunderstorms and to forecasts before setting out are important safety precautions. Avoid committing yourself to a location from which quick escape will be difficult if such conditions threaten.

Northern Arizona Slot Canyons: Flash Flooding (11)

Thunderstorms produced by the summer monsoon can trigger rapid to extreme rises in water levels, particularly in the slot canyons so popular with backpackers in the Four Corners area. Drownings from such flash floods are unfortunately common. Walls of water a dozen or more feet high may move through such narrow canyons, sweeping large boulders (and certainly hikers) with little warning. Pay close attention to the sky for evidence of swelling cumulus that may develop into thunderstorms. Just the appearance of a threatening sky is reason enough to move out of a slot canyon. Even thunderstorms several miles away can produce flash floods. Review Chapter 4 and pay close attention to weather forecasts.

Northern New Mexico Slot Canyons: Flash Flooding (12)

Thunderstorms produced by the summer monsoon can trigger rapid to extreme rises in water levels, particularly in the slot canyons so popular with backpackers in the Four Corners area. Drownings from such flash floods are unfortunately common. Walls of water a dozen or more feet high may move through such narrow canyons, sweeping large boulders (and certainly hikers) with little warning. Pay close attention to the sky for evidence of swelling cumulus that may develop into thunderstorms. Just the appearance of a threatening sky is reason enough to move out of a slot canyon. Even thunderstorms several miles away can produce flash floods. Review Chapter 4 and pay close attention to weather forecasts.

Grand Canyon: Heat (13)

The highest temperatures in this region will be found along the floor of the Grand Canyon. Relief can be found (short of jumping in the river, and that will cool you off) by ascending to the rim. Temperatures will cool approximately 4°F to 5°F for every 1000 feet of elevation gain.

THE CENTRAL U.S. ROCKIES: COLORADO AND UTAH

It's tough country to visit. It's even tougher country to live in. So powerful is the sun in summer, one adopts a perpetual squint. Summer can bring biblical periods of forty days of heat well over 100 degrees, reducing you to a lizard state of mind: no thought and very little action.

Terry Tempest Williams,
Red: Passion and Patience in the Desert

On the 30th we left the encampment at our accustomed early hour, and at eight o'clock were cheered by a distant view of the Rocky Mountains. For some time we were unable to decide whether what we saw were mountains, or banks of cumulus clouds skirting the horizon and glittering in the reflected rays of the sun.

Dr. Edwin James, *Diary of the Long Expedition, Volume 15*, 1820

Ask anyone east of the Mississippi to describe their image of the American West, and odds are they will describe a scene from either Colorado or Utah. Set in the heart of the Rockies, the largest range in North America, both states offer plentiful icons: the Maroon Bells of Aspen, the technicolor needles of Bryce National Park, and the slickrock fantasyland of Arches National Park. This region exhibits astonishing diversity in geology, as well as plant and animal life. The canyonlands in southwestern Colorado and southern Utah feature water-conserving cacti and yucca, with willow, cottonwood, and greasewood near streams and rivers. The tiny kangaroo rat manages to obtain all its water needs from plant matter. Its larger neighbors include jackrabbits, coyotes, mountain lions, and mule deer. Move higher and farther north, and new species appear: black bear, bighorn sheep, and elk, the latter famous for their unrestrained autumn rut. Hike through stands of ponderosa pine and aspen to about 8000 feet, emerging then into subalpine spruce and fir. Gnarled krummholz

both reflects and adapts to the demanding environment at and above 11,000 feet.

With more than fifty peaks topping 14,000 feet and scores of others just slightly shorter in Colorado alone, this region plays havoc with the jet stream. Normally a well-ordered river of air, the skyscraping spires of this region deflect the jet stream into a confusing maelstrom, an atmospheric version of turbulent whitewater rapids. Because the jet stream has already traversed the Cascades and the Sierra, storms have dropped much of their moisture by the time they arrive in Colorado and Utah. The result in winter is what has been called *champagne powder:* snow with a liquid water content of just 7 percent, compared to about 14 percent in the Cascades. That fuels the dreams of skiers and snowboarders during the off-season, months before the first flakes begin to fly. Those dreams can be quickly transformed into a nightmare, though, when swift winds aloft produce strong crest-level winds, which sometimes are accompanied by strong downslope or chinook winds, typically between November and March. These winds can damage forests and residential areas, and they also can reduce snowpack at an astonishing rate. (See Local Weather Patterns You Need to Understand later in this chapter.) Even winds of lesser magnitude can cause extensive drifting, which complicates the picture for backcountry skiers and snowboarders. Avalanche activity can be particularly difficult to anticipate early in winter, because of extensive snow accumulating on lee slopes and, particularly, because of the internal weakness that develops within the relatively shallow snowpack. This weakness is the result of a strong temperature *gradient* in the snowpack, which means a big change in temperature through the depth of the snow.

Snow can arrive in the high country as early as September and occasionally along the Front Range near Denver, which once received 4 inches as early as September 3. It more typically arrives in October. The colder air and shorter days transform the aspens into shimmering torches of gold. The communal stands of these trees so valued for their beauty in autumn are also prized by beaver, elk, moose, and deer, both for browsing and construction material. The shorter hours of daylight that gild the aspen also result in less heating and fewer thunderstorms.

Although soggy snow may fall anytime (generally above 6000 feet), thunderstorms are the prime weather consideration in summer. The seasonal monsoon that produces almost daily thunderstorms over much of Arizona and New Mexico extends into this canyon country and beyond.

Such thunderstorms may begin as early as 11:00 A.M. (Remember: A lack of rain from a dark, towering cloud does not necessarily mean a lack of lightning.) It is best to plan climbs and excursions to exposed peaks and ridges for early in the day, and to be off ridges by 1:00 P.M. at the latest. Lightning detection equipment has shown as many as 10,000 strikes on a single day of thunderstorm activity in Colorado. Some of those strikes trigger wildfires, which are most common in late summer and early autumn.

Flash floods are another hazard stemming from thunderstorm activity. The rapidity with which river levels rise in slot canyons can be unbelievable, even when the thunderstorms are miles away. While specific advice is offered for some areas in the Trail Notes section that follows, it is crucial to remember that flash flooding is a threat in summer in most narrow canyons and that rain can also produce quicksand along some riverbanks. The hazard for such flash floods is greatest from mid-July through early September in both Utah and Colorado. These cautions aside, many more achingly beautiful days occur here for enjoying the alpine meadows and soaring peaks than farther north in the Rockies.

Colorado and Utah: The Big Picture

Keeping a close eye on forecasts has no substitute, but a discerning look at satellite images (or even the direction high clouds are moving) will offer clues to important details that may be missing in more general forecasts issued for public consumption. The movement of clouds can mirror the movement of winds aloft, as well as the shifts in such steering currents. These winds aloft will give backcountry skiers important guidance on which slopes will be lee slopes, tending to load up with drifting snow and resulting in a high avalanche hazard. Experienced forecasters and guides pay close attention to these shifts, as well as to the paths smaller disturbances travel. So does anyone who spends much time outdoors, particularly skiers venturing off piste—off the beaten trail—which is why the examination of this region's weather begins with a look at the big picture: the major storm tracks and their influence on the weather. These are shown in the illustrations that follow, together with the areas that tend to get the most precipitation and the least. The illustrations mirror what you would be likely to see in a satellite image. A brief description follows, including the duration and intensity of each pattern.

A northerly storm track can drive powerful cold fronts in mere

Storm track, or surface winds, from the north

Storm track from the northwest

Storm track from the west

"Future" storm track/developing low east of the Rockies

Storm track from the southwest

Storm track, or flow, from the south to south-southwest

hours from Montana through Wyoming and into Colorado and beyond. This is associated with a ridge of high pressure extending from British Columbia and Alberta down into the Great Basin. The air that arrives with the cold front usually is truly cold. Temperatures may drop into single digits as early as mid October in Denver, and even earlier than that in the mountains to the west.

A *northwesterly storm track* brings plentiful moisture from the Pacific. Although the Cascades and Sierras are both adept at wringing out considerable moisture from the clouds, this track can bring large snowfalls to both the Wasatch Mountains and the Continental Divide. Northwesterly winds can also create "lake-effect" snow over the Wasatch Mountains: A foot of snow in 24 hours is not uncommon. Think "Northwesterly wind, skier's friend."

A *westerly storm track* drops much of its moisture over the Cascades and Sierras to the west, but enough moisture usually remains to drop significant rain or snow over the Wasatch Mountains and the Continental Divide to the west of the Front Range. The old saw describes the impact on Colorado well: "Pacific front, mountains get the brunt; southeast low, Denver gets the snow." The movement of the jet stream over Utah and Colorado also tends to produce strong winds aloft.

A *future storm track* perhaps best describes the lows that develop just east of the Rockies in winter. Southeastern Colorado and northern New Mexico are the favored locations for such lows. Eventually such lows move northeast toward the upper Midwest, but they drop their heaviest snow along the Front Range as they develop. The ski areas farther west get a few inches, if any. Cold rain may initially fall over southeastern Colorado, followed by snow. This is the second part of the aphorism stated previously as "southeast low, Denver gets the snow." Such developing lows typically occur with a westerly jet stream, and a cold front dropping from the north.

A *southwesterly storm track* from late fall through winter tends to have more of an impact on Utah than on Colorado. When it does occur, which is not often, this pattern tends to focus precipitation from north of Ogden into southeastern Idaho with relatively high snow levels. Such southwesterly flows are more common during El Niño winters; in Colorado, this pattern brings the heaviest snow to the San Juan Mountains.

A *southerly to south–southwesterly storm track* occurs during the summer monsoon season. This carries moisture northward from the Gulf of Mexico, and at times from the Gulf of California, as the Bermuda high drifts westward in the Atlantic. As intense summer sun heats mountain slopes, that moisture rises, fueling thunderstorms, usually in the afternoon. Such afternoon thunderstorms are common throughout the region. Keep a careful eye on the sky, and plan climbs to exposed locations for early in the day. During winter months, this storm track tends to deposit the heaviest snow in the high country of southern Utah, such as the Brianhead Ski Area, as well as the San Juan Mountains of Colorado.

Colorado and Utah: Local Weather Phenomena You Need to Understand

I refer again to one of cowboy artist Charles Russell's most famous works, *Waiting for a Chinook*. A skeletal steer, weakened by hunger to the point of collapse, is shown staggering through the snow: Wolves patiently await the animal's almost certain demise. The title refers to the hope that a chinook will bring rapid warming and snowmelt, exposing enough vegetation for the beleaguered creature to survive. *Chinook* is just one name for *downslope winds,* which do in fact bring rapid warming and snowmelt (see the illustration on page 96). Native Americans living in or near the Rockies used to call such winds "Snow Eaters," since the warming could melt several inches of snowpack in a single day, even leading to flooding. In Utah, such winds are commonly referred to as "canyon" or "Wasatch" winds. Whatever their name, such warm winds can be unpleasantly strong, leading to weakening of both snow bridges and the overall snowpack, which in turn leads to increased avalanche hazard. This surprises backcountry travelers in general and ice climbers in particular, placing them in unexpected danger. These winds are most frequent from November through March: Boulder, Colorado, for example, may experience more than a dozen chinook episodes per season.

Such downslope winds are the result of a strong difference in surface air pressure across a mountain range, and strong winds aloft crossing that range, aided by precipitation falling over the upwind slopes. In Utah, watch for strong reported or forecast winds aloft from the east and higher surface air pressures east of the Wasatch than in Salt Lake City or Ogden. In Colorado, the reverse is usually true: Winds in a chinook pattern move most frequently from west to east, and can cause trouble in such places as Boulder and Fort Collins. Watch for strong reported or forecast winds aloft from the west and higher surface pressures west of the Continental Divide than to the east in Fort Collins or Boulder. When such conditions exist, anticipate damaging winds, abrupt warming (a

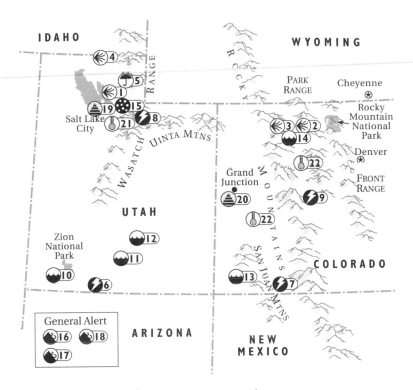

Colorado and Utah (icon locations are approximate)

rapid increase of 20°F to 40°F is possible), an elevated avalanche hazard, and unsafe ice climbing conditions. Avoid lee slopes.

Colorado and Utah: Trail Notes
Utah: Easterly Downslope Winds (1)

Easterly winds aloft will produce downslope winds along the west slopes of the Wasatch, especially from Provo and Salt Lake City north to Ogden, most especially through the canyons. Weber Canyon along Interstate 84 is a prime example. Checking winds aloft at crest elevation for a moderate or strong easterly flow (25 knots or more) or for higher pressure to the east are both ways of anticipating the possibility of strong canyon and downslope winds in this area. Higher pressure at Evanston, Wyoming, compared to either Salt Lake City or Ogden, by 4 to 6 millibars or more, is a good indication.

Colorado: Westerly Downslope Winds (2)

Strong westerly winds aloft will produce strong downslope winds along the east slopes of the Rockies, particularly in or near Boulder, Golden, and Fort Collins. If the jet stream is moving directly over Colorado, or forecast winds aloft are strong (50 knots or more), expect gusty and possibly damaging winds in these areas; hurricane-force winds have been recorded in southern Colorado. Rapid warming and snowmelt frequently occur, though occasionally the movement of cold air overwhelms the warming of downslope winds. The result can be miserably cold winds that chill travelers to the bone. Damaging winds rarely extend more than 15 miles out onto the Plains, although winds will still be strong.

Colorado: Easterly Downslope Winds (3)

Although strong downslope winds are typically associated with westerly winds aloft, occasionally strong easterly winds can produce gusty winds to the west of the Continental Divide. If high pressure over the Plains states and low pressure over the Four Corners area is developing, be prepared for the possibility of strong downslope winds along the western slopes of the Continental Divide. Winds exceeding 100 miles per hour resulted in extensive blowdown of timber along the west side of the Park Range in 1997, when a large low-pressure area settled just east of the mountains and Denver was nailed by a blizzard.

Snake River: Outflow (4)

Higher pressure to the north over Idaho and the Snake River plain can produce strong canyon winds between the Bannock and Aspen Ranges into northern Utah. Check for higher pressure at Pocatello compared to Logan, with a difference of 6 to 8 millibars or more.

Ogden Area: Convergence Zone (5)

A confluence or convergence of winds can produce sharply increased rainfall or snowfall upwind or generally to the west of the Wasatch. Precipitation may be double that found in the lowlands just upwind of the zone. Prior to the arrival of a trough in the upper atmosphere, such increased precipitation may be 12 to 24 miles upwind of the Wasatch. Once the trough moves through, the heaviest precipitation will shift toward the Wasatch: Little and Big Cottonwood Canyons will tend to receive the heaviest snow with northwesterly winds, while Park City and Deer Valley will get their heaviest snows when winds are from the south to southwest.

Utah Canyonlands: Monsoon Thunderstorm (6)

Expect increased thunderstorm activity over southern Utah during the summer monsoon, a northward circulation of moist air off the Gulfs of Mexico and California. Such thunderstorms are preceded by small puffs of cumulus clouds that rapidly swell into towering cumulo-nimbus by afternoon. Watch carefully for such upward growth. For safety, plan to be descending from ridges or peaks by afternoon. Such storms can produce lightning, lightning-sparked wildfires, damaging winds even in the absence of rain, and flash flooding from rain.

San Juan and Sangre de Cristo Mountains: Monsoon Thunderstorms (7)

Expect increased thunderstorm activity over southern Colorado during the summer monsoon, a northward circulation of moist air off the Gulf of Mexico and the Gulf of California. Such thunderstorms are preceded by small puffs of cumulus clouds that rapidly swell into towering cumulo-nimbus by afternoon. Watch carefully for such upward growth, and for safety plan to be descending from ridges or peaks by afternoon. Such storms can produce lightning, lightning-sparked wildfires, damaging winds even in the absence of rain, and flash flooding from rain.

Wasatch and Uinta Mountains: Thunderstorms (8)

Although not subject to the same frequency of thunderstorms as the canyonlands farther south, both the Wasatch and Uintas see increased thunderstorm activity during summer. Such thunderstorms are preceded by small puffs of cumulus clouds that rapidly swell into towering cumulo-nimbus by afternoon. Watch carefully for such upward growth. For safety, plan to be descending from ridges or peaks by afternoon. Such storms can produce lightning, lightning-sparked wildfires, damaging winds even in the absence of rain, and flash flooding from rain.

Colorado Rocky Mountains: Thunderstorms (9)

The Colorado Rockies (including Rocky Mountain National Park) see markedly increased thunderstorm activity during summer. Such thunderstorms are preceded by small puffs of cumulus clouds that rapidly swell into towering cumulo-nimbus by afternoon. Watch carefully for such upward growth, and for safety plan to be descending from ridges or peaks by afternoon. Such storms can produce deadly lightning, lightning-sparked wildfires, damaging winds even in the absence of rain, and flash flooding from rain.

Zion National Park Area: Flash Flooding (10)

Thunderstorms during the summer monsoon can produce flash flooding in minutes. The thunderstorms do not even have to be directly over Zion or the Virgin River, as this area drains a large region. Be very cautious during summer if thunderstorms are forecast. If cumulus clouds build, do not enter slot canyons. After thunderstorm activity in the area, remain out of the canyons for 24 hours. (Re-read the section on flash flooding in Chapter 4.)

Escalante River Area: Flash Flooding (11)

Thunderstorms during the summer monsoon can produce flash flooding in minutes. The thunderstorms do not even have to be directly over the Escalante River, as this area drains a large region. Be very cautious during summer if thunderstorms are forecast, particularly if you are planning to enter Harris Wash. If cumulus clouds build, do not enter this area. After thunderstorm activity in the area, remain out of the canyons for 24 hours. (Re-read the section on flash flooding in Chapter 4.)

Capitol Reef National Park Area: Flash Flooding (12)

Thunderstorms during the summer monsoon can produce flash flooding in minutes. The thunderstorms do not even have to be directly over Capitol Reef or the Fremont River, as this area drains a large region. Be very cautious during summer if thunderstorms are forecast, particularly if you are planning to enter Grand Wash or nearby slot canyons. If cumulus clouds build, do not enter this area. After thunderstorm activity in the area, remain out of the canyons for 24 hours. (Re-read the section on flash flooding in Chapter 4.)

Mesa Verde National Park Area: Flash Flooding (13)

Thunderstorms during the summer monsoon can produce flash flooding in minutes. The thunderstorms do not have to be directly over the park, as this area drains a large region. Be very cautious during summer if thunderstorms are forecast, particularly if you are planning to enter nearby slot canyons. If cumulus clouds build and rain falls, do not enter this area. After thunderstorm activity in the area, remain out of the canyons for 24 hours. (Re-read the section on flash flooding in Chapter 4.)

Rocky Mountain National Park Area: Flash Flooding (14)

Thunderstorms during the summer monsoon can produce flash flooding in minutes. The thunderstorms do not have to be directly over the park, as this area drains a large region. Be very cautious during summer if thunderstorms are forecast, particularly if you are near the Big Thompson River or Virginia Canyon at or below treeline. (Re-read the section on flash flooding in Chapter 4.)

Great Salt Lake: Lake-Effect Snow (15)

Cold air moving over the relatively warmer waters of the Great Salt Lake can produce substantial snow over the western slopes of the Wasatch Mountains, with a foot of snow falling in a day or less. Anticipate this if temperatures are well below freezing and winds are moving across the lake toward the Wasatch. While it is snowing in the mountains, the sun may be out in Salt Lake City.

Colorado and Utah: Early-Season Avalanche Risk (16)

If substantial snow—roughly 2 to 3 feet—falls in October and November, the Wasatch in Utah and the Rockies in Colorado will tend to develop a more stable early-season snowpack if snow continues to fall at fairly regular intervals. However, snowfall of less than 2 feet followed by clear and cold weather will promote dangerous depth hoar formation and an unstable snowpack. Northern and eastern slopes will typically experience the highest danger. Ski pole, shovel shear, or Rutschblock tests are strongly recommended. Carefully seek updated guidance from local avalanche forecasts.

Colorado and Utah: Main-Season Avalanche Risk (17)

Assessing avalanche hazard in the Rockies is never easy, due to the complex snowpack structure that typically evolves. Backcountry travelers should pay close attention to avalanche forecasts issued by a local office, seek advice from the local ski patrol office, and perform shovel shear, ski pole, or Rutschblock tests on their own. Snow falling at a rate of 1 inch per hour (roughly 2 centimeters) or more, along with moderate to strong winds aloft that cause extensive drifting, should lead to particular caution, and a delay of at least 24 to 48 hours before venturing into the backcountry.

Colorado and Utah: Late-Season Avalanche Risk (18)

Springtime warming brings a shift in avalanche hazard. The south and western slopes that typically were safer during the core winter months often experience the greatest hazard. North and eastern slopes tend to be safer if snowpack temperatures remain below freezing. As always, seek guidance from local avalanche forecasts.

Salt Lake: Fog (19)

A ridge of high pressure or a split in the winds aloft can promote the development of fog near the Great Salt Lake, including Salt Lake City. If winds aloft are westerly but weak, anticipate this condition. However, climbing to 5000 or 5500 feet should put you in the clear.

Grand Junction: Fog (20)

A ridge of high pressure can produce persistent radiation fog from Grand Junction in Colorado to Vernal, Utah. This may last a week or more, requiring a storm with significant winds to break up the temperature inversion and the fog trapped below.

Peter Sinks and Bear River Range: Cold Pooling (21)

A combination of light winds, clear skies, and snow-covered ground produce very cold temperatures in low spots. Such bone-chilling cold can be avoided by remaining on adjacent slopes. Peter Sinks holds the record for the second-coldest temperature in the continental United

States (–56°F/C). As an example, on one occasion when the basin recorded 17°F, it was still 42°F on the rim.

Colorado: Cold Pooling (22)

A combination of light winds, clear skies, and snow-covered ground produces very cold temperatures in low spots. Such bone-chilling cold can be avoided by remaining on adjacent slopes. This pool of cold air may deepen to 1500 feet 3 to 5 hours after sunset. Areas most prone to such deep cold include Eagle Valley, Gunnison, Alamosa, Taylor Park, and Fraser.

THE NORTHERN APPALACHIANS: NEW YORK TO QUEBEC

There is a sumptuous variety about the New England weather that compels the stranger's admiration . . . and regret.

Mark Twain, *The Family Mark Twain*

Fine feathery snow crystals drift down. There is not a breath of moving air. The sharp clean smell of this new snow prickles my senses and excites. Within a minute I stand at the edge of the pond feeling peace.

Bernd Heinrich, *Winter World*, on the arrival of winter in Vermont

The Appalachians may not match the Rockies, Sierras, or Cascades in height or grandeur, but the smoothed shoulders of this ancient range speak not only of its age but also the severity of its weather. Storms here can equal anything found west of the Mississippi. The highest winds recorded on this planet—yes, anywhere on Earth—were recorded at the summit of Mount Washington in New Hampshire's White Mountains. That was a peak gust of 231 miles per hour.

The Appalachians stretch 1500 miles, paralleling the Atlantic coast. The central and southern Appalachians are comprised of a more or less continuous series of ridges and valleys, extending from central Alabama to Pennsylvania. New York's Catskills are included by some in the central Appalachians, but for ease of reference they are included here with their northern relatives, the Adirondacks and in the northern Appalachians. Although the northern Appalachians are less continuous than their neighbors farther south, the weather is just as rugged. Mount Washington, which holds the global wind record, stands 6288 feet high. The challenging and often severe weather in the northern Appalachians is not largely a function of elevation, as is the case in western ranges. Rather it is the result of high latitude, together with proximity to the North Atlantic, the convergence of the Gulf Stream and Labrador currents just offshore, the Great Lakes to the west, and the frequent visits of the jet stream during the long winter. Five major ranges comprise the northern Appalachians: the Catskills in southeastern New York State and the Adirondacks to the north, the Green Mountains in Vermont, the White Mountains in New Hampshire, and the Longfellow Mountains of Maine. All pose major challenges to visitors on trail, lake, and river. Visualize the seasons of the year as a pie chart, and the supersized slice would be winter-snow season. Fall, the season of glorious color, and spring, aptly termed "mud season," would be slices for the diet-conscious. They are both but brief transitions into or out of winter. Summer can be a hazy, hot, and humid season—prone to stretches of beautiful weather but also violent thunderstorms.

Two basic types of thunderstorms develop in the northern Appalachians. The first is air mass or "popcorn" thunderstorms, which are most common during the summer months of July and August. The risk factors for air mass thunderstorms include the three H's: hot, humid, and hazy weather. A fourth could be called "high terrain." The latter offers a big assist in triggering such storms. The greatest threat posed by this variety of thunderstorm is lightning. The second basic pattern is that of severe convection, organized clusters or systems of thunderstorms that typically move from the Great Lakes into Quebec. Such thunderstorms can generate hurricane-force winds capable of flattening entire mountainsides of forest and woodland. It has happened. Be aware that heavy rain from these thunderstorms can turn hiking trails into small streams, leading to potentially dangerous falls. Thunderstorms in this second pattern often develop during the morning with the arrival of warm air, then redevelop in the afternoon with the approach either of a squall line or a cold front and sometimes both. If you wake up to thunderstorms, expect more of them later in the day. While tornadoes generally are not common in the mountains, small tornado corridors exist in the Northeast, such as in the Berkshires. Several key ingredients work together to produce these stronger thunderstorms: a ridge of high pressure over the Midwest resulting in a northwesterly flow aloft with winds of 40 to 50 miles per hour (or more) and moisture streaming from the Gulf of Mexico in a southerly flow at lower levels. Even moisture evaporating from crops can contribute to the mayhem. Small approaching disturbances in the upper atmosphere can set off severe thundershowers to the north and northeast of the ridge in what is sometimes called "a ring of fire."

Winter produces the storms for which the northern Appalachians are justly famous. *Nor'easters,* lows tracking up the Atlantic coast, can generate blizzard conditions that send two- and four-legged creatures searching for secure cover. Such blizzards are most common along or near the coast, or in the larger valleys such as the Hudson or Champlain. The name "nor'easter" comes from the fact that winds circulate counterclockwise around a low that drives northeasterly winds into the coastal side of these storms. Arctic air sliding over the Great Lakes to the west produces heavy lake-effect snows along the western slopes of this range. It can become astonishingly cold. Meteorologist Anton Seimon, who graciously served as a resource for this section, reports seeing the mercury freeze on his thermometer at −47.5°F. That is not a record. The record is −52°F, set in two places: Old Forge in the western Adirondacks on February 18, 1979, and Stillwater Reservoir just to the northeast on February 9, 1934. Hypothermia is definitely a problem in the Northeast, and not just during winter. Deaths from hypothermia have occurred on the major peaks every month of the year, particularly in the Presidential Range of New Hampshire and on Mount Katahdin in Maine. Rain, the colder temperatures, and higher winds above treeline can be a lethal mix even in summer. Carry extra clothing in your pack, and be willing to turn back rather than trying to tough it out.

Although this region lacks the potential for the large avalanches that occur in the western United States and Canada, smaller but still lethal avalanches can and do occur. Such slides are most common in the White Mountains of New Hampshire, specifically at Tuckerman and Huntington Ravines in the Presidential Range. Strong westerly winds following a front typically load the east-facing slopes, resulting in the highest risk. Such elevated avalanche hazards typically follow immediately after heavy snowfall—that is, snow falling at a rate of 1 inch or more per hour or when temperatures warm and the snow becomes progressively warmer, possibly even changing to or becoming mixed with rain. The combination of heavy, wet snow, high winds, and bitter cold prompted the late Paul Petzoldt to call Mount Washington "the great booby trap of the East."

New York to Quebec: The Big Picture

Keeping a close eye on forecasts has no substitute, but a discerning look at satellite images (or even the direction high clouds are moving) will

Storm track, or surface winds, from the north

offer clues to important details that may help you select the area most likely to offer the best weather for your planned activity. It goes without saying (but is worth a reminder here) that this is not a substitute for acquiring the latest pertinent local forecasts from a trusted forecast source, such as the local office of the National Weather Service. The movement of clouds can mirror the movement of winds aloft, and the shifts in such steering currents. These winds aloft will give backcountry skiers important guidance on which slopes will be lee slopes, tending to load up with drifting snow with the resulting higher avalanche hazard. In this region, that primarily would be either Vermont or New Hampshire. Experienced forecasters and guides pay close attention to these shifts, as well as the paths that smaller disturbances travel. So does any-

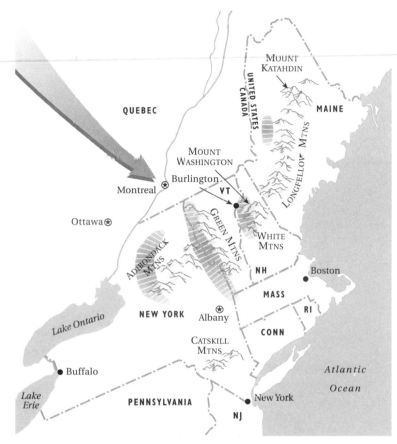

Storm track from the northwest

one who spends much time outdoors, particularly skiers, climbers, and backpackers venturing off piste—off the beaten trail. Thus our examination of this region's weather begins with a look at the big picture: the major storm tracks and their influence on the weather. Those are shown in the illustrations that follow, together with the areas that tend to get the most precipitation and the least. The illustrations mirror what you would likely see in a satellite image. A brief description follows, including the duration and intensity of each pattern.

A *northerly storm track or flow* does not tend to bring storms in the sense of rain or snow. However, it can bring frigid air originating from a Siberian high that streams over the North Pole and through Ontario and Quebec, largely unmodified by movement over the Great Lakes. Such

Storm track from the southwest

deep cold may last for just a few days or for a week or more. Contrary to popular opinion, the coldest temperatures may not occur in hollows or valleys on cold, clear, windless nights but at higher elevations. The coldest temperatures often occur in the Adirondacks, as already cold air forced upslope onto the plateaulike base of the range leads to further cooling. The combination of frigid temperatures and high winds result in dangerous wind chills. Normal safety precautions and equipment often fail to offer sufficient protection in such Arctic conditions: Extreme caution is mandatory. The arrival of Arctic air is usually well forecast.

A *northwesterly storm track* brings what are called "Alberta clippers" because such lows tend to develop along the east slopes of the Canadian Rockies. Typically, these lows swing over the Great Lakes

Storm track from the southeast

and then hook back into southern Quebec. This produces significant lake-effect snow on the windward slopes of the Adirondacks. Occasionally, these lows will move out over the Gulf of Maine and be transformed into a nor'easter. When this occurs, the significant snow tends to shift to the windward (usually western or southwestern) slopes of the Green Mountains of Vermont, the White Mountains of New Hampshire and the Longfellow Mountains of western Maine. This occurs because the air is forced upward over those slopes, wringing additional precipitation from the clouds. Valley floors often see very little snow in such a pattern. During the summer months, this track, if paired with southerly winds closer to the ground, frequently generates severe thunderstorms. Thundershowers in the morning are

Storm track, or surface winds, from the northeast

often followed by even stronger thunderstorms later in the afternoon.

A *southwesterly storm track* is less common. Because it brings warm and rather moist air from the Gulf coast up into the western Appalachians, it tends to be unpopular with skiers and other winter sports enthusiasts. The warm, moist air mass produces either wet snow, a mix of rain and snow, or—to the south of the low—sleet. Storms passing to the west produce rapid warming and strong southerly winds in the Champlain Valley of Vermont and the upper Connecticut Valley of New Hampshire. The exceptions include western Maine, southeastern Quebec, northern New Hampshire, and northern Vermont. Entrenched cold air in those areas can produce snow, and usually drier snow than in other spots just slightly farther south. This is especially true of Vermont—even when freezing rain is glazing over eastern New Hampshire and western Maine. Keep in mind that the higher peaks and ridges may extend above the surface cold air mass and receive warmer temperatures and possibly rain. If weather maps show a trough near Pittsburgh, the approaching low will tend to hook up the coast, maintaining colder temperatures and snow in this region. If that upper trough is west of Pittsburgh, although precipitation may begin as sloppy snow, odds strongly favor a change to rain.

A *southeasterly storm track* that zips up the Atlantic coast gives rise to the infamous nor'easter. These produce the thigh-deep or even waist-deep snow that children treasure and adults abhor (at least that is what they claim). Maximum precipitation occurs when the storm track keeps the low just offshore of Cape Hatteras and Nantucket Island. If the low moves too far offshore, the precipitation over land will be reduced. The resulting northeasterly surface flow around the low combines cold air with copious moisture to produce epic snowfalls—hence the name "nor'easter." Such a track often directs a sequence of lows up the coast.

A *northeasterly storm track or surface flow* is most common when high pressure is located to the Northeast, over Quebec or the Canadian Maritimes. Such a pattern brings cool, moist air off the North Atlantic. The result is low-level clouds, light rain, or ocean-effect snow with fog along the coast.

New York to Quebec: Local Weather Phenomena You Need to Understand

The legendary nor'easter requires only a quick glance at a satellite image to convince you of its capacity to wreak absolute meteorological havoc. The death spiral of clouds stretching from over the open Atlantic into a rapidly constricting curve over land could do a python proud. Nor'easters look like trouble, even to those innocent of their storied specifics. Relatively rare during the summer months, these storms most frequently rip up the eastern seaboard from September to May. The result can be the stuff of lore and legend, passed from one generation to the next. *The Perfect Storm* of screen and literary fame is but one example. Others include the Great Blizzard of 1888, which produced up to 50 inches of snow around Albany, New York. That total was approached as recently as 1978, when the combination of heavy snow and howling winds built drifts of up to 10 feet in the Boston area.

Nor'easters are not homegrown: They are typically born along Colorado's Front Range or the Gulf of Mexico, but can even develop over the waters of the southeast Atlantic coast. As the original low

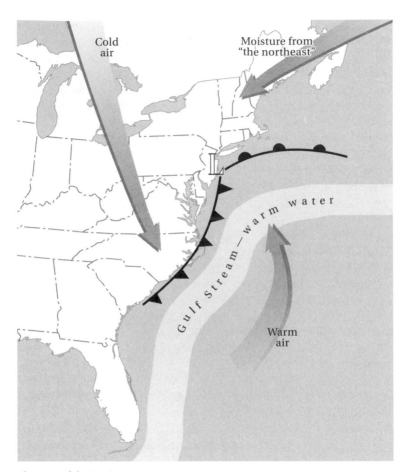

Elements of the Nor'easter

approaches the Atlantic coast, or develops there, the contrast between colder land temperatures (especially in winter) and the warm Gulf Stream can cause explosive deepening, or even the development of an additional low. This often occurs near Cape Hatteras. Add a trough of low pressure over the eastern United States with swift winds aloft and high pressure farther north over eastern Canada to direct cold air into the low, and all the ingredients needed for a major nor'easter are present. As noted, the name "nor'easter" comes from the fact that winds circulate counterclockwise around a low that drives northeasterly winds into the coastal side of these storms. The combination of careful research and improved computer-modeling and forecast skills usually results in few unanticipated nor'easters, but even the best meteorologists still have their hands full estimating where the heaviest snow and rain will hit. Know that the exact track of such storms can make a world of difference: A track up the west side of the Appalachians into the St. Lawrence River Valley will result in more rain or sleet over the region, while a track to the east of the mountains will result in colder air and, therefore, more snow. Once in the backcountry on extended trips, keep a close eye on the sky. The appearance of cirrus streaming from the south or southeast while broadening and thickening should set you thinking about returning to civilization—soon.

New York to Quebec: Trail Notes
Longfellow Mountains (Maine): Downslope Winds (1)

When winds at or below about 4000 feet are out of the east (typical with a nor'easter pattern), the resulting downslope winds over the western slopes will produce warmer temperatures, though not nearly as pronounced as the chinooks in the western United States and Canada. However, when winds at or below about 4000 feet are out of the west, the resulting downslope winds over the eastern slopes will produce milder temperatures along the east slopes of the Green Mountains. Precipitation enhanced by the initial movement of air over the Great Lakes will be much reduced along and near these eastern slopes, with a better chance of sunshine.

Green Mountains (Vermont): Downslope Winds (2)

When winds at or below about 4000 feet are out of the east (typical with a nor'easter pattern), the resulting downslope winds over the western slopes will produce warmer temperatures, though not as pronounced as the chinooks in the western United States and Canada. However, when winds at or below about 4000 feet are out of the west, the resulting downslope winds over the eastern slopes will produce milder temperatures along the east slopes of the Green Mountains. Precipitation enhanced by the initial movement of air over the Great Lakes will be much reduced along and near these eastern slopes, with a better chance of sunshine.

Berkshire Mountains: Downslope Winds (3)

When winds at or below about 4000 feet are out of the east (typical

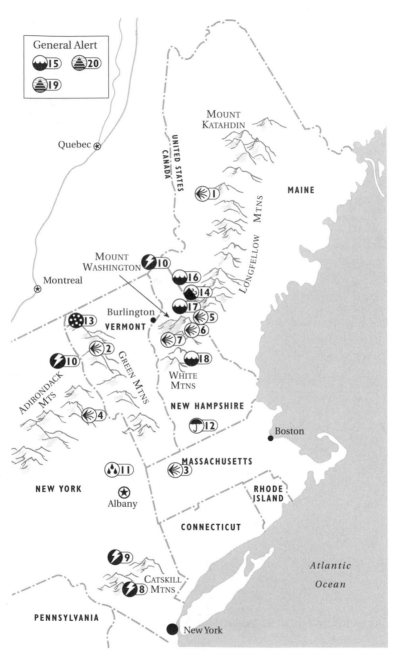

Northern Appalachians: New York to Quebec trail notes reference map (icon locations are approximate)

with a nor'easter pattern), the resulting downslope winds over the western slopes will produce warmer temperatures, though not as pronounced as the chinooks in the western United States and Canada. However, when winds at or below about 4000 feet are out of the west, the resulting downslope winds over the eastern slopes will produce milder temperatures along the east slopes of the Berkshires into the Connecticut River Valley. Precipitation enhanced by the initial movement of air over the Great Lakes will be much reduced along and near these eastern slopes, with a better chance of sunshine.

Adirondack Mountains: Downslope Winds (4)

When winds at or below about 4000 feet are out of the west, the resulting downslope winds over the eastern slopes will produce milder temperatures along the eastern and southeastern slopes of the Adirondacks. Moderate to heavy lake-effect snow will be much reduced along and near these eastern or southeastern slopes, with a better chance of sunshine.

Pinkham Notch: Gap Winds (5)

Moderate to strong southerly winds will result in locally stronger and gusty winds in Pinkham Notch and just to the north of it. Wind speeds at Whitefield will offer a good clue, but if prevailing winds are forecast to be southerly at speeds of 20 miles per hour or more, expect blustery conditions in Pinkham Notch.

Crawford Notch: Gap Winds (6)

Moderate to strong southeasterly winds will result in locally stronger and gusty winds in Crawford Notch and just to the northwest of it. If prevailing winds are forecast to be southeasterly at 20 miles per hour or more, expect particularly blustery conditions in the Crawford Notch.

Franconia Notch: Gap Winds (7)

Moderate to strong southerly winds will result in locally stronger and gusty winds in Franconia Notch and just to the north of it. If prevailing winds are forecast to be southerly at 20 miles per hour or more, expect particularly blustery conditions in Franconia Notch.

Shawangunk Mountains: Air Mass Thunderstorms (8)

Because of the lower elevation of the Shawangunks, thunderstorms tend to develop later in the day here. Keep an eye to the north: If you see towering cumulus developing in that direction, odds are good they will begin developing here as well, though a bit later.

Catskill Mountains: Air Mass Thunderstorms (9)

Because of the higher elevation of the Catskills, thunderstorms tend to develop earlier in the day here: late morning or early afternoon. Watch carefully for the appearance of flat-bottomed cumulus. If they begin to show steady, upward growth, it is time to seek shelter.

Upstate New York, Northern New England, Southern Quebec: Severe Thunderstorms (10)

If you awake to thunderstorms in the morning from May through summer, stronger thunderstorms are likely to follow later in the day with the approach and passage of a squall line and cold front. Watch for brief, hazy clearing followed by increased clouds, wind, and decreasing pressure. Anticipate damaging winds, extensive lightning, and heavy rain. Such storms can generate tornadoes even in the mountains. Seek shelter well before the afternoon storms hit.

Hudson and Mohawk Valleys: Freezing Rain (11)

High pressure over southern Quebec and low pressure near or over New Jersey can funnel cold air from Montreal between the Adirondacks and the Green Mountains over Lake Champlain and into the Hudson River Valley. If this happens at the same time warmer air aloft is carrying moisture from over the Great Lakes, the result can be fierce ice storms. Such storms can persist for several days from the east slopes of the Catskills into the lower Hudson and Mohawk Valleys in downstate New York. Watch for northerly winds carrying below-freezing air from Quebec, with west winds crossing Lakes Huron and Ontario at temperatures above freezing.

Monadnock Mountain: Back Door Cold Front (12)

A back door cold front brings localized bad weather—everything from fog, drizzle, and rain to a mix of snow and freezing rain. This is most common when a surge of cold air from Quebec encounters moist air flowing onshore from coastal Maine and New Hampshire east of the Green Mountains and south of the Whites. Watch for northerly winds in southern Quebec and northern New Hampshire and Vermont, with generally onshore winds along the coast. Typically, the worst weather occurs near popular Monadnock Mountain in southern New Hampshire. Better weather will be found farther north in the Presidential Range. A more general example occurs when a low to the west directs warm air over the trapped cold air. This can occur throughout the Northeast and be especially persistent over western Maine.

Adirondack and Green Mountains: Lake-Effect Snow (13)

Cold air crossing the unfrozen sections of Lakes Huron and Ontario and also Lake Champlain can produce heavy snow over the western slopes of the Adirondacks and the Green Mountains. Snowfall rates of up to 13 inches an hour have been measured. Such heavy snow usually does not reach very far to the east, although the weaker remnant snow bands can reach as far as Boston. Such snows typically occur about 12 hours after a strong cold front passes through, as the colder, drier air begins streaming across the warmer lake water and becomes charged with moisture. Lake-effect snow from Lake Champlain can produce considerable powder snow from Mount Mansfield to Jay Peak in Vermont. Watch for forecasts of northwesterly winds.

Northern New England: Avalanche Threat (14)

The focus of avalanche danger in the Northeast is Mount Washington—particularly Tuckerman and Huntington Ravines and the all too aptly named Gulf of Slides on the lee or east side. Key indicators of a rising and dangerous avalanche hazard include moderate to heavy snowfall rates of an inch or more an hour, especially with strengthening westerly or northwesterly winds. Hazard levels are typically highest within 24 hours of a storm, usually decreasing to low or moderate by 48 hours. A shift to rain should definitely lead to extreme caution, as it increases loading on the slope. Also be aware of the potential for falling ice, particularly in May and June. Check with the snow rangers based at Mount Washington for updated information.

New York to Quebec: Flooding and Ice Jams (15)

Heavy rain falling onto frozen ground can lead to rapid flooding, together with ice jams that amplify such flooding. Be particularly careful in narrow stretches of river valleys: Water levels can rise abruptly.

Wild and Androscoggin Rivers: Flash Flooding (16)

Summer thunderstorms or heavy rains in early spring or late autumn can result in rapid rises in water levels and flash flooding. Be particularly careful in the most narrow stretches of these rivers.

Peabody River: Flash Flooding (17)

Summer thunderstorms or heavy rains in early spring or late autumn can result in rapid rises in water levels and flash flooding. Be particularly careful in the most narrow stretches of the Peabody River.

Pemigewasset River: Flash Flooding (18)

Summer thunderstorms or heavy rains in early spring or late autumn can result in rapid rises in water levels and flash flooding. Be particularly careful in the most narrow stretches of the Pemigewasset.

Northern New England: Advection Fog (19)

Onshore winds directing warm air over the colder water of the Labrador current can result in thick fog that persists for days. Such fogs are most common in July and August and typically will not dissipate until the wind changes direction, no longer blowing onshore. The coastal— or eastern—slopes of the Green, White, and Longfellow Mountains are most prone to such fogs.

New York to Quebec Valley: Radiation Fog (20)

Late September and October bring radiation fog, particularly to the river valleys of the Appalachians. When high pressure settles over the

Northeast, the combination of moist ground, light winds, clearing skies, and longer nights allows moist air near the ground to condense into thick but typically shallow fog. Heating from the sun usually evaporates such fog by midday.

THE CENTRAL AND SOUTHERN APPALACHIANS: PENNSYLVANIA TO ALABAMA

The windes here are variable, but the like thunder and lightning to purifie the aire, I have seldome seene or heard in Europe. From the Southwest come the greatest gustes with thunder and heat. The Northwest winde is commonly coole and bringeth faire weather with it.

John Smith, *A Map of Virginia*, 1612

"The venerable finished beauty of these mountains tells a story beside which that of the Alps is like the raw roughness of a new-quarried block compared to a finished statue.

Geologist Henry Sharp,
quoted in *Wild America*

The Appalachians rank among the most ancient mountain ranges on Earth. Formed two to three hundred million years ago, the forces of rain, wind, and snow have had ample time to erode and soften these once-soaring peaks and ridges. Now heavily forested with hardwoods, any hiker can attest that the Appalachians are still fully capable of turning even well-conditioned legs into  quivering, rubberlike posts incapable of further forward motion. The spine of the southern Appalachians is rooted in northern Georgia and central Alabama. Paralleling the Atlantic coast, the range extends northward into Tennessee and the Carolinas, with the Great Smokies to the west and the Blue Ridge Mountains to the east. The apex of the range is North Carolina's Mount Mitchell, which reaches a height of 6684 feet. Ascending from the east or west, visitors encounter changes in climate similar to what they would find traveling northward from Georgia to Maine. Few travelers would suspect that the Appalachians once served as home to the American bison, elk, eastern timber wolf, and beaver. All had disappeared by the late

1800s (and some well before). Yet the diversity of plant and animal life in this range remains stunning. The central Appalachians served as the terminus of the great glaciers during the last ice age ten thousand years ago; the halt of the ice sheets to the north turned the Great Smoky Mountains of eastern Tennessee and western North Carolina into a botanical and wildlife refuge. Plants and animals incapable of surviving in the austere, icy climate farther north were able to thrive in this area. The result today is a concentration of species numbering in the thousands, unmatched in mountain ranges anywhere else in the continental United States.

The central Appalachians undulate through Virginia, West Virginia, and Maryland to the more pronounced backward-S–shaped curves of the Alleghenies in Pennsylvania and the Poconos to the northeast. A place of gentle beauty, these mountains have also served as a contentious battleground—and still do. The conflicts are no longer between Northern and Southern armies of blue and gray but between Arctic and tropical air masses. The battle lines, or fronts, are capable of triggering fireworks that easily eclipse any human-made bombardments, and they are further amplified by the uplifted Appalachians.

The presence of the Bermuda high off the Atlantic coast circulates copious water vapor inland, mainly during the summer months, resulting in air bearing easily twice the moisture of that found over the Rockies. Average annual rainfall in or near the Smokies ranges from more than 50 inches in the valleys to more than 80 inches on the larger peaks, amounts second only to that of the lush rain forests of the Pacific Northwest. Lake Toxaway averages roughly 90 inches per year. This moisture, together with substances called *terpines* that are emitted by pine trees, is the source of the haze that led to the names "Blue Ridge" and "Smokies." Of course, industrial activity has added another ingredient: pollution. A single heavy thunderstorm or slow-moving low can dump 6 or more inches of rain, resulting in flash flooding that can quickly overwhelm campsites near streams.

The collision of that moisture with colder air from the north can generate vigorous storms from late October into April. (The behavior of these storms is more fully explored in the next section.) Significant snow can fall as late as May on the highest peaks but typically disappears from most hiking trails by late April. However, keep in mind that one good cold front can quickly turn the highest trails white— often after days of sunny, springlike weather. The availability of warm, moist air also fuels thunderstorms. Like the northern Appalachians, two basic types of thunderstorms develop here. The first is air mass or "popcorn" thunderstorms. Those typically develop first during the late morning hours along the highest, east-facing slopes, which is where the rising sun first generates the valley breezes that drive the moist air upslope. The three H's that lead to such thunderstorms are frequently present during summer: hot, humid, and hazy weather along with a fourth "H"—high terrain—which offers a big assist in triggering such storms. The greatest threat posed by this variety of thunderstorm is lightning. The problem in the central and southern Appalachians is that the pervasive haze makes it difficult to see thunderstorms form. Usually, little evidence of them is found in the backcountry other than gradual darkening until you hear thunder or feel the rushing, cooler air from the gust front—good reason to check the forecast carefully.

The second basic pattern is *severe convection:* organized clusters or systems of thunderstorms that are most common in the southern Appalachians during March and April, and occasionally early May. A secondary peak of severe thunderstorms occurs occasionally in November. Keep in mind that if conditions are right, dangerous thunderstorms can and do occur anytime. The slow movement of these storms can cause localized flash flooding. Farther north in Pennsylvania, strong thunderstorms start around the spring equinox, peak near the summer solstice, and fade by the autumnal equinox. Such thunderstorms are extremely dangerous, capable of generating winds in excess of 60 miles per hour, flash flooding, large hail, and frequent lightning. Late summer and early autumn can bring tropical storms or even hurricanes from the Atlantic or Gulf of Mexico. Although winds diminish as such storms move ashore, damaging winds can persist into the Appalachians, along with the potential for flooding rains and mudslides. While such storms can strike as early as June, records indicate a peak of activity in mid-September, specifically September 10, in the Atlantic basin. Aside from these relatively rare storms, September and October produce some of the most delightful weather throughout the central and southern Appalachians. April and May can also offer delightful weather in the southern Appalachians, with less heat and humidity.

A final word to visitors accustomed to the drier environment of the Rockies: Moss, fallen leaves, and other vegetation can make the ground quite slippery, so good footwear and trekking poles are important considerations.

Pennsylvania to Alabama: The Big Picture

Keeping a close eye on forecasts has no substitute, but a discerning look at satellite images on television weather broadcasts, Internet weather sites, or even the direction high clouds are moving overhead will offer important clues that may help you select the area most likely to offer the best weather for your planned activity. It goes without saying (but is worth a reminder here) that this is not a substitute for acquiring the latest pertinent forecasts from a trusted forecast source, such as the local office of the National Weather Service. The movement of clouds can mirror the movement of winds aloft and the shifts in such steering currents. Experienced forecasters and guides pay close attention to these shifts, as well as the paths smaller disturbances travel—as should anyone who spends much time outdoors, particularly backpackers venturing into the backcountry for an extended trek. Thus our examination of this region's weather begins with a look at the big picture: the major storm tracks and their influence on the weather. Those are shown in the illustrations that follow, together with the areas that tend to get the most precipitation and the least. While a single storm track is most common, occasionally a split in the jet stream, occasionally appearing as two cloud streams, will occur. This is not easy to discern from satellite photos. Where those jets rejoin can be a zone of intense storm development. The following illustrations mirror what you would likely see in a satellite image. A brief description follows, including the duration and intensity of each pattern.

A *northerly storm track* in winter can drive cold, stable air south from a zone of high pressure in New England. This case does not describe the winds in the upper atmosphere as much as it refers to the direction of winds at and near the surface. As the cold air is forced up or "dammed" against the eastern slopes of the Appalachians, the result can be extensive and persistent low clouds and drizzle at lower elevations, even into western North Carolina. Warmer, sunnier conditions can occasionally be found at higher elevations along the eastern slopes just to the west of Asheville, usually at or above 3000 feet. Regionally, however, this clearing is more common along the western slopes. A disturbance passing over the Appalachians following such an Arctic push can produce a mix of snow, freezing rain, and rain both in the interior valleys and along the eastern slopes. This sort of pattern tends to be most frequent from northeastern Georgia into Virginia, especially from late December into early March, though it can occur even during the spring months. During some long-lived events, the cold air dammed against the east slopes will push far enough southward, allowing it to loop around the south end of the range and back up along the western slopes into Tennessee. This, however, is a fairly rare event.

A *northwest to westerly storm track* can drive vigorous cold fronts and squall lines through the region. During winter, this is the source of "Alberta clippers," lows moving off the Canadian Rockies into the eastern United States. Clippers generate lighter snowfall than the southwest or southerly tracks described elsewhere: Precipitation tends to occur within a 100-mile-wide band focused just to the north of the storm center. Even after a cold front passes, significant rain or snow can occur as

Storm track or surface winds from the north

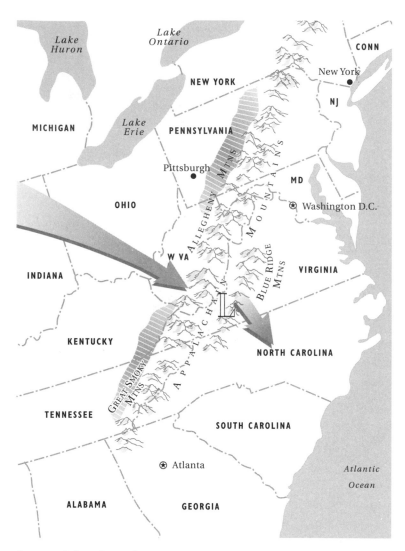

Storm track from the northwest to west

air is forced upward along the western slopes of the Appalachians. This is especially true from the Cumberland Plateau in eastern Tennessee into western North Carolina and Virginia. Some of the coldest air in this region occurs when Arctic air moves from the Canadian prairies into the southeast. Occasionally, Alberta clippers can jump to the middle Atlantic coast and redevelop into nor'easters, resulting in fierce winter storms.

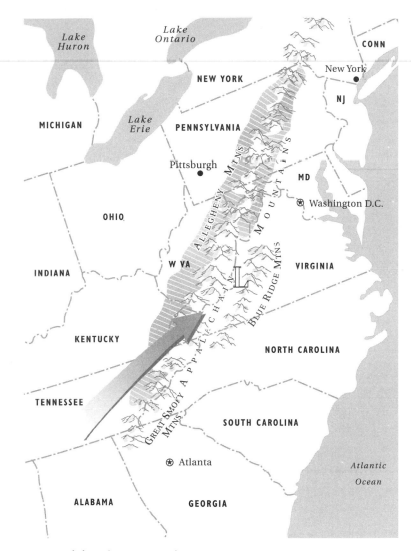

Storm track from the west to southwest

A northwesterly or westerly storm track is infrequent during the summer months, as the jet stream is usually much farther north. During spring, lows are preceded by a moist flow off the Gulf of Mexico. When that is coupled with the energy of the jet stream and cold air behind the system, the result can be awe-inspiring thunderstorm systems capable of torrential downpours, flash flooding, baseball-sized hail, damaging winds, and even occasional tornadoes. It can also carry what are called *closed lows,* which on satellite photos resemble whirlpools. They too can produce prolonged, heavy rainfall. Evidence of this kind of storm track should suggest it is not a time to commit to exposed locations. The eastern slopes of the Appalachians will offer sunnier and warmer weather with a westerly flow. However, camp close to one of the numerous gaps, and you may find yourself chasing your tent. Winds channeled through such gaps accelerate, often producing winds 50 percent stronger than nearby areas. Steer clear of such gaps for more tranquil campsites.

A *west to southwesterly storm track* during late fall and winter is often called a "Gulf runner." Although such lows may originate along the east slopes of the Colorado Rockies, those typically steer farther north, toward Pennsylvania and West Virginia. More frequently, lows steered by this track originate along the Gulf coast from Texas to Alabama, eventually moving into the Carolinas and Virginia. Whatever their origin, it is the warm, moist air drawn from the Gulf of Mexico that can help to strengthen these storms, resulting in a nasty mix of snow, rain, and even sleet or freezing rain; all within a small area. If such lows track northward along the west slopes of the Appalachians, the heaviest precipitation is typically to the north and west of the low along the western slopes of the range, or in the Ohio Valley. Precipitation may begin as snow, but then change to rain as it erodes the cold air trapped below. Freezing rain may occur during the transition from snow to rain. Lows moving to the east of the Appalachians will drop the heaviest precipitation along the east slopes, but both sides can get a thorough soaking. Significant snow can occur, particularly along the Blue Ridge, if temperatures are cool enough. In fact, long after such lows track well north, northwesterly winds at the surface can generate persistent upslope snow in winter that may linger for days on the west side of the Appalachians. Lows that track offshore usually generate the heaviest precipitation from Shenandoah National Park northward.

A *southwesterly or southerly storm track* is called a *coastal track* for obvious reasons. During the summer months when the primary jet stream is typically located to the north of this region, this pattern produces thunderstorms in the warm, moist air flowing off the Gulf of Mexico or the Atlantic. Such a flow pattern may also direct a tropical storm or hurricane into the region (or the remnants of one) from summer into autumn. The greatest potential for such storms is usually from August through October. This is obviously a situation to monitor carefully through updated weather forecasts and definitely is not a time to venture into the backcountry, given the threat of flash floods from heavy downpours. This general south to southwesterly storm track can also generate severe thunderstorms from March through June, before the jet stream retreats northward. During winter, a low originating along the east slopes of the Colorado Rockies or from the western Gulf of Mexico may cross the Appalachians, redevelop or even form a new low as it encounters the warm, moist air and water of the Gulf Stream,

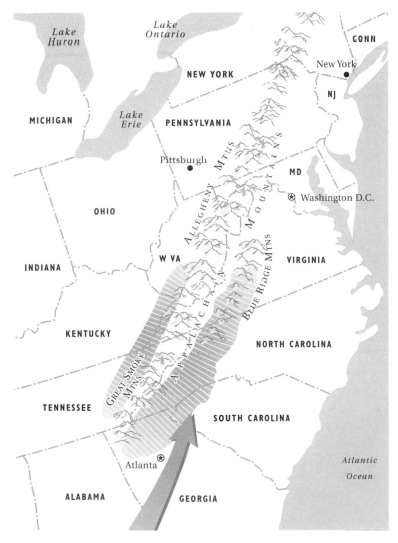

Storm track from the southwest to south

then swing northward while generating heavy rain and occasionally snow, as well as strong winds. These are the infamous nor'easters. One such megastorm in 1993 produced 60 inches of snow at Mount Mitchell. The heaviest snow tends to occur roughly 150 miles northwest of the center of the low. On other occasions, some low centers may track northeastward from the northeastern Gulf of Mexico or

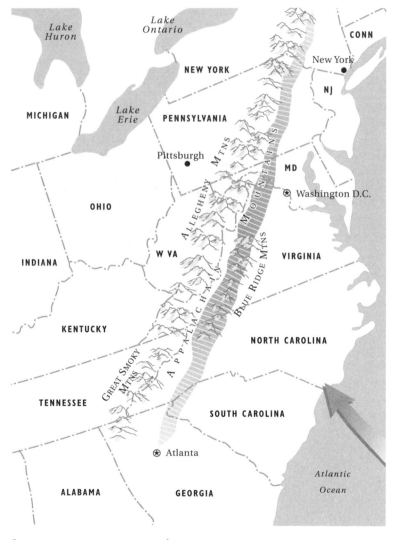

Storm track from the south to southeast

east of Florida, bringing inclement weather to much of the eastern seaboard.

A south or southeasterly flow, typically around the Bermuda high in summer, will pump warm, humid air into the region, resulting in almost daily thunderstorm activity, particularly along ridges and major peaks. Such thunderstorms typically develop first along east-facing slopes from late morning through early afternoon, with activity reaching a maximum in July and August.

Pennsylvania to Alabama: Trail Notes
South Mountain: Gap Winds (1)

This break in the Appalachians west of Gettysburg can experience winds 50 percent stronger than surrounding areas thanks to winds accelerating through the gap. Expect blustery conditions when prevailing winds are moderately strong from the west and northwest and surface pressures are significantly higher to the north and west.

Shade Gap: Gap Winds (2)

Very strong gap winds can occur in this break in the Appalachians to the west of Harrisburg in the Jacks Mountain Range. Expect blustery conditions when prevailing winds are moderately strong from the west and northwest and surface pressures are significantly higher to the north and west. Stake your tent well in this area.

Blue Ridge Mountains: Downslope Winds (3)

Strong west to northwesterly winds at or above ridge elevation (check the winds aloft forecasts) often produce fairly strong downslope winds along the east slopes of the Blue Ridge Mountains in Virginia and North Carolina. "Flying saucer" or lenticular clouds, as well as racing cirrus clouds, provide a good warning of such winds.

The Narrows: Gap Winds (4)

Rapidly building high pressure and west to northwesterly winds following a strong cold front can generate winds 50 percent stronger than those reported upwind of the Narrows along the New River on the state line between Virginia and West Virginia.

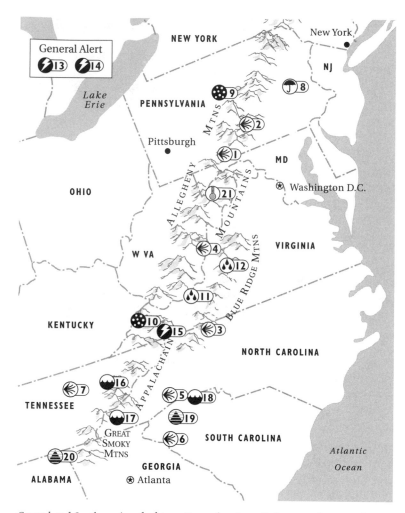

Central and Southern Appalachians: Pennsylvania to Alabama trail notes reference map (icon locations are approximate)

Mine Hole Gap: Gap Winds (5)

High pressure building to the west of the Appalachians following a strong cold front can generate especially blustery gap winds through Mine Hole Gap just east of Asheville, North Carolina. Wind speeds may be 50 percent stronger than those reported upwind of the gap.

North Carolina and South Carolina: Downslope Winds (6)

When a very strong jet stream crosses the Appalachians in the Carolinas from the west to northwest, strong downslope winds can result along the east slopes into the western Piedmont, moving as far as Greensboro in North Carolina and Columbia in South Carolina. Watch for racing cirrus clouds, and check winds aloft forecasts (as discussed in Chapter 7).

Eastern Tennessee: Downslope Winds (7)

Strong west to northwesterly winds off the Cumberland Plateau following a vigorous cold front can generate rapid warming and strong downslope winds in the Great Valley from Chattanooga to Knoxville.

Pocono Mountains: Precipitation Maximum (8)

A nor'easter will generate some of the heaviest precipitation along the eastern slopes of the Poconos. Heading to the western slopes of the Poconos, or particularly the western slopes of the Bald Eagle Mountains, will bring drier conditions. However, if it is snow you are looking for after the passage of such a storm, go to the eastern slopes of the Poconos.

Allegheny Mountains: Lake-Effect Snow (9)

While lake-effect snow is heaviest over the northwestern corner of Pennsylvania in its gradual rise toward the Alleghenies, heavy snow will also occur in the southwest corner along Chestnut Ridge and the Laurel Highlands. Westerly winds off Lake Erie following an Arctic front will focus the heaviest snow in the northwest, while northwesterly winds off the lake will focus the heaviest snow toward Chestnut Ridge and the Laurel Highlands.

West Virginia to North Carolina: Upslope Snow (10)

While cold air streaming over the Great Lakes following an Arctic front produces the most extensive upslope snow over the western slopes of the Alleghenies in Pennsylvania, such snow can even extend as far south as northern North Carolina. When winds over Ohio and western Pennsylvania are expected to blow more from the north or northwest, anticipate upslope snow along the west slopes of the Alleghenies in West Virginia and the Smokies in Tennessee, even to the Blue Ridge Mountains in Virginia and North Carolina. This is most common from late December through early March.

New River, Roanoke, and Shenandoah Valleys: Freezing Rain (11)

Cold air trapped in these valleys after a push of Arctic air tends to be very persistent, making them prime spots for long-lived freezing rain as a warmer weather system approaches from the general direction of the southwest. Another disturbance is needed to scour out the cold air trapped in these valleys.

Blue Ridge Mountains: Upslope Rainfall and Flooding (12)

Storms tracking along the east slopes of the Blue Ridge Mountains will tend to produce the heaviest rainfall along the higher terrain of the Blue Ridge, with the heaviest flooding potential from just north of Roanoke through Shenandoah National Park.

All Areas: Severe Thunderstorms (13)

Spring is the prime season for severe thunderstorms. Watch forecasts especially carefully this season. Be very cautious when temperatures and humidities are high, a cold front lies to the west, and a fairly strong jet stream is dipping south. (Review the safety guidelines in Chapters 3 and 4.)

Pennsylvania to Alabama (East Slopes): Air Mass Thunderstorms (14)

When the Bermuda high is driving warm, humid air up from the south to southeast, expect thunderstorms to develop during the late morning hours over the eastern slopes of the Appalachians, with peak activity during the early to midafternoon hours. Such thunderstorms may tend to drift westward as the day progresses. Overall, such "popcorn" thunderstorms are most frequent over the central Appalachians in July and August. (Be familiar with the guidelines in Chapter 4.)

Mount Rogers: Air Mass Thunderstorms (15)

The typical summer "popcorn" or air mass thunderstorms tend to form earliest in the vicinity of Mount Rogers, usually in the late morning or early afternoon. A heavy shower developing there offers early warning of similar showers elsewhere in the nearby Blue Ridge Mountains.

French Broad River: Flash Flooding (16)

The French Broad River, which originates in North Carolina and drains into Tennessee, can rise rapidly when thunderstorms or a slow-moving low dump heavy rain. Select campsites on higher ground when such conditions threaten.

Tuckasegee River: Flash Flooding (17)

The Tuckasegee River in the Smokies of the Carolinas can rise rapidly when thunderstorms or a slow-moving low dump heavy rain. Select campsites on higher ground when such conditions threaten.

Hickory Nut Gorge: Flash Flooding (18)

Heavy rains can generate flash flooding along the Hickory Nut Gorge in North Carolina. Select campsites on higher ground when such conditions threaten.

Virginia to Georgia: East Slope Fog (19)

High pressure driving cold air south from New England can generate extensive fog, low clouds, and drizzle along the lower eastern slopes of the Appalachians. Know that low clouds in locations such as Raleigh, North Carolina may mean fog in the mountains. Such conditions can be avoided by changing to a destination along the western slopes, or even at higher elevations along the eastern slopes. Locations at 3000 to 4000 feet should typically put you above the murk. Radiation fog in the late summer through fall usually tops out at about 2500 feet.

Alabama to Tennessee (West Slope): Fog (20)

The same high pressure directing cold air from New England that can generate extensive fog, low clouds, and drizzle along the east slopes can occasionally generate the same conditions along the western slopes. Such conditions are usually confined to Alabama and Tennessee. A forecast plunge in temperatures in northern Georgia is a good early indicator, and of course visible satellite pictures illustrate this pattern once it occurs. Either head farther north, or simply hike to elevations at or above 3000 feet. If a disturbance is expected from the west, be aware of the possibility of freezing rain or mixed rain and snow at lower elevations.

East Slopes: Arctic Outbreak (21)

Severe cold can follow an Arctic outbreak when north to northeasterly winds drive air from the plains of Quebec along the east slopes of the Appalachians in Pennsylvania, western Maryland, and Virginia. A disturbance approaching from the west that brings warmer air as well as moisture can produce freezing rain or drizzle both along the east slopes and also in the interior valleys where the cold air is trapped.

Conclusion

A person starts to live when he can live outside himself.
Albert Einstein

By day, mountains demand much of our attention—whether austere rock or lush forest, meadows brimming with wildflowers, or shining glaciers. The sky is usually but a backdrop, not commanding the expanse it does over the plains, prairies, or ocean. Sunset with its alpenglow, however, signals the shift of focus to the sky: the indescribable beauty of the star-encrusted heavens. There is usually less water vapor at altitude, which lends an almost touchable brilliance to the night sky. Now, the peaks and ridges can be sensed if not seen directly, serving more as a framework for the show above. It is a sight I have enjoyed countless times—while reclining on boulders until the last vestiges of the summer sun's warmth has drained from the stone and I finally shiver with the cold, or perched on benches sculpted from snow until my fingers are numb, almost matching the temperature of my backside, finally driving me into the dark recesses of my tent, snow cave, or igloo for the remainder of the long winter night.

Most of the preceding pages have focused on the sky, and for good reason. Together with the information gathered before we hit the trail, the sky is rich with clues to the weather ahead. In the high country, after all, the sky is not merely above us but also around and even beneath us. Coming to understand such clues, and acquiring the desire to search for them should not strip the wonder from the wilderness but add to our appreciation of it. It is my hope this book will encourage you to seek and savor the beauty of the high country, and to do so with greater confidence and safety. It is all too easy to become transfixed by the many issues and demands of daily life. As important as those matters may be, it is equally important to take time to recharge our spirits, to balance our technology-driven lives with hours spent in the easy enjoyment of wild places. A simple walk in the mountains can erase time. The great peaks that give a sense of such permanence at once reduce us and our concerns to insignificance but also elevate us by association, intoxicating us with wonder as we mindfully become part of something much greater than ourselves. May our trails cross some day.

Jeff Renner
Sammamish, Washington

Appendix I: Wind Chill

	40°	35°	30°	25°	20°	15°	10°	5°	0°	-5°	-10°	-15°	-20°	-25°	-30°	-35°	-40°
calm	40	35	30	25	20	15	10	5	0	-5	-10	-15	-20	-25	-30	-35	-40
5 mph	36	31	25	19	13	7	1	-5	-11	-16	-22	-28	-34	-40	-46	-52	-57
10 mph	34	27	21	15	9	3	-4	-10	-16	-22	-28	-35	-41	-47	-53	-59	-66
15 mph	32	25	19	13	6	0	-7	-13	-19	-26	-32	-39	-45	-51	-58	-64	-71
20 mph	30	24	17	11	4	-2	-9	-15	-22	-29	-35	-42	-48	-55	-61	-68	-74
25 mph	29	23	16	9	3	-4	-11	-17	-24	-31	-37	-44	-51	-58	-64	-71	-78
30 mph	28	22	15	8	1	-5	-12	-19	-26	-33	-39	-46	-53	-60	-67	-73	-80
35 mph	28	21	14	7	0	-7	-14	-21	-27	-34	-41	48	-55	-62	-69	-76	-82
40 mph	27	20	13	6	-1	-8	-15	-22	-29	-36	-43	-50	-57	-64	-71	-78	-84
45 mph	26	19	12	5	-2	-9	-16	-23	-30	-37	-44	-51	-58	-65	-72	-79	-86
50 mph	26	19	12	4	-3	-10	-17	-24	-31	-38	-45	-52	-60	-67	-74	-81	-88
55 mph	25	18	11	4	-3	-11	-18	-25	-32	-39	-46	-54	-61	-68	-75	-82	-89
60 mph	25	17	10	3	-4	-11	-19	-26	-33	-40	-48	-55	-62	-69	-76	-84	-91

Average Frostbite Time

30 minutes
10 minutes
5 minutes

Appendix II: Heat Stress

Relative Humidity	0%	5%	10%	15%	20%	25%	30%	35%	40%	45%
120°F	107	111	116	123	130					
115°F	103	107	111	115	123	127	135	143	151	
110°F	102	105	108	112	117	123	130	137	143	15
105°F	95	97	100	102	105	109	113	118	123	12
100°F	91	93	95	97	99	101	104	107	110	11
95°F	87	88	90	91	93	94	96	98	101	10
90°F	83	84	85	86	87	88	90	91	93	9
85°F	78	79	80	81	82	83	84	85	86	8
80°F	73	74	75	76	77	77	78	79	79	8
75°F	69	69	70	71	72	72	73	73	74	7
70°F	64	64	65	65	66	66	67	67	68	6

Shaded Areas: Extreme Caution

90–130°F   Sunstroke/heat exhaustion possible
106–130°F Danger. Sunstroke/heat exhaustion likely
130°F+   Extreme danger. Sunstroke or heatstroke imminent

50%	55%	60%	65%	70%	75%	80%	85%	90%	95%	100%
135	142	149								
120	126	132	138	144						
107	110	114	119	124	130	136				
96	98	100	108	106	109	113	117	122		
88	89	91	91	93	95	97	99	102	105	
81	83	83	86	86	86	86	88	88	89	
75	75	76	76	77	77	78	78	79	79	
69	69	70	70	70	70	71	71	71	71	

Appendix III:
Cloud Identification Chart

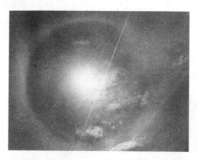

Halo. Commonly seen 24–48 hours ahead of precipitation.

Lenticular cloud. Wavelike clouds over mountains often suggesting approaching precipitation.

Cirrus clouds. High clouds often seen before the arrival of a warm front.

Cirrostratus clouds. High clouds often seen before the arrival of a warm front.

Altostratus clouds. Mid-level clouds often seen after cirrus clouds and before the lower stratus clouds when a warm front is approaching.

Stratus clouds. Flat, layered clouds often seen with the approach of a warm front and precipitation, or the arrival of ocean air.

Nimbostratus. Stratus clouds producing widespread precipitation and often lowered visibility.

Altocumulus. Mid-level cumulus clouds marking unstable air that often indicate the potential for thunder or rain showers later in the day.

Cumulus. Lower clouds that mark unstable air. With continued growth, these often indicate the potential for thunder or rain showers later in the day.

Cumulo-nimbus. Cumulus clouds producing rain, snow or thunder, lightning and hail.

Stratocumulus. Lumpy, layered clouds that can produce showers.

Appendix IV: Useful Conversions and Guidelines

Equivalent Distance Measurements
1 statute mile = 0.87 nautical mile = 5280 feet = 1.6 kilometers
1 foot = 0.30 meter = 30.48 centimeters
1 nautical mile = 1.15 statute miles= 6072 feet = 1.85 kilometers
1 degree Latitude = 60 nautical miles = 111 kilometers
1 minute Latitude = 1 nautical mile = 1.85 kilometers
1 kilometer = 3280 feet = 0.62 mile
1 meter = 3.28 feet = 39.37 inches
1 centimeter = 0.39 inch

Equivalent Air Pressure Measurements
1 inch of Mercury = 33.8 Millibars
1 Millibar = 0.03 Inch of Mercury
Standard Air Pressure = 29.92 Inches of Mercury = 1013.2 Millibars

Equivalent Wind Speed Measurements
1 knot = 1 nautical mile per hour = 1.15 statute mph = 1.85 kilometers per hour
1 statute mile per hour = 0.87 knot = 1.6 kilometers per hour
1 kilometer per hour = 0.62 mile per hour = 0.55 knot

Equivalent Volume Measurements
1 gallon = 3.786 liters
1 liter = 0.264 gallon
1 cubic meter = 35.31 cubic feet
1 cubic foot = 0.029 cubic meter

Actual Conversion from Fahrenheit to Celsius
(Degrees Fahrenheit-32) x 5/9 or (Degrees Fahrenheit-32) x 0.556

Actual Conversion from Celsius to Fahrenheit
(9/5 x Degrees Celsius) + 32 or (1.8 x Degrees Celsius) + 32

Appendix V:
Internet Resources

American Avalanche Association
www.avalanche.org

Appalachian Mountain Club
www.outdoors.org

Canadian Avalanche Association
www.avalanche.ca

Jackson Hole Area Mountain
Weather
www.mountainweather.com

Mount Washington Observatory
www.mountwashington.org

National Oceanic and
Atmospheric Administration
www.noaa.gov/wx.html

National Weather Service
www.nws.noaa.gov

North Carolina State University,
Atmospheric Sciences
www.meas.ncsu.edu/01-about.html

Northwest Avalanche Institute
www.avalanche.org/~nai

Northwest Weather and
Avalanche Center
www.nwac.noaa.gov
www.nwac.us

Penn State University/
Department of Meteorology
web.met/psu.edu/weather/index.html

The Mountaineers
www.mountaineers.org

University at Albany, State
University of New York/
Department of Earth and
Atmospheric Sciences
www.atmos.albany.edu

University of Utah/Meteorology
Department
www.met.utah.edu

University of Washington/
Department of Atmospheric
Sciences
www.atmos.washington.edu

Appendix VI: Bibliography

Bailey, Harry, *Weather of Southern California,* University of California Press, Berkeley, 1975.

Branch, Michael, and Philippon, Daniel, *The Height of Our Mountains,* The Johns Hopkins University Press, Baltimore, 1998.

Cox, Steven M., and Fulsaas, Kris, eds., *Mountaineering: The Freedom of the Hills,* 7th edition, The Mountaineers Books, Seattle, 2003.

Critchfield, Howard, *General Climatology,* Prentice Hall, Englewood Cliffs, NJ, 1983.

Daffern, Tony, *Avalanche Safety for Skiers and Climbers,* The Mountaineers Books, Seattle, WA, 1998.

Ferguson, Sue, and LaChapelle, Edward, *The ABCs of Avalanche Safety,* 3rd edition, The Mountaineers Books, Seattle, 2003.

Fleagle, Robert, and Businger, Joost, *An Introduction to Atmospheric Physics,* Academic Press, Orlando, FL, 1980.

Gilliam, Harold, *Weather of the San Francisco Bay Region,* University of California Press, Berkeley, 2002.

Huschke, Ralph, *Glossary of Meteorology,* American Meteorological Society, Boston, 1986.

Johnson, Kent, and Mullock, John, *Aviation Weather Hazards of British Columbia and the Yukon,* Minister of Environment, Canada, 1996.

LaChapelle, Edward, *Field Guide to Snow Crystals,* International Glaciological Society, Cambridge, England, 1992.

————. *Secrets of the Snow: Visual Clues to Avalanche and Ski Conditions,* University of Washington Press, Seattle, 2001.

Martin, Jason, and Krewarik, Alex, *Washington Ice: A Climbing Guide,* The Mountaineers Books, Seattle, 2003.

McClung, David, *The Avalanche Handbook,* 2nd edition, The Mountaineers Books, Seattle, 1993.

Nelson, Mike, *The Colorado Weather Book,* Westcliffe Publishers, Englewood, CO, 1999.

Ortenburger, Leigh, and Jackson, Reynold, *A Climber's Guide to the Teton Range,* 3rd edition, The Mountaineers Books, Seattle, 1996.

Ray, Peter, *Mesoscale Meteorology and Forecasting,* American Meteorological Society, Boston, 1986.

Renner, Jeff, *Lightning Strikes: Staying Safe Under Stormy Skies,* The Mountaineers Books, Seattle, 2002.

————. *Northwest Mountain Weather: Understanding and Forecasting for the Backcountry User,* The Mountaineers Books, Seattle, 1992.

Selters, Andy, *Glacier Travel and Crevasse Rescue,* The Mountaineers Books, Seattle, 1990.

Wallace, John, and Hobbs, Peter, *Atmospheric Science: An Introductory Survey,* Academic Press, Orlando, FL, 1977.

Whiteman, C. David, *Mountain Meteorology: Fundamentals and Applications,* Oxford University Press, Oxford, 2000.

Woodmencey, Jim, *Weather in the Southwest,* Southwest Parks and Monuments Association, Tucson, AZ, 2001.

Index

A

advection fog 43, 44
air pressure 24-26
Alberta clippers 268
Aleutian low 168, 169, 183
American Avalanche Association
    118
anemometers 138
avalanches 123-132, 149, 190,
    191
Avalanche Assessment Triangle
    123
Avalanche Hazard Scale 130

B

barometers 137
Beaufort Scale 97, 98
bora 94, 95

C

channeled winds 99
chinook 94, 95, 216-218, 256
cirrus clouds 32
cold air avalanche 174, 191
cold fronts 38, 39, 62, 63
condensation 29, 50
convection 50
converging winds 100
corner winds 101
cumulo-nimbus 54, 55, 59-65,
    106, 107
cumulus clouds 38, 51, 52, 54

D

depth hoar 127
direct action avalanches 123
diverging winds 100

downbursts 107
downslope winds 104
downdrafts 107

E

equilibrium metamorphism 128,
    129

F

faceting 127
fair weather cumulus 51, 52
flash floods 76-80
flash to bang principle 70, 71
foehn 94
fog 41-47
freezing level 121, 122
fronts 25, 26, 31

G

gap winds 99
glaciers 95, 105, 130, 131
glacier wind 95, 104, 174
Grand Teton National Park
    11-19
gravity winds 103
gulf runners 287-288
gust fronts 107

H

hailstone 53, 55
Heat Stress Index 298
hypothermia 80, 81

I

ice blowout 174, 175
ice fog 47
inversion 42

J
jet stream 28, 90

L
land breezes 103, 105
lapse rates 121, 122, 123
lee waves 92, 93
lee wave clouds 33, 34
lightning 56-59
lifting condensation level 51

M
melt-freeze metamorphism 129
microbursts 108
monsoon 243-245

N
NOAA/National Weather Service
    135, 136, 139, 141, 143-148,
    150, 151
nor'easters 271-273

O
occluded fronts 40, 41, 62, 63
orographic effect 61, 62
orographic thunderstorms 62

P
Pineapple Express 172-173,
    186-189, 197-199, 216-217
"popcorn" thunderstorms 49
precipitation fog 45, 46
post frontal thunderstorms 64
Puget Sound Convergence Zone
    202-204

R
radar 153
radiation fog 41, 42
relative humidity 30, 31, 51

S
Santa Ana winds 230-232
satellite images 152, 153
sea breezes 103, 104, 105
slab avalanches 124, 127
snow 118-126
snow level 122, 123
solar heating 23
stability 34
stationary fronts 41, 62, 64
steering currents 27
stratus clouds 34
sublimation 31
sundowner winds 232-234
super cooled droplets 53, 119,
    120, 121
surface hoar 127

T
terrain blocking 101, 102
thunderstorm safety 67-81, 108,
    109, 110, 111

U
upslope flow 61, 104
upslope fog 46, 47

V
Valley winds 103

W
warm frontal fog 45
warm fronts 31, 34-36, 62
warm sector 37
weather watches, warnings 68,
    144, 145, 146
wildfires 81- 86
wind Chill Chart 297
wind loading 124
winds aloft 27, 89-92, 151, 152
windstorms 112, 113, 114

About the Author

Jeff Renner is the chief meteorologist for the NBC television station in Seattle, KING-TV, and also prepares daily forecasts for the *Seattle Times*. An award-winning weather forecaster and science writer, he's written *Lightning Strikes, Northwest Mountain Weather,* and *Northwest Marine Weather* and is a contributing author to *Mountaineering: The Freedom of the Hills*—all published by The Mountaineers Books. Having earned his degree in atmospheric sciences from the University of Washington, Jeff enjoys doing frequent "field research" in and above the mountains as a skier, climber, hiker, and flight instructor to enhance his understanding of

The author ski touring in the Cascades with Kiana, the fastest family member on the snow (© Creative Indulgence)

mountain weather. He endeavors to improve the quality and scope of weather information for all who work or play in the great outdoors.

THE MOUNTAINEERS, founded in 1906, is a nonprofit outdoor activity and conservation club, whose mission is "to explore, study, preserve, and enjoy the natural beauty of the outdoors. . . . " Based in Seattle, Washington, the club is now one of the largest such organizations in the United States, with seven branches throughout Washington State.

The Mountaineers sponsors both classes and year-round outdoor activities in the Pacific Northwest, which include hiking, mountain climbing, ski-touring, snowshoeing, bicycling, camping, kayaking, nature study, sailing, and adventure travel. The club's conservation division supports environmental causes through educational activities, and by sponsoring legislation and presenting informational programs.

All club activities are led by skilled, experienced instructors, who are dedicated to promoting safe and responsible enjoyment and preservation of the outdoors.

If you would like to participate in these organized outdoor activities or the club's programs, consider a membership in The Mountaineers. For information and an application, write or call The Mountaineers, Club Headquarters, 7700 Sand Point Way NE, Seattle, WA 98115: 206-521-6001. You can also visit the club's website at *www.mountaineers.org* or contact The Mountaineers via email at *clubmail@mountaineers.org*.

The Mountaineers Books, an active, nonprofit publishing program of the club, produces guidebooks, instructional texts, historical works, natural history guides, and works on environmental conservation. All books produced by The Mountaineers Books fulfill the club's mission.

Send or call for our catalog of more than 500 outdoor titles:

The Mountaineers Books
1001 SW Klickitat Way, Suite 201
Seattle, WA 98134
800-553-4453
mbooks@mountaineersbooks.org
www.mountaineersbooks.org

The Mountaineers Books is proud to be a corporate sponsor of The Leave No Trace Center for Outdoor Ethics, whose mission is to promote and inspire responsible outdoor recreation through education, research, and partnerships. The Leave No Trace program is focused specifically on human-powered (nonmotorized) recreation.

Leave No Trace strives to educate visitors about the nature of their recreational impacts, as well as offer techniques to prevent and minimize such impacts. Leave No Trace is best understood as an educational and ethical program, not as a set of rules and regulations.

For more information, visit *www.LNT.org,* or call 800-332-4100.

ALSO IN THE MOUNTAINEERS OUTDOOR BASICS SERIES

WILDERNESS NAVIGATION:
Finding Your Way Using Map, Compass, Altimeter, & GPS, 2nd Edition
Bob & Mike Burns
A classic handbook for learning to navigate.

THE OUTDOOR KNOTS BOOK
Clyde Soles
A guide to the ropes and knots used in the outdoors by hikers, campers, paddlers, and climbers.

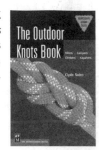

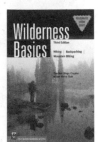

WILDERNESS BASICS, 3rd Edition
San Diego chapter of The Sierra Club
A classic handbook for the outdoor novice interested in hiking, backpacking, paddling, and mountain biking.

MOUNTAINEERING FIRST AID:
A Guide to Accident Response and First Aid Care, 5th Edition
Jan Carline, Martha J. Lentz, and Steven MacDonald
The classic text on mountaineering first aid includes the latest treatment protocols for backcountry injuries.

OTHER TITLES YOU MIGHT ENJOY FROM THE MOUNTAINEERS BOOKS

LIGHTNING STRIKES:
Staying Safe Under Stormy Skies
Jeff Renner
Lightning kills more people in North America than any other weather phenomenon. Renner provides clear, practical strategies for everyone who recreates or works outdoors.

DON'T FORGET THE DUCT TAPE:
Tips and Tricks for Maintaining and Repairing Outdoor & Travel Gear, 2nd Ed.
Kristin Hostetter
Pack this little guide with you and be an outdoor fixit guru!

Mountaineers Books has more than 500 outdoor recreation titles in print.
Receive a free catalog at
www.mountaineersbooks.org.